ADVANCED INDUSTRIAL PSYCHOLOGY

VOLUME – I

RAM NATH SHARMA
S.S. CHANDRA

ATLANTIC
PUBLISHERS & DISTRIBUTORS

Published by
ATLANTIC PUBLISHERS AND DISTRIBUTORS
B-2, Vishal Enclave, Opp. Rajouri Garden, New Delhi-110027
Phones : 25413460, 25429987, 25466842

Sales Office
7/22, Ansari Road, Darya Ganj, New Delhi-110002
Phones : 23273880, 23275880, 23280451
Fax : 91-11-23285873
web : www.atlanticbooks.com
e-mail : info@atlanticbooks.com

Printed in India at
Nice Printing Press, Delhi

Preface

Advanced Industrial Psychology is that branch of Psychology which examines human behaviour under modern industrial circumstances. The study of human behaviour covers both external behaviour and inner feelings in which research is carried out on the concerned behavioural problems that arise in an industrial environment. The Advanced Industrial Psychology plays an important role in industry in increasing production, promoting harmonious relationship among workers and in creating better understanding between labour and management.

This book covers the undergraduate and postgraduate syllabi of all the Indian Universities. Its subject matter has been planned and treated according to the weightage given to different topics in the University syllabi. Based upon standard books, it studies industrial psychology in the setting of Indian conditions. While data have been gathered from standard books and reputed research journals published in the West, an attempt has been made to give the reader an insight into the problems of Indian industrial conditions and Indian labourers. Causes of their problems have been explored and suggestions advanced for amelioration of their conditions. Thus, the book is equally useful for all those concerned with industry and labour. It includes a discussion of the problems of industrial management and their solutions, and illustrates psychological tests and methods of measurement along with vocational guidance to the reader so that he may develop an understanding for the choice of a career and achievement of job satisfaction.

The method of presentation in this landmark publication is lucidly analytic with central headings, side headings and sub-headings given in different types to facilitate understanding. Each point has been discussed in a separate paragraph. Illustrations have been given wherever required.

The book will be an indispensable source for all professionals, researchers and students in the field of Psychology and for anyone working in the related areas for acquiring an up-to-date overviews.

Although we have done our best to make this book an ideal textbook, yet suggestions are invited for improvement of the book in its next edition.

RAM NATH SHARMA
S.S. CHANDRA

Contents

1

IMPACT OF INDUSTRIALIZATION

The interweaving of human relations results in society. The human relations are determined by human attitudes. The pattern of human relations and the nature of human civilization and culture mutually determine each other. The pattern of human relations in an agricultural society is quite different from that of the industrial society. The measure of social relations in the primitive society is widely different. In short, the structure of society is determined by the trade and profession of the society and the attitudes of the members towards these. The social relations found in modern industrial society are very complex and intricate compared to the simple and straightforward social relations found in ancient societies. The industrialization has affected the society in every respect. The customs and traditions, the fashion and manners, the ways and modes of living all have been deeply influenced by industrialization. The processes of industrialization are intimately related with scientific processes. Therefore, the attitude of the members of industrial society becomes scientific. In an industrial society, the superstitions and blind faiths have no place. People expect and demand rational explanation of every phenomenon. The reason and not faith is the touchstone of every action and belief in the industrial society. The freedom of thought and individualism are the cornerstones of the industrial society. The methods and means of social control have changed. The ancient institutions of marriage and family have also changed. The old values and rules pertaining to religion and morals are undergoing radical changes. The new patterns of social stratification are being established. The caste system is being replaced by the class system. Even the means of recreation and entertainment are undergoing change in industrial urban society. Thus it is apparent that industrialization has influenced every aspect of society. It is not quite easy to judge if this impact is good or bad; but it is possible to study the consequences flowing from industrialization. The following discussion is an attempt to make an in-depth study of the impact of industrialization upon various aspects of society.

IMPACT UPON SOCIAL INSTITUTIONS

The institutions of marriage and family are to be found in every society. With the changes in the structure of society, these institutions also undergo changes. Traditionally the Indian society has recognized marriage to be a sacred and religious institution but in the modern industrial society, it has been reduced to a contract. In the past marriage was considered to be a permanent and inalienable bond which could not be terminated at will. But now, under the impact of industrialization, divorce and marriage go side by side. Now it is not considered an evil to terminate the contentious and miserable marriages. The following discussion will make explicit the impact of industrialization upon marriage :

(1) Marriage is a social contract. Prior to heavy industrialization of India, marriage in this country was considered to be a religious and sacred institution. It was commonly believed by Hindus that marriage was necessary for emancipation or salvation and that anyone who did not marry could not find salvation in this life. Besides, marriage was regarded to be a permanent bond. Marriages were supposed to be made in heaven and only God could sever a marital bond. But with the advance of industrialization, these beliefs are considered superstitious and anyone holding them is frowned upon. Today marriage is regarded to be only a social contract between a man and a woman. The aim of marriage in modern times has ceased to be spiritual and now its aims are economic, social and biological only.

(2) Higher age of marriage. In Indian society only a few decades back, parents used to marry their children at very early age. Child-marriages were quite common. But with the industrialization, the age of marriage is advancing; it is getting higher and higher. In metropolitan towns of India today, boys and girls are generally marrying at the ages of 25 to 35.

(3) Practice of non-marrying. As we have referred to above the aim of marriage in India is no longer spiritual; the marital bond is no longer looked upon as sacred or inviolable. As a consequence of rejection of the traditional beliefs and attitudes, many young men and women in big towns prefer to live single. According to the thinking and beliefs of these young persons, the major need filled by marriage is biological and this can be easily satisfied out of wedlock.

(4) **Practice of love marriages.** In industrial society men and women usually work together. In mills, factories, offices and other places men and women work together. Under these circumstances they get a chance of coming together, meeting and exchanging ideas and opinions. As a result of this human concourse, individuals become intimate and the intimacy becomes love which ultimately blossoms in marriage.

(5) **Increase in divorce cases.** The industrial society is becoming more and more complex everyday. The philosophy of individualism is flourishing in society. Even husband and wife have different outlook and attitude. Both of them as a rule work in separate social spheres. As a result of this, marital bonds are from time to time rent by discord. The mental conflict increases and the situation of divorce develops. In all industrial societies today there is legal sanction for divorce.

The foregoing discussion makes plain the influence of industrialization upon marriage. Besides affecting the institution of marriage, the industrialization produces effects upon the institution of family. Following are some of the important effects of industrialization upon family.

(1) **Difference regarding function of family.** As a result of industrialization the function of family has changed considerably. Compared to today the family had much more functions in the past. Now a number of functions which used to be performed by families in the past have been taken over by other institutions. Traditionally an Indian family used to be a centre of birth, rearing and education of children. The children used to get training in the ancestral profession. The function of socialization of children, too, used to be performed by the family. But in the industrialized society of today, the family is not required to fulfil these roles. Today children are born in hospital. Even for the nurture of the children, there are today a number of official and non-official institutions. In big towns we find today a number of Infant-Care Centres and Children Homes. The education of children today is done in schools and not in homes. The professional training also is no longer the obligation of the family. What is even more, even feeding is no longer the exclusive obligation of the family. Many people in metropolises eat out of homes. In almost all big cities, people rarely take lunch at home except on Sunday and holidays. In many families both husband and wife go out for work. In these circumstances the functions of a modern family are more formal than real.

(2) Breaking-up of joint family. Traditionally most of the Indian families were joint families. As a result of industrialization, most of these joint families are breaking up and are being replaced by nuclear families. There are a number of reasons for this. Firstly, in industrial towns there is acute shortage of residential accommodation. Most of the people have to content themselves with a single- or two-room accommodation. In these circumstances it is physically exceedingly difficult if not impossible to retain the joint family system. Secondly, as a sequel to industrialization, family trades and profession have been eliminated. The sons of the same parents differ widely in respect of economic and social levels. This has given rise to individualism. As a result of all these conditions, joint family is all but finished in industrial towns.

(3) Small families. As a result of industrialization, the cost of living has gone up. At the same time standard of living has also gone up considerably. Everybody wants good clothes, houses and other comforts of life. Obviously, it is not possible to maintain the standard with a big family. Therefore, people these days want to keep small families. The prevalence of contraceptives and abortion has made this goal easily attainable. Thus we find that there is a strong trend towards small families in industrialized towns.

(4) Change in the status of women. In past the status enjoyed by women in Indian society was rather low. Women were shut up in the four walls of the home. From economic and social points of view, woman was subject to man. The woman enjoyed no independence. Without husband the condition of a woman was miserable. As a result of industrialization there has been much improvement in the status of women. Along with men, women today work in all walks of life. They are therefore becoming independent economically. Their status and respect in society have therefore improved considerably. Nowadays women consider themselves equal, even superior, to men. As a result of this feeling, many women today do not like to marry. They wish to assert their independence by defying the laws of the society.

(5) Disintegration of family. As a result of industrialization, the outlook of intense individualism has grown. Everyone wants to have his own way; no one likes to be subject to anybody. Nobody these days appreciates the need for adjustment and give and take. Thus we find in modern society families cracking up under least strain. There is continuous tension and conflict in the minds of family members. As a consequence of this situation, it is small wonder that families are breaking up fast in urban society.

(6) Difference in family goals. The goals and ideals which nourished the traditional Indian family were spiritual and religious. The housewife used to regard her husband as a god or divine being. They willingly subjected themselves to each and every whim of their husbands. Even children used to give unqualified respect to their parents. The father was regarded to be the head of the family and his command was rarely defied. In Indian homes Ram and Sita were ideals of paternal devotion and wife's dedication to husband respectively. In industrial society there is no room for such ideals. For a modern wife, the husband can be at best an honourable colleague and, under no circumstances, a god. The status of father in a family is being lowered as a result of industrialization. Compared to parents, children now have more say in the family affairs. In the past, the functions which were regarded sacred duty and ideals are now considered acceptable only from utilitarian point of view. The father no longer holds sway over family members.

Impact of Industrialization upon Social Stratification

From times immemorial human society has been riddled with inequalities and discriminations. From the very beginning of civilization we find some or other form of hierarchy in society. The society has always been divided into various classes having different rights and privileges and each enjoying a unique distinction and status in society. The classification and stratification in society have always been governed by some definite principles. As a matter of fact, neither all persons in a society are equal nor are the various functions in the society of equal value. Therefore, in order to maintain some system and order in society, it is necessary to establish a hierarchy of functions in society. In different societies the principle behind the hierarchical arrangement of functions is different. In some societies the distinction between classes is based on the relationship of master and slave while in others it is based upon the ideas of high, low and middle classes. Still in some other societies the governing principle of this distinction is caste system. In the modern industrial society, the classification and stratification of society are based upon the concept of economic classes. The society today is divided into the classes of capitalists and labour.

As referred to above, the basis of distinction between classes in society is different in different countries and at different times.

This basis is sometimes biologic, sometimes historic and sometimes religious. As a matter of fact, in the stratification of any society, are reflected its values and ideals. In a religious society the gurus and godmen enjoy a place of pride. In a martial society warriors and conquerors occupy top positions. On the other hand, in a capitalist society, the wealthy persons are on top. In some industrialized societies like Japanese, the technocrats occupy privileged positions. Thus, it is apparent that in different societies, the basis of distinction among classes is different.

Basis of Stratification in Industrial Societies

In industrial societies there is a unique kind of social stratification. In industrial society the different strata of society are known as social classes. The basis of stratification in an industrial society is different from that of other societies. Generally social stratification in an industrial society occurs on the following fourfold bases :

(1) Occupation (2) Education
(3) Income (4) Birth

Now we shall study these in a little detail :

(1) Occupation. In industrial societies the main basis of social stratification is occupation. In these societies the status and prestige of an individual are determined by the position and rank he occupies, the nature of his profession and his rank and status in that profession. What is meant is that rank and status are of crucial importance in industrial society. Indeed in an industrial society, rank and occupation are indicative of one's ability. The rank and status and occupation are not hereditary in industrial society; one has to strive and struggle for these. In a society where caste system is prevalent, the occupations and professions are hereditary. The son of a Brahmin does the job of a Brahmin and enjoys the same status and respect in society as were being enjoyed by his father. The son of a Brahmin becomes automatically entitled to respect and status of his father. On the contrary, in an industrial society, the son of a manager cannot claim the post of manager after the retirement of his father. He must possess all the necessary qualifications for it, that is, he must earn the managership. In order to gain status in an industrial society one has to strive hard. In an industrial society, there is no value for heredity but one has to strive for status.

(2) Education. In an industrial society education is an important determinant of the status of a person. The better educated are regarded more highly than the less educated. Of course, in every society, the poets, writers and learned have got top rank and status. However in industrial society there is some difference in this regard from other societies. The industry has closer relation to science and technology than formal learning. This is why a person who is highly learned is not regarded so well as a person who is proficient in science and technology. In an industrial society it is not literary learning but the scientific learning that commands respect. As a consequence of industrialization the importance and value of subjects like philosophy and literature have gone down. The formal learning has been replaced by utilitarian subjects. The predominant outlook in education today is pragmatic. Naturally training in science and technology is conducive of industrial advance. It is applied science that is responsible for industrialization. On account of the utilitarian nature of science and technology, the scientists and technologists enjoy places of prestige in industrial society.

(3) Income. Nowadays in industrial societies, the measuring rod of one's social status is one's income; the higher one's income, the higher one's social status. In materialistic societies, one's material possessions are indeed the exclusive determiner of one's worth in the society. The rich are worshipped and poor are hated. According to the materialistic outlook, the possession of material comforts and luxuries is the paramount aim of life and the more are one's material possessions nearer is one to the *summum bonum* of life. For acquisition of material comforts, money is needed. Therefore a person's income or salary determine his status in the society.

There is another reason also for regarding money and wealth as criterion of social status. In the industrial societies, the various types of qualifications are needed for earning money; without these qualifications it is not possible to earn wealth. A man must be laborious and hard-working in order to earn lots of money. It is natural in that background that one's wealth should be regarded as a measure of one's abilities and qualifications. It is but natural to accord high status to a man of ability. Thus, from both points of view, money and income are the determiner of one's social status.

(4) Birth. In the determination of social status, one's birth and pedigree have always been kept in view. In different societies the family into which one is born has been regarded important in various ways. In the caste-based societies, the son of Brahmin was accorded the status of Brahmin without the slightest consideration of his actual merit. In feudal societies, the family had great importance in determining one's social status. In industrial society, too, the family has unique importance in determining the social status of a person. However, the reasons for the importance of family in social stratification in industrial society are not the same as in caste-based or feudal society. In an industrial society it is recognized that in order to develop or flower one's talents, the family plays an important role. A successful manager and technocrat needs especial opportunities of training, etc.; only those families which can provide such facilities produce successful persons in industrial societies. A man born in a high class family naturally gets more opportunities of development than a person who is less fortunate in this respect. In socialisation the family plays an important role. Thus from the above discussion, the role of family becomes apparent.

IMPACT ON CASTE SYSTEM

In Indian society the caste system has had a unique role and importance. The social status of a person was determined by his caste. The industrialization has diminished the role of caste. Following are the salient features of the impact of industrialization upon Indian caste system :

(1) Disintegration of caste system. The industrialization in India has led to breakdown of caste system; under the impact of industrialization the traditional caste-based structure of society is collapsing. Traditionally, the social status of a person in Indian society was determined by the caste into which he was born. As a result of industrialization, the caste-based criterion of social classification has changed. In the industrial society it is the class and not the caste which fixes the social status of a person. Now the society is split into classes. Man gets social status according to his class. Thus the caste system is now disintegrating.

(2) Reduction in brahmins' influence and power. In the traditional social structure the Brahmins enjoyed the highest status in the society. But as a result of industrialization, the influence of Brahmins is on wane; it is gradually losing its traditional hold on Indian society. Now there are other criteria of social stratification. It is no longer necessary that one should be a Brahmin in order to attain high social status. As a matter of fact, the traditional role of Brahmins in society is all but finished. Those who are unable to adapt themselves according to the changed circumstances have a parasitic existence in modern industrialized society. That is why a Brahmin today is looked down upon.

(3) Rise of shudra. In the traditional Indian society, a shudra enjoyed the most inferior status in society. Indeed, his plight was miserable and he was treated no better than a slave. The shudras were subjected to all kinds of calumny and obliquity. They enjoyed little respect in society. As a result of industrialization there is some improvement in the condition of shudra. In the industrial society the criterion of social status is works and not birth. Anyone proficient in industrial know-how is bound to get a place of pride in society irrespective of the fact that he is a Brahmin or a shudra. Today a number of persons born into shudra family are occupying high-ranking positions in society.

(4) Abolition of caste-based functions. In the traditional caste-based society each caste had some functions. Generally the entertainment was also caste-based. The Brahmin had the role of teacher, the Kshatriya that of warrior. Now all this has changed. It is no longer obligatory upon a shudra to do menial jobs for upper castes. Due to these changes the traditional functions of the castes stand abolished.

(5) Division of labour : Non-Proficiency-oriented. Under the caste system the division of labour was based upon caste and upon the consideration of efficiency. A Brahmin was to perform the function of learned even if he was poor in learning. Under the influence of industrialization, the criterion of division of labour has changed. The industrialization has encouraged specialization. Nowadays a person is not given a task unless he is specially trained for it. In every department of society a specialized training is needed for the successful performance of a job. The shudras are today doing teaching jobs. On the other hand, Brahmins can be seen to be doing the menial jobs. A proficient shudra can now easily attain the position of an industrial manager and a number of Brahmins may be working under him.

(6) End of control of castes. In traditional society the caste system was an effective instrument of social control. Each caste had its own code of conduct which was strictly adhered to, any violation thereof attracting strong social reprobation. The violation of caste-based code of conduct used to result in excommunication. In modern industrial society the control of caste has become loose and lax. The industrial society is highly intricate and complex. Nowadays persons of all castes work together and it is, therefore, well-nigh impossible to observe the separate caste-based codes of conduct. In modern industrial societies the instruments of effective social controls are provided by law and law enforcing agencies.

(7) Hold of untouchability loosening. Under the caste system there used to be no inter-caste social mixing. The persons belonging to different castes did not get together and share a common board. As far as shudra was concerned, he could not even sit, stand or walk near the persons of upper castes. A shadow of shudra was scrupulously avoided. On the other hand, there are cases where shudras themselves did not welcome the opportunity of being in the company of Brahmins. They forbade Brahmins from entering their quarters. As a result of industrialization, the spectre of untouchability is relaxing its grip upon the thought and imagination of people. Today members of all castes work together in mills and factories and eat foodstuff from the same canteens and tuck-shops. Many a waiter in restaurants are shudra. Even Brahmins willingly partake of food prepared and served by these people. Besides in parks and public places there are no restrictions on the entry of shudra. Thus, industrialization can be said to have come as a boon for the low castes.

(8) Prevalence of inter-caste marriages. Under the caste system, the inter-caste marriages were a strict taboo. Hardly anyone dared to defy this taboo and marry with a spouse of any other caste except one's own. The punishment for such marriages was nothing less than complete excommunication. In modern societies these taboos are giving way. Though inter-caste marriages are not very common, people do marry into other castes without much disapproval. In mills and factories persons belonging to different castes come together, develop common interests and form friendships. Some of these contacts bloom and flower into mutual love and attraction. The mutual attraction breaks the caste barriers and such persons marry. There is another reason for prevalence of inter-caste marriages. Due to frequent encounters with members of other communities, one comes to realize the fundamental oneness of all human beings. One begins to appreciate that stereo-typed thinking with regard to other castes is not valid. Thus, the factors like caste pride and hatred for other castes which help accentuate caste barriers become inoperative. Consequently there emerges a rational outlook. The factor of mutual regard and love comes to be considered as the only relevant consideration in regard to marriage.

IMPACT ON RELIGION

Some persons are of the view that religion prospers and flourishes only in ignorance. Even if this view is not altogether true, it does contain an element of truth. It is true that religion prospers most in societies where ignorance is rampant. On the contrary as the areas of science and knowledge spread, the hold of religion weakens. Generally science and religion are considered to be mutually opposed. In the absence of scientific explanation, small and insignificant things and events become pillars of religious faith and dogma. When the scientific explanation of any thing is wanting, it is replaced by dogmatic explanation. In pre-scientific days the phenomenon of rain, storm, etc., was linked with the religious phenomenon and it was imagined that there are gods of rain, thunder, etc. Thus, it is quite evident that the extension of scientific knowledge proves detrimental to religion. Industrialization is intimately related to science and technology and with the growth of industrialization there is spread of science and technology. The widespread use of science and technology engenders a scientific outlook. The scientific outlook is quite opposed to religious and dogmatic outlook. Therefore it is pretty clear that the growth of industrialization proves detrimental to religion. In Indian society religion and morals are intimately linked. The moral principles are grounded in religious faith and belief. Morality is based upon religion. This is the reason why with the decline in religion there is change in moral principles as well. The following discussion will make clear how industrialization has influenced our religious and moral thinking.

Industrialization has deeply influenced the course of religion. Following are some of the important features of influence :

1. Decline of orthodoxy and superstitions. Under the garb of religion, orthodoxy and superstitions flourish. As a matter of fact the whole edifice of religion is built out of bricks of superstition and blind faith. Superstitions are due to ignorance. In practical life, belief in superstitions and orthodoxy proves harmful. For material and industrial progress it is very essential that men should be free from the clutches of superstitions. They must have rational and scientific outlook. The process of industrialization helps the spread and dissemination of science and practical knowledge. As a result of industrialization people learn the truth of physical reality. They begin to appreciate and value the practical results and are prepared to give up irrational beliefs. The knowledge disseminated and spread on account of industrialization subverts religious orthodoxy.

2. Development of religious tolerance. As a result of industrialization, the outlook of general masses in respect of religion has become broad. Generally orthodox religious persons are of narrow and parochial outlook. On account of their parochial outlook, they regard their own religion as supreme and infallible. Their attitude towards other religions is that of contempt. As a consequence of industrialization, the persons of different faiths come together and get an opportunity of knowing and understanding the truth about each other. This results in dispelling of wrong notions about other faiths and an appreciation of basic unity of all faiths. Therefore as a result of industrialization, there is development of religious tolerance.

3. Founding of secular states. Previously the states used to be theocratic; each state subscribed to some or other faith. Each nation had a national religion. The citizens professing faiths different from that of the state did not enjoy full rights and privileges; they were treated as second-rate citizens. But as a result of industrialization, the concept of theocratic states has become obsolete. Due to industrialization every state now has a sizeable number of minorities whose claims cannot be ignored. Therefore, nowadays it is a practice for almost all states not to consider any religion as special or state religion. The states today subscribe to the ideology of secularism, according to which state is neutral in matters of religion but accords equal status to all religions. This is secularism.

4. Social aspect of religion. Religion and religious functions have dual aspect. The first is its spiritual aspect and the second is its social aspect. In an industrial society, the spiritual aspect of religion is not very important. Its social aspect, however, is quite important in industrial societies. Nowadays, festivals are celebrated not so much as religious affairs but as social functions. Even going on pilgrimage to-day is more of a social necessity than a spiritual need. A visit to temple or mosque even has come to assume social overtones.

IMPACT ON MORALS

Following are the ways in which industrialization has influenced morals :

1. Development of rational outlook. The Indian society has been traditionally based upon morality and religion. In India there has been little critical thinking in regard to moral principles and beliefs. The moral principles were accepted as universal truths beyond the sphere of doubt and reason. As a result of industrialization, the outlook of common man has changed. Now people demand rational justification as to why a particular action is considered right or wrong. In industrial societies it is believed that the moral principles are man-made and that morality is for the sake of human life and society and not vice versa. The tendency to examine and evaluate every moral principle before acquiescing to it is graining around in modern society.

2. Development of materialist outlook. On account of industrialization, the importance and value of physical progress and development have enhanced. An average citizen of to-day does not appear to be satisfied and contented. The maximum material acquisition seems to have become the aim of modern life. It is for this reason that common man of today is averse to religion and spirituality. Today there is a strong competition for acquiring as much wealth as possible.

3. Individualism. The industrial societies are increasingly becoming complex and in all spheres of life there is reign of specialisation. Due to industrialization, large metropolises are coming up. In large communities there is decline in fellow-feeling. In such societies therefore the community feeling or the feeling of mutual belongingness is rather missing. Life becomes rapid and mechanical and people have little opportunity to look after the welfare of others. Life in industrial societies becomes self-centred. As a result of this, there is growth and development of individualism in these societies.

4. Permissiveness in sex morals. As a result of industrialization, the sexual mores have become lax. There are numerous reasons for this laxity. Firstly, the opportunities for the mixing-up of sexes have increased. Nowadays boys and girls can meet without much difficulty and social opposition. In mills, factories and offices, men and women work together. As a result of this frequent encounter of sexes there is laxity in sexual morals. Moreover, industrialization has given rise to materialistic thinking and according to the materialist outlook of life, the traditional taboos on sex are harmful and that free sex is consistent with healthy and sane life. This is why that today premarital sex is not considered to be criminal or immoral. Indeed sex without marriage is coming to be considered quite normal, healthy and moral. In Western society all taboos on sex have broken down. A new highly permissive sex morality is the order of the day.

5. Increase in Crimes. As a result of industrialization, there is an all-round rise in the incidence of crime. It is a common observation that the rate of crime is very high in industrial towns. In large metropolises family life is subject to many pressures. It is very difficult to have normal family life in those towns. On account of disintegration of family life, the control of family over individuals is becoming lax. Due to absence of this control, there is encouragement of crime. In every industrial town, prostitution and liquor consumption are rampant. Besides theft and dacoity also are commonplace in industrial towns. The incidence of violence and murder is also high in industrial towns.

6. Loosening of social control. In industrial towns labourers and artisans from places far and wide come in search of jobs. Having found jobs, they settle in these towns. In industrial towns like Delhi, Kanpur, Bombay, Calcutta, etc. workers from all over India are settled. As most of these workers are outsiders, they are not subject to usual social controls. Moreover, caste and clan considerations are almost non-existent in big metropolises. On account of all these factors, the social control becomes loose and lax. In industrial towns it is neither the family nor caste and clan nor society in general that exercises social control. It is exercised by law and law enforcing agencies like police, courts, etc.

IMPACT ON ENTERTAINMENT

The entertainment and relaxation are essential to life. Relaxation is indispensable for the health of everyone. The means of relaxation and entertainment keep changing with time and circumstances. There is a big difference between the means of entertainment in pre-industrial and post-industrial societies. In India there has been significant change in means of entertainment as a result of industrialization. Following are the important influences upon entertainment due to industrialization :

1. Entertainment outside family. Traditionally, in India family was the centre of entertainment. All entertainment was focussed upon family. Generally all families used to be joint and therefore were very large. A single family used to have about a dozen adult members and a dozen children. On account of large families it was possible to find all kinds of entertainment within the family itself. The adult male members used to beguile themselves by playing cards or chess and females used to gossip, swing or sing. As there were very many children in every family, the entertainment of children was easy. In the modern industrial societies, the situation is just the opposite of the old state of affairs. The families today are not joint. The size of families has shrunken. A family today consists of husband and wife and their two or three children. Besides, in many families both husband and wife are employed. Under these circumstances there is no scope of entertainment within the family. Today almost everyone goes out for entertainment. The entertainment today has become institutionalized.

2. Professional entertainment. In industrial societies the entertainment has become a business and a profession. Today there are a number of institutions of entertainment. The cinemas, clubs, dance and gambling dens are all centres of entertainment. We buy entertainment today. Throw money and have fun is the situation today.

3. Artificial entertainment. Due to industrialization entertainment has become a business and profession. A professional entertainment however lacks the true spirit of entertainment. It is artificial and usually debases the man instead of relaxing him.

Besides, entertainment in industrial societies is not only artificial but is base and low also. Today classical music and dance are little appreciated. Moreover these days entertainment by liquor and drugs is becoming common. In bigger towns prostitution is also a big source of entertainment. From all this it is apparent that the standard of entertainment has fallen steeply as a result of industrialization.

QUESTIONS FOR EXERCISE

1. Explain impact of industrialization on human behaviour.
2. Write short note on Impact of industrialization on entertainment.

2
INDUSTRIAL PSYCHOLOGY

WHAT IS INDUSTRIAL PSYCHOLOGY?

Industrial psychology, as the name indicates, is that branch of psychology which studies human behaviour under industrial circumstances. Psychology is a normative science of behaviour which can be observed in the social, economic, educational and other spheres. In the modern period, the different branches of psychology have developed during the study of human behaviour in these various fields. Educational psychology has been developed to study human behaviour in a social environment. This is an age of industrial progress, in which each progressive nation is expanding the scope of its industries. But industries cannot be made to function without human beings, because individuals are required in the capacity of managers, administrators, programmers, etc. And, wherever there are human beings, their behaviour will be influenced by their relationship. If, in the industrial field, human relations deteriorate, then the result is strikes and lockouts which have a widespread impact upon the economy of the nation. Since the future of every nation depends upon its industrial development and progress, this particular field of human behaviour becomes extremely important. It is the aim of industrial psychology to study the principles governing behaviour in the industrial field and to undertake research.

A Branch of Practical Psychology

Psychology is not merely a theoretical science for it not only enunciates general laws concerning human behaviour but also tries to improve human life by applying these principles. Like any other science, therefore, psychology also has two aspects — the theoretical and the practical. Industrial psychology is naturally a branch of practical psychology because it is fundamentally a study evolved for the improvement of human relations in the industrial sphere. The knowledge provided by it is used to solve the problems of people who work in industry, as well as to solve those non-human problems which emerge from time to time in industries. Nowadays psychologists are appointed to study the problems which arise in the field of industrial psychology. A glance at the history of industrial psychology will show us that universities have been responsible for the research concerned with it, but even more important research has been carried on in big industries under actual conditions. It is, therefore, more appropriate to consider industrial psychology as a branch of practical psychology. It is the application of psychological facts and principles to the problems concerning human relations in business and industry. Psychological facts and principles are used in human relations in the field of business and industry and this constitutes industrial psychology. Industrial psychology provides practical solutions to the problems that arise in the industrial society and its economic organisation. The industrial psychologist makes a study of the behaviour of people working under conditions of business and industry. The subject matter of the industrial psychologist is always the human being, because it is the human being who is the object of a psychological study. Even in a business or industrial environment, this continues to be true. Just as social psychology studies the human being under social circumstances, industrial psychology studies the individual in a business environment. Whereas it has been called the study of conduct, but it would be better to substitute the word 'behaviour' for this term because conduct is more properly the concern of ethics, not of psychology.

Briefly, then, in defining industrial psychology, it can be said that it is that branch of psychology which studies human behaviour under business and industrial conditions, and in which research is carried on concerning the behavioural problems that arise in an industrial environment. It should be clearly kept in mind that the study of behaviour covers both external behaviour and inner feelings.

HISTORY OF DEVELOPMENT

The development of psychology as a science began particularly in the nineteenth century but by the twentieth century its scope had been extended so much that independent branches of it emerged soon after. Psychological studies in the sphere of industry became important enough to be constituted as an independent branch called industrial psychology. Hence the development of industrial psychology should be said to begin in the twentieth century.

Even before the twentieth century, certain researches were carried out, which could be useful to industrial psychology. For example, during the sixteenth, seventeenth and eighteenth centuries, much important research was carried out on dynamics, the most noticeable being the work of Galileo, Borelli, Columb and Marey. In France in the nineteenth century, Mary and Mosso carried out research on muscular work and the problem of fatigue. In the beginning of the twentieth century, Ioteyko and Imbert did much research work on important methods in industrial psychology. Kraepelin did important work on the work curve, the training and selection of employees. Lahy located many important psychophysical factors which influenced the development of skill in typewriting.

Apart from these above researches, Lahy, Book,[1] Imbert and Scott[2] published valuable works on different aspects of industrial psychology.

Contribution of Munsterberg

Yet, the most important contribution to industrial psychology was the research work of Hugo Munsterberg, a German psychologist. He was the director of the psychological laboratory at Harvard University, from where he retired. Munsterberg was particularly interested in the study of individual differences. He established a correlation between individual differences and psychological tests. In his book *On the Witness Stand,* Munsterberg explained the role of psychological principles in finding out the causes of crime. In another book *Psychology and the Teacher,* Munsterberg elucidated the value of applying psychological principles to teaching. In 1910-11 he described some psychological discoveries in the field of industry. He had already started his work on industrial psychology when he was a lecturer in Berlin. In 1912 he published a book on this subject in German, which was later published in America in 1913 under the title *Psychology and Industrial Efficiency.* In 1914 Munsterberg published another book in German on the subject of the psychology of technical personnel.

In the sphere of industrial psychology, Munsterberg worked upon the possibility of improving adjustment and efficiency. He showed the great benefit of utilizing psychology in this field. He pointed out that psychology can help in three ways. In the first place, psychology can help in the selection of the best qualified individual for a particular job. In the second place, the psychologist

1. Book, W.F., *The Psychology of Skill,* University of Montanna.
2. Scott, W.D., *Influencing Men in Business,* New York.

can help in the creation of such psychological conditions in industry under which every employee can be encouraged to produce as much as he can. Thirdly, in industry the psychologist can give useful suggestions by which those employees who can make useful contributions to the work can be given special training. On the basis of these researches, Munsterberg gave many valuable suggestions about the use of psychology in the sphere of industry. He suggested that psychological tests should be employed in the recruitment of employees. He also showed that the process of learning can be speeded up by industrial training. He pointed out the importance of the conditions of work, the morale of the employees and the conditions of fatigue. Munsterberg's suggestions were not mere verbal jugglery because he demonstrated the value of recruiting motormen, telephone operators and naval officers by psychological tests. He thus made it clear that there is much advantage to be gained by using psychological principles and theories in the sphere of industry.

At the same time, great importance was attached to Taylor's plan for scientific organisation in the field of industrial organisation and administration. Munsterberg related his own theories with Taylor's plan and stressed the fact that in industries, manpower should be properly utilised for industrial and economic progress. He demonstrated that both industrialists and workers stand to benefit by the application of psychological theories to industry. By using psychological research it is possible to cut down the time consumed in industrial work, to increase the work done by labourers, to improve the standard of living of all concerned. Briefly, Munsterberg made it clear that the economic, cultural and social level of a country can be raised by using psychological principles in the sphere of industry because it becomes possible to provide every person with the kind of work in which he can take interest and do well. Munsterberg's books influenced much of the thinking in the industrial sector, and in the more advanced countries his ideas were soon put into practice. Not only in Germany but in all Europe and America there was almost a flood of research in the industrial sphere. For these reasons Munsterberg is believed to be the father of industrial psychology.

The First World War played an important role in emphasizing the work of Munsterberg because with the beginning of war it became necessary to make extensive use of psychological testing. Within a short period of the publication of Munsterberg's work, the war started leading to a very large scale recruitment of soldiers. Countries in which Munsterberg's thinking had an influence quickly realised that by using psychological testing techniques, it would be possible to find the fittest individuals for the different branches of the armed forces. In England the psychologists were called in to help in the selection of army, navy and air force personnel. These psychologists devised techniques of testing adaptability of individuals for the armed forces. In Germany and France psychologists like Anderson,[3] Moede, Benary and Gamelli propagated the importance of psychological testing through the medium of their books. Later, psychological testing was adapted to the selection of people for different professions, and this helped the industry enormously.

Development of Industrial Psychology in America

In 1917 U.S.A. also entered the arena of war, and established a society for the purpose of administering psychological tests for people joining the armed forces. These tests were used on a very large scale in the recruitment to the armed forces. As a result, research in industrial psychology was encouraged and the literature connected with it started growing rapidly. Between 1916 and 1918 H.L. Hollingworth, A.T. Poffenberger and A.W. Kornhauser did valuable research work in industrial psychology. All of them were teachers in universities. In addition to their work, considerable research work was done by other people who were directly connected with industry. In 1919 H.C. Link wrote a book *Employment Psychology* on the psychology of employees. It included information on professional training, the prevention of accidents, analysis of work methods and means of removing indifference to work, and other industrial problems. The following are the more important works published during this period :

1. Hollingworth, H.L., *Vocational Psychology,* 1916.
2. Hollingworth and Poffenberger, *Applied Psychology,* 1917.
3. Kornhauser, A.W., and F.A. Kingsbury, *Psychological Tests in Business,* 1924.
4. Kitson, H.D., *The Psychology of Vocational Adjustment,* 1925.
5. Laird, D.A., *The Psychology of Selecting Men,* 1927.

---

3. Anderson, H.G., *The Selection of Candidates for the Air Service, Reports of the British Medical Society.*

6. Bingham, W.V., and M. Freyd, *Procedures in Employment Psychology,* 1926.
7. Moore, B.V., and G.W. Hartmann, *Readings in Industrial Psychology,* 1931.

In 1922 W.V. Bingham started the publication of *Journal of Personnel Research,* connected with the working class. He also published an important book on the psychological analysis of the various aspects of accidents, entitled *Personality and Public Accidents.*

In addition to the research work and the published work of different scientists, the American interest in industrial psychology went on to the establishment of many industrial associations which further encouraged research in the field of industry. In 1916 an association called the Bureau of Salesmanship Research was established to carry out research on the problems of distribution of goods. The year 1917 saw the establishment of a Research Bureau for Retail Training to study and analyse training in selling. The Psychological Corporation was established in 1921. In 1922 Bingham headed an association called the Personnel Research Corporation, which was later assisted by the National Research Council, the Engineering Foundation and the American Federation of London. From this brief account of the development of industrial psychology in America, it is clear that the Americans have made a very extensive and valuable contribution to its development.

Development of Industrial Psychology in Germany

Much has already been said about the contribution of Munsterberg to the development of industrial psychology. He was a German scientist who did his work in America, but many other German scientists also made valuable contributions to industrial psychology. In 1961 W. Moede and Miorkowski conducted research on the use of psychological principles in the selection of motor drivers. Taking inspiration from their work, almost fourteen research centres were opened in Germany in the same year. Next year the Saxon Railway Company established a research centre in Dresden to conduct research on the use of psychological principles for the selection of locomotive engineers and other employees. The General Electric Company used psychological tests in the selection of individuals for mechanical work. The Greater Berlin Tramways Company established a research centre in Dresden to conduct research on the use of psychological principles for the selection of locomotive engineers and other employees. After the war Germany went through a period of industrial reorganisation, during which many psychological laboratories were also established to help in the work of most industrial complexes. By 1922 some twenty-two industrial complexes had their own psychological laboratories, and within four years the number went up to 100. The universities also helped in researches in industrial psychology. As a result Germany produced much valuable literature on the subject of Industrial psychology, both in the form of books and journals.

Development of Industrial Psychology in England

Most of the important work in industrial psychology in England was done by two institutions, a brief description of which is given here :

1. **Industrial Health Research Board.** The institution was established to find out means of increasing production, improving the efficiency of the workers, and overcoming fatigue, etc. In 1918 it was called the Industrial Fatigue Research Board, but it was later given its present name. The English scientific and industrial research department and the Medical Research Council provided valuable assistance to the development of this institution, while the government accorded it recognition. It conducted important and beneficial research on the psychological aspects of the health of workers, hours of work and physical conditions, wages, promotion and transfer, etc.

2. **National Institute of Industrial Psychology.** This was established in 1921 with the help of industrial organisations. Its director was C.S. Myers, also the director of the psychological laboratory at Cambridge University. As a result this organisation got the assistance of industrial houses as well as universities and succeeded in doing considerable work in different spheres of industrial psychology.

Development of Industrial Psychology in Russia

Communist Russia, too, did not lag behind the other advanced nations in the development of industrial psychology because the Russian government paid great attention to all the developments in the field of industry. In 1920 Central Institute of Labour was established in Moscow under the direction of Gesteve. While in 1907 there were 60 research centres looking into the various problems of industry, their number rose to 100 within four years in Moscow alone. All of them were aligned to the central institute mentioned above. The chief objective of the institute was to carry out research on the use of tools and machines, the use of file, etc. Hence it did extensive studies in the defects and advantages of all kinds of machines and machine tools. In addition, it also did much work on the working conditions for the employees and on work methods. This institute employed the Taylor system for scientific organisation. In 1922 a laboratory for industrial psychology was established to conduct research on problems of workers. Even the Neurological Institute of Moscow University was conducting research into these problems to keep step with the progress of communism in all other spheres. Russia laid stress on research in ways of improving human relations in the industrial field because under the communist system, the differences between employer and employee were eliminated.

Development in other European Countries

Most of the other European countries also fell in step with the leaders and encouraged research in industrial psychology. Many institutes for this work were established in Holland, Belgium, Poland, Italy, Spain, Austria and other countries. The International Congress of Applied Psychology was established in Geneva, Switzerland. It conducted important research in vocational guidance and selection of personnel. At the same time, a research institute was established in Zurich, where research for training in industries and professions, in work method, etc., was done. In 1920, in these conferences, there was an exchange of opinion on the subjects of vocational guidance and the use of psychological principles in the field of industry. The third conference of this kind took place in Milan in 1922. In this conference, the interest centred on work analysis, the importance of psychology and physiology in the prevention of accidents, Taylor's plan, etc. In 1931 a conference was organised in Moscow in which different aspects of industrial progress and the economic progress of employees came under review.

It will be obvious from the above account that most of the European nations took a keen interest in research into various aspects of industrial psychology at the turn of this century, leading to the publication of numerous books and journals. At almost every place, universities, individual organisations, government and industrialists combined to work for the development of industrial psychology. On the other hand, the Asian countries developed interest in Industrial psychology at a much later stage. Japan is the sole exception because it went through a period of remarkable industrial progress which necessitated research in industrial psychology at about the same time as Europe. In 1921 Japan saw the establishment of an Institute of Industrial Efficiency.

Industrial Psychology in India

Interest was taken in industrial psychology in India only after Independence. Some research in industrial psychology began with the establishment of psychological laboratories in universities. Psychological research was then encouraged in industrial complexes because of the development of large scale industries and the increasing tempo of the labour welfare movement. Most of the big industries took the help of psychologists for the recruitment of personnel, but the most important and consistent work done was in the recruitment of armed forces personnel. Psychological testing by the psychologists became an essential part of recruitment to every branch of the armed forces. The government itself was responsible for the establishment of numerous psychological laboratories in which emphasis was laid on vocational guidance. At Allahabad, in Uttar Pradesh, considerable vocational guidance is provided to people after psychological testing at the State Bureau. There are approximately twenty-five school psychologists in various government schools whose task is to give vocational guidance along with other psychological help. Psychologists are consulted by big industrialists for their advertisement campaigns. The advice of the psychologists is sought by the industrialists not only in the recruitment of personnel but even in the sale of the goods produced by them. In this way, industrial psychology is steadily growing in this country but the progress here cannot be compared with the progress in Europe and America. In the last few years, many books on industrial psychology have been published in India, but they are textbooks, not concerned with any original research. No journal of industrial psychology is published in the country. Most of the university laboratories also conduct little, if any, research on industrial problems. And only in very few of the industrial organisations is the help of the psychologist sought. From this point of view, the country is far behind the Western nations but this backwardness is part of the lack of development in other spheres. Hence, there is hope of progress in this direction too. Most of the young educated industrialists are now trying to use psychological principles in such spheres as physical and psychological working conditions, the selection of employees, advertisement, sales, etc. Hence, there is reason to expect more development in industrial psychology in the near future.

INDUSTRIAL PSYCHOLOGY AND GENERAL PSYCHOLOGY

Psychology is a science of behaviour, the term behaviour being interpreted most liberally, for it comprehends not only both objective and subjective forms of human behaviour, but also the behaviour of the higher animals. Human behaviour includes man's behaviour under all kinds of conditions and circumstances, normal, abnormal, social, industrial, legal, in childhood, in adolescence, in old age. Psychology studies behaviour in all these conditions, but with reference to the environment and situations.

What is General Psychology?

Psychology is a positive science in which facts are studied. It tries to find out causal relations in behaviour by using the methodology of science. As a science, psychology finds out the principles of human behaviour and once it has established some causal relations, it makes predictions about behaviour. General psychology is the most extensive branch of psychology. Perhaps it is better called "Source" or "Ground" rather than a branch as aspect for it involves the study of all the general principles used in all its other branches. It studies all processes of human behaviour such as learning, thinking, memory, sensation, perception, emotion, feeling and personality. It also makes a study of the origins, the well-springs of human behaviour such as motivation, nervous system — the various levels of consciousness, etc. It even outlines the methodology of psychology. It differs from industrial psychology because its explanations are more concerned with the practical application of psychological principles.

Distinctions from General Psychology

From the above elucidation of general psychology, it is amply clear that industrial psychology differs from general psychology. The major differences are the following :

1. Difference of nature. As has been pointed out, industrial psychology is a branch of practical psychology while, on the other hand, general psychology is more theoretical.

2. Difference of scope. The scope of industrial psychology is more limited and, in, fact different. General psychology studies, in general, human behaviour under all kinds of situations. Industrial psychology, on the other hand, studies human behaviour only in industrial and business situations.

3. Different Points of view. The point of view of general psychology is more theoretical but that of industrial psychology is chiefly practical.

Relation with General Psychology

Despite the above-mentioned differences between the two, there is an intimate relationship between general and industrial psychology. In industrial psychology, the psychologist makes use of those principles in an industrial situation which he has learnt from general psychology. For example, the conclusions of general psychology about such psychological processes as learning, perception, attention, memory and association, etc., are utilized under industrial conditions in order to improve the skills concerned with these processes. The psychology of interest and attention is much used in the field of advertisement. In this manner, the industrial psychologist must have extensive knowledge of general psychology, although the opposite is not true. The general psychologist does not need knowledge of industrial psychology.

NATURE OF INDUSTRIAL PSYCHOLOGY

It is easier to understand the nature and scope of industrial psychology by analysing its definition. Industrial psychology is a science, hence its nature is scientific. It employs scientific techniques to study the social aspect of human behaviour. It is a science in the same way in which general psychology and sociology are sciences. Along with the study of individual behaviour, industrial psychology also makes a study of group dynamics. The aim of this study also is to find facts and establish causal relations between them, to derive universal laws based on these causal relations and then to apply these laws to concrete situations and solve problems of a social nature.

What is a Science?

In order to test the validity of the statement that industrial psychology is a science, it is necessary to find out what science is. Science is the study of a limited field. If a study is to be called scientific, then its scope must be limited and also systematic. Yet a study cannot be called science only if its subject matter possesses both these traits, for the study must also make use of the scientific method. In fact, science differs from the arts and philosophy on account of its method, and its peculiar nature depends more upon the method than upon the subject matter.

Characteristics of the Scientific Method

It is, therefore, necessary to understand the scientific method if we are to understand the nature of science. In the scientific method, the subject matter of a limited sphere is studied systematically. It needs the use of great patience, courage, hard work, creative imagination and objectivity. In the absence of this scientific attitude or scientific spirit, no person can derive the full benefit of using the scientific method. Before starting his work, a person conducting research should make a detailed analysis of the problem which he wants to study, because if the analysis is detailed enough, the study itself becomes more facile. The scientific method is constituted by the following steps :

1. Observation. The first step in the scientific method is a careful and detailed observation of the subject matter, often, by the use of apparatus. The apparatus itself must be accurate and dependable.

2. Recording. The second step in the scientific method is the careful and systematic recording of all the observed facts. Objectivity is a necessary element in recording.

3. Classification. Now the recorded information has to be classified and organised. This is an important and serious step. In Karl Pearson's words : "The classification of facts, the recognition of their sequence and relative significance is the function of science." Classification must be done in such a way that one can see some pattern and relationship between the scattered facts which have been observed. For this it is essential that the information is arranged on a logical and coherent basis.

4. Generalisation. The next important step in the scientific method is the derivation of general laws on the basis of patterns observed in the organised matter. This general law, which is arrived at, is called a scientific law.

5. Verification. Verification is the fifth stage because the scientific method does not conclude with the derivation of a universal law. It is necessary to test and verify the truth of this law. Validity is an essential condition of a scientific law, for without validity, the law cannot be called scientific.

Essential Elements of Science

We have now seen the elements that are necessary for any study to be classed as a science. Simply stated, a study must possess the following characteristics to be called scientific :

1. Scientific method. As has been pointed out above, a study is called scientific not because the subject matter is of a particular kind but because it makes use of the scientific method.

2. Factual. Science is the study of facts; it searches for facts. Its subject matter is constituted by facts, not ideals.

3. Universal. Scientific principles are universal for they are found to be true everywhere if their basic conditions are fulfilled.

4. Veridical. Scientific laws have a validity which can be put to test at any time. Whenever they are tested, they are proved correct.

5. Discovery of cause-effect relationship. Science aims at the discovery of cause and effect relations between the various facts of the subject. Having found the cause-effect relationship, it pronounces certain facts universal and valid laws.

6. Prediction. Science can make predictions about the future on the strength of the universal laws enunciated by it, because these laws are based on cause-and-effect relationships, between facts-relationships, which are always true. Science itself is based on faith in causality. The scientist believes that what will happen in the future can be determined on the basis of what is, because the law of causality is incontrovertible and universal.

Industrial Psychology is Scientific

We will find all the above elements in industrial psychology, and hence we can conclude that industrial psychology has a claim to be considered as scientific.

1. Industrial psychology uses the scientific method. All the methods of industrial psychology are scientific. It makes the greatest possible use of the experimental method. In the experimental method, the subject of study is placed in predetermined conditions and then studied. After careful observation, the industrial psychologist records all the facts observed, follows this up by a logical classification and the derivation of universal laws by generalization. It is these universal laws which make up the principles of industrial psychology. In this way, it is obvious that industrial psychology makes use of the scientific method. Although the other methods employed by industrial psychology are not as scientific as the experimental method, every effort has been made to invest them with a factual and scientific character, and much success has been achieved in this direction. Industrial psychologists may have many different opinions about the value and the utility of a particular method, but all of them agree that the method of study must be scientific.

2. Industrial psychology is factual. Industrial psychology makes a factual study of behaviour, its conclusions are objective and impartial. Its conclusions about behaviour are not normative. It describes behaviour and tries to find out laws which govern it. Hence it is concerned with facts, not value.

3. The Laws of industrial psychology are universal. The laws enunciated by industrial psychology produce the same results everywhere, under identical conditions. These rules prove to be the same at all times and places, irrespective of the differences in character of the persons involved. For example, the law that in industrial organisation, the conditions of work and wages will influence the quality and quantity of production, will prove to be true wherever it is tested.

4. The principles of industrial psychology are valid. Upon verification and even reverification, the principles of industrial psychology prove to be valid. Their validity can be tested by anyone and at any time. For example, the fact that there is always some dissatisfaction, repression or maladjustment at the root of all labour tensions can be tested anywhere.

5. Industrial psychology analyses cause-effect relationships. Industrial psychology discovers the laws of behaviour and explains the causal relations existing between them. In industries, the psychologist tries to discover the causal relations underlying human relationship, advertisement and development, etc. He can thus discover very useful facts and laws. In this way, industrial psychology aims at finding out not only the 'what' of behaviour but also its 'how'.

6. Industrial psychology can make predictions. Because industrial psychology can find out the causal relations that exist in human behaviour, it can make predictions about it, and these predictions also turn out to be true. For this reason, in all modern industrial nations, the predictions made by industrial psychologists are taken into account by the industrialists in solving industrial problems and disputes. These predictions have proved of much value.

It is clear from the above explanation that industrial psychology is an exact science, but one must not conclude from it that it is as exact as the physical sciences. In fact, it is a mistake to expect the same degree of precision and exactness from every science, because in every science the precision depends upon the nature of its subject matter. Obviously, a science which studies human behaviour in industrial conditions cannot be as exact as a science which studies physical things, because human behaviour is a complex, dynamic and changeable phenomenon. Hence, in calling industrial psychology an exact science, it is necessary to keep in mind its limitations, although these limitations cannot be fixed or determined with precision. And it is hoped that the precision of industrial psychology will improve with the development of more modern techniques of study.

INDUSTRIAL PSYCHOLOGY AND INDUSTRIAL SOCIOLOGY

Industrial psychology, as the name indicates, is that branch of psychology which studies human behaviour under industrial circumstances. Psychology is a normative science of behaviour which can be observed in the social, economic, educational and other spheres. In the modern period, the different branches of psychology have developed during the study of human behaviour in these various fields. This is an age of industrial progress, in which each progressive nation is expanding the scope of its industries. But industries cannot be made to function without human beings, because individuals are required in the capacity of managers, administrators, programmers, etc. And, wherever there are human beings, their behaviour will be influenced by their relationships. If, in the industrial field, human relations deteriorate, then the result is strikes and lockouts which have a widespread impact upon the economy of the nation. Since the future of every nation depends upon its industrial development and progress, this particular field of human behaviour becomes extremely important. It is the aim of industrial psychology to study the principles governing behaviour in the industrial field and to undertake research. According to M.L. Blum, "Industrial psychology is simply the application or extension of psychological facts and principles to the problems concerning human relations in business and industry."[4]

Industrial sociology also studies problems concerning human relations in business and industry though from the sociological point of view. This common subject matter naturally creates a close relationship between industrial sociology and industrial psychology. Even when working in an industry, the individual is never alone because he constantly comes into contact with other workers, supervisors, managers and industrialists. In business, the worker has to deal with all kinds of people. For this reason it also

4. Blum, M.L., *Industrial Psychology and Its Social Foundation*, Harper & Bros., New York, p. 3.

becomes necessary to study the social foundations of industrial psychology. Efforts are being made to bring industrial organisation to a scientific level. The more progressive countries try to improve the social life of the worker by organising various kinds of social programmes. The following points need to be considered in a study of the relationship of industrial sociology and industrial psychology :

1. Worker and social progress. The progress of the industrial workers is a part of the general social progress. Hence the movements for social progress were accompanied by movements for an improvement in the conditions of industrial workers. It was accepted as a general principle that the work of social emancipation would remain incomplete so long as nothing was done to improve the conditions of industrial workers. For this reason social workers turned their attention in this direction. Bills were passed in parliament to this effect. Social workers directed the attention of industrialists towards the bad condition of the workers and insisted that they should be given human rights and their conditions changed so that the workers could improve their standards of living. Exploitation of workers was violently objected to and decried. Great stress was laid on providing social security to the workers. Political parties also began to pay attention to the amelioration of the lot of workers. In this manner the progressive nations linked the improvement of the industrial worker with the movements for general progress. This humanistic attitude is spreading rapidly in industry in all modern nations.

2. Workers' department and welfare schemes. As a result of this humanistic approach, most modern nations have created workers' departments which undertake the task of safeguarding the rights of workers and working for their betterment. Labour welfare is now accepted as an important element in social welfare. Labour welfare includes the improvement in the social, economic and psychological conditions of the worker. In most large industries labour welfare officers are appointed to look after the workers and to help solve any disputes that may arise between them and the employers. The modern state is a welfare state the object of which is to enhance the welfare of the citizens in every sphere. The worker is an important part of the population and the government which does not undertake measures for labour welfare cannot hope to achieve its ideal of social welfare. After achieving Independence Indian Government, too, has begun to pay attention to the question of labour welfare. It has, from time to time, enacted laws to secure the rights of workers in various industries. Although even now many industrialists avoid the clutches of the law by various means, the pressure exerted by the trade unions is steadily changing the situation.

3. Industrial management. Today efforts are being made to raise industrial management to the level of a science. The suggestions of Taylor and Thurston have been particularly valuable in this respect. A scientific industrial management implies the establishment of a management under which all the elements of production are most efficiently employed, thus eliminating the exploitation of any one element and the exhaustive use of any other. In a scientific industrial management system, a humanistic approach is adopted to deal with the workers and efforts are made to provide them with more facilities. The advanced countries are continuously making rapid strides in this direction.

Thus, both industrial sociology and industrial psychology are applied sciences engaged in study and research in the field of industry and the areas connected with it. The similarity between the two, however, ends here. They undoubtedly study common material but from a different viewpoint. In the words of R.M. MacIver, "It is a difference of attitude in regard to a common material."[5]

SCOPE OF INDUSTRIAL PSYCHOLOGY

Pointing out the scope of industrial psychology,[6] Harrell has laid stress on the following things :

1. Industrial psychology is concerned with the physical aspect of the environment of work, for example, the effect of light and temperature on work and safety.

2. It is primarily a study of the principles and behaviour of human relationships.

3. It is a study of the causes that lead to indifference and disinterest and the motives and attitudes that influence zeal and high morale.

4. It is a study of the methods by which neurotic people can be brought back to a level of normal mental health.

---

5. MacIver, R.M., *Community : A Sociological Study*, Macmillan and Co. Ltd., London, p. 65.

6. Harrell, T.W., *Industrial Psychology*, p. 1.

5. It is a study of the factors that create cooperation between labourers and the management, a study of the relations between the supervisor and his subordinates and of industrial conflicts.

It is clear from the above exposition that industrial psychology studies, apart from the physical environment, the principles of human relationships, the factors which lead to and maintain mental health, and bases of high morale. Briefly, then, the scope of industrial psychology is the following :

1. **Economic, social and psychological aspects of industry.** Industrial psychology is concerned with human behaviour in the entire industrial environment. Consequently, it studies the economic, social and psychological aspects of human behaviour. In the modern age, most economic factors have some psychological influence. The various factors in the communal life of workers living in an industrial environment also influence the psychology of the worker. Industrial psychology studies this also.

2. **Study of the physical aspect of work's environment.** In an industry the worker is greatly influenced by the conditions under which he works. If the conditions are to his liking, the worker feels satisfied and remains healthy while on the other hand if the conditions are not good the number of accidents goes up and workers become dissatisfied. Working conditions include a number of factors such as clean air and water, arrangement for necessary rest, less noise, clean atmosphere, sufficient light, good relations between the worker and the management. In all these, guidance by the psychologist can prove of immense value. For example, it is better to consult the psychologist about the arrangement for lighting, about the quantity or intensity of the light and the angle from which it should come. Even the colour of the walls, floor and ceilings of the factory psychologically influence the worker. It has been seen in experiments that, if the colour scheme of the environment is good, there are fewer accidents and the atmosphere remains good. And it is for the psychologist to say what should be the colour of the machines, roofs, floors and ceilings. It can thus be said that industrial psychology studies the physical working conditions in industrial environment.

3. **Principles of human relationships.** Irrespective of the automation introduced in any industry, the human element cannot be eliminated. Even the biggest and the most efficient machine needs an engineer to run it, and because the engineer is a human being, the importance of the psychological element in the running

of the factory cannot be denied. The efficiency of the man will depend very much upon the nature of his relations with the management. In the last century most industrialists behaved like autocrats and considered the workers as nothing more than tools. But in that period the level of efficiency was never very high. It has been seen that an industrialist can achieve a higher rate of production if he behaves sympathetically with his employees. In the present age, the industrialist can no longer do as he wills, because of the existence of labour unions. An industrialist who cannot maintain good and cordial relations with his workers does not succeed for long. Being the science of behaviour, Industrial psychology tries to discover principles for improving human relationships in an industrial environment. At the root of most of the lockouts and strikes, two common forms of expressing discontent seen so frequently in most industries today, are distorted and injured human relationships. Industrial psychology helps to solve these problems.

4. Study of aptitudes and motives. As in any other circumstance, human behaviour in the industrial environment is influenced and formed by attitudes and motives. Behaviour changes with the change in stimuli. Hence it is necessary to study the rules pertaining to correct attitudes and motives. Industrial psychology pursues this kind of study. One example of a study of this kind is the study conducted by the Hawthorne Works Western Electric Company into the effect of the attitudes of workers upon production. This study is known as the Hawthorne Studies.

5. Study of principles of mental health. Today, all intelligent people realise the importance of maintaining the proper health of workers. The worker's mental health is profoundly influenced by the conditions under which he works and by the attitude of other people towards him. Industrial psychology studies the factors influencing the mental health of industrial workers and tries to discover principles for maintaining their mental health. Industrial psychology also gives suggestions for improving the mental health of those who are suffering from mental disease or are otherwise unbalanced.

6. Study of human relation. Industrial psychology is the study of human behaviour in an industrial context. As has been pointed out earlier, the physical conditions of work have a direct and strong influence upon human behaviour. The manner in which the supervisor or the manager behaves towards the worker has a direct influence upon the efficiency, attitudes and motives of the worker. Some employees try to spread maladjustment among industrial workers for purely personal reasons. Even this is a problem of human relations. Being a branch of psychology, industrial psychology is particularly concerned with the observation and study of human relations about which it reaches conclusions through experiment and other study. On the basis of these conclusions it tries to discover general principles which can help in improving social relations between the workers and the management.

Briefly, all Industrial situations are within the scope of industrial psychology because every one of them influences human behaviour. The scope of industrial psychology expands with expansion of the sphere of industrial activity.

Problems of Industrial Psychology

In his book *Industrial Psychology and its Social Foundations,* the psychologist Blum has stated, "Industrial psychology offers a dynamic solution to the perplexing problems which confront an industrial society and economic system."[7] What are these problems concerned with industry or profession? These are the problems psychological in nature that arise in any sphere of industry. Briefly, the problems of industrial psychology are as follows :

1. Selection of the right man for the right job. If success is to be achieved in any industry, it is essential that the right man should be found and appointed to the right job. This involves first an accurate work study and also the selection of the most qualified individual from among the applicants to suit that particular job. This is basically a problem for the psychologist because the selection involves many kinds of psychological tests to discover the various abilities of the individuals. It also happens sometimes that an individual working on a particular post cannot work efficiently for personal reasons, even though he is otherwise perfectly qualified to hold that post. In such a situation, the industrial psychologist is faced with the problem of giving suggestions which will once again render the individual fit for work.

2. Training of workers. Although different individuals have varying degrees of ability to perform different kinds of functions, training can be useful in improving these abilities to such an extent that the individual becomes capable of doing work which he could not have done without training. The kind and length of

---

7. Blum, M.L., *Industrial Psychology and its Social Foundations*, New York, p. 5.

training required to train a particular individual to bring him up to a certain level of efficiency can be determined by the psychologist. Hence, another problem for the industrial psychologist is the training of workers.

3. Morale in industry. Despite the best possible working conditions in an industry, the highest efficiency cannot be achieved unless the workers also have a high morale. Morale can be seen on one hand in the enthusiasm and zeal with which work is tackled and on the other hand in the mutual cooperation extended to others in group activities. How a proper morale can be maintained in an industry and what steps are necessary to create it, is a problem of psychology, and it is the industrial psychologist who solves it.

4. Human relations in industry. The problem of human relations in industry has assumed greater importance and complexity with the formation of trade unions, which have channelled the power of the workers into a single direction. Now, no industry can run successfully and smoothly for any length of time in the absence of good relations between the management and the workers' union. If the relations deteriorate, the level of production falls, accidents increase, and lockouts and strikes are the result. This problem of human relations is primarily the concern of social psychology and the person best equipped to solve it is the industrial psychologist.

5. Fatigue and boredom. In industry, as in any other sphere of human activity, individuals become tired and bored after a long spell of mechanical work. Their psychological fatigue increases with this. Fatigue is both physiological and psychological. Scientifically viewed, the work and the instruments used in an industry should be so designed and planned as to result in the least possible amount of fatigue and the highest possible quantity of work. Specialists of engineering psychology have designed various kinds of machines and tools with this objective in view. They have also given many suggestions about the improvement of methods of work. Industrial psychologists also have conducted many experiments on mental fatigue and boredom, and given many valuable suggestions on the basis of their results. It has been observed, for example, that if there is arrangement for music and light entertainment in certain kinds of mechanical work, the extent of fatigue and boredom is greatly reduced.

6. Industrial accidents. If we want a machine to function without any accident, two things are necessary. In the first place the machine itself should be in a good working order. In the second place, the worker manipulating it should be using it correctly, and his mental condition must be normal. For the first factor, engineering psychologists have given useful suggestions for keeping the machines functioning properly and without accidents. Regarding the second factor they have given some suggestions for the development of safety habits, proper maintenance and the maintenance of normal mental health. Hence, one important problem before industrial psychology is the prevention of accidents.

7. Responses towards physical environment. It has already been pointed out that the physical conditions existing in an industry, conditions such as the quantity, quality and direction of light, arrangement for fresh and clean air, proper ventilation, hygiene, level of noise, the amount of humidity in the air, etc., have an important influence upon the efficiency of the worker. In order to find out the kind of conditions that should exist in a particular industry, it is necessary to find out the workers' response to their environment. Clearly, it is the industrial psychologist who can find out and determine the quantity and quality of these physical conditions which are desirable.

8. Problems of production. Maximum production in any industry can only be achieved under certain circumstances. Even if the machines are the best, it is essential that the workers handling them must also be capable. How can this ability be tested? In every factory many machines are installed. How can one find the particular person best suited to operate each particular machine? And out of the many people who apply for a job in a factory how can one discover the few who may prove to be really capable? In order to achieve maximum production it is necessary that machines should be so designed as to induce the minimum fatigue and the lighting so arranged as to give the least possible strain to the workers. Besides, most people soon become bored with their work. How can their enthusiasm be reawakened? How should the factory work be designed so as to reduce the number of accidents? Psychology is needed to solve all these problems which beset every industry.

9. Problems of selling. The work of an industry does not end with the production of things, but carries on till the produced goods are sold. If one does not get success in selling the final produce, its quality and quantity matter less than nothing. And in order to sell things, it is necessary that people should be acquainted with the product, its qualities, and should develop the need to buy them. Advertisement serves this purpose, and successful advertisement is based on appeal. Hence, the value of psychology in the field of advertisement can hardly be disputed.

10. Prevention and solution of industrial conflicts. No industry is completely free from quarrels and conflicts of a minor or major kind. At times these conflicts get out of hand lead to strikes by the workers or lockouts by the management. There are extreme cases in which such conflicts lead to widespread arson, murder and wilful destruction of public and private property. Although some economic demands or political factors may be at the root of such industrial conflict, the most important factor influencing the actions of workers and management alike is the psychological element. That is why sometimes even great issues are overlooked so that no conflict occurs while relatively insignificant incidents like the impolite words of a manager to a worker may lead to strikes and violent conflicts. It is the psychological factor which results in strikes and conflicts becoming extremely violent. If, then, such conflicts are to be resolved, the mere satisfaction of economic demands is not enough. It is necessary also to remove those factors which, from the psychological standpoint, are responsible for the occurrence of such conflicts. If these psychological factors are kept in view from the beginning, it is possible to reduce the number of conflicts. And it is the task of industrial psychology to study these factors.

11. Problems of personal conduct. While the majority of workers are inspired to revolt and conflict because of some defect in the environment, there are a few workers in whom the root cause of misconduct and conflict is some defect of personality and character. In such cases, it is necessary to consult the industrial psychologist who can trace the cause of the individual's maladjustment and offer a solution.

The importance and value of the industrial psychologist's advice in big industrial complex is evident from the above exposition of his role in solving various problems of industry. It is for this reason that in all progressive countries, industrial psychologist are employed in all large industries.

OBJECTIVES OF INDUSTRIAL PSYCHOLOGY

"The aim of Industrial psychology," according to Myers, "is not primarily to obtain greater output but to give the worker greater ease at his work. Ease does not mean mere physical ease but also mental ease."[8] As a branch of applied psychology, industrial psychology has the following objectives :

1. Personnel selection. Industrial psychology tries to find out how a suitable individual can be selected to perform a particular task. If this can be done, then the work gets the correct worker while the worker himself gets the work he can do best.

2. Care of worker's health. If the worker does not have good mental and physical health, the work of the industry cannot progress smoothly. His mental and physical health is profoundly influenced by the conditions under which he is required to work and by his relations with the management. The objective of industrial psychology is to discover the ideal conditions in which the best mental and physical health of the worker can be maintained.

3. Protection of worker's economic interests. Mental health cannot be maintained unless a person's economic interests are secure. Besides, the worker cannot be encouraged to give of his best, if he is uncertain about his economic condition. Hence industrial psychology evaluates the efficiency of the worker and determines an adequate salary or suggests scientific principles on the basis of which an adequate salary can be determined.

4. Search of proper methods of work. One important reason of accidents and mishaps in factories is the improper methods of work. Improper working also promotes fatigue and boredom. Hence, another objective of industrial psychology is to find out the proper methods of work so that accidents are prevented, and fatigue and boredom reduced to the minimum.

5. Removing maladjustment. Another important factor which causes industrial conflicts is the lack of adjustment between the worker and his circumstances and the conditions in which he works. This maladjustment is primarily psychological in nature. It is the task of the industrial psychologist to locate the cause of maladjustment and to suggest means of rectifying it. This is another objective of industrial psychology.

6. Reform of working conditions. It is the task of the industrial psychologist to find out the ideal conditions in which the highest efficiency can be attained and the worker maintained at the peak of mental and physical health. The most important working conditions are — arrangement for adequate and proper lighting,

---

8. Myers, C.S., *Industrial Psychology*, pp. 14-15.

proper ventilation, absence of noise, provision for periodical rest, normal conveniences for the male and female employees, etc.

7. Reform in machines. The worker and the machine are equally responsible for the number of accidents and amount of fatigue induced in the worker. Prevention of accidents and reduction in fatigue can be achieved by the proper designing of machines. Industrial psychologists give useful suggestions for the improvement of machines and tools.

8. Reform in human relationships. In order to maintain a proper atmosphere and a high degree of morale among the workers in an industry, it is necessary to have proper and cordial human relations between the workers and the management. One objective of the industrial psychologist is to suggest means of improving human relations.

9. Humanistic approach in industry. Psychological studies have established that human relations in industry cannot be good unless a humanistic approach is adopted. Hence the relations existing between the management and the various levels of workers should be improved and the barriers between them removed. Industrial psychologists' help is spreading the humanistic approach in industry.

FUNCTION AND VALUE OF INDUSTRIAL PSYCHOLOGY

Progress in the field of industry depends not only on advances in technology but also upon the cordiality and pleasantness of human relations. In the field of industry, these human relations are also the industrial relations, and are fundamentally psychological in nature. They depend upon the interest, motives, sentiments and passions of individuals. If their nature is to be understood and they are to be made more profitable, it is necessary to undertake a study of interests, motives, sentiments and passions, which is the task of psychology. For this reason, psychological study in the sphere of industry is of great value. The following facts can be pointed out about the contribution of industrial psychology to industry :

1. Solution of labour problems. Conflicts between management and workers is almost a normal feature of every industry and can be caused by almost any factor. Often they become so violent that they result in severe losses in terms of money and lives to both the management and the workers. At the root of all such conflicts are some psychological tensions. It is the task of psychology to study these conflicts, and for that reason psychology can help in the solution of these problems. Most of the means adopted today to improve the relations between the management and the worker are in fact evolved from psychological observation and testing under actual industrial conditions over a long period. They cannot be changed by the wish of any one individual. The truth of the matter is that a conflict can be resolved only if the various factors inherent in it are separated and analysed. Even in the sphere of industrial conflicts, only the psychologist can do this. One major cause of conflict, for example, is the individual differences between individuals which are studied by psychology. Just as a doctor is consulted in the case of bodily disease, and the sociologist consulted about social problems, the industrial psychologist should be considered as a specialist on psychological problems in industry and his help should be sought.

2. Prevention of accidents. Psychology has provided valuable suggestions not only in the solution of conflicts but also in the prevention of accidents. Psychologists have discovered the kinds of machines that should be designed, the manner in which they should be operated and the plan according to which they should be arranged in a factory. The purpose of this study is to find means of preventing accidents. The psychologist finds out how much accident-prone the workers are and suggests methods of getting rid of this propensity.

3. Study of aptitudes. Irrespective of the quality and nature of the physical conditions prevailing in a factory, it depends upon the worker's aptitude to make the best use of them. If the worker has a favourable attitude towards the work it will be done but if his aptitude is not suitable then even the best conditions cannot persuade the worker to work. The study and measurement of aptitude is the subject of psychology and it is the psychologist who can help the industrialist here.

4. Maintaining morale. In order to maintain a certain level of production and to improve the quality of production, it is necessary in every industry and profession to maintain a high level of morale among the workers. Morale is influenced by a large number of psychological factors such as affection and freedom, the desire to make sacrifices, availability of proper leadership, etc. By studying these, the psychologist can give suggestions for maintaining morale.

5. Creating proper leadership. The study of leadership is the responsibility of social psychology. In the field of industry, the supervisor must not only be an official but also a capable leader because otherwise he cannot guide the workers properly and encourage them to work hard. Social psychology can help in the field of industry by pointing out the qualities that are necessary for leadership and by explaining how such qualities can be developed. It can also tell the industrialist about the person who has such qualities or who is capable of developing them.

6. Measurement of individual differences. Success in industry or a profession can be achieved only if the most capable workers are assigned jobs which they are best capable of performing. If this can be done, the workers perform their functions with greater interest and can thus increase production and improve its quality. And individual differences can only be discovered by a wide variety of psychological tests. Hence, the assistance of the psychologist can prove of great value in this sphere.

7. Study of efficiency. In an industry all the workers do not have the same degree of efficiency. Nor is this required, because there are many different kinds of functions to be performed, for which varying levels of efficiency are needed. The psychologist finds out which person has the requisite efficiency to perform a particular job. In addition to this, the psychologist can also give suggestions for improving efficiency by removing those obstacles which hinder efficient working.

8. Use of psychological tests. In the present day psychological tests are being extensively employed to select the most qualified individuals for particular jobs in industry. The chief tests are those of intelligence, interest, aptitude and personality. Sometimes several of these tests are included in a single test battery. Some of these tests are used on individuals while others are used to study the group qualities of workers. All of these tests have their own limitations but even then they are successfully used in the recruitment of employees in the industry.

9. Motion and time studies. Different people take varying amounts of time to complete a specific job because they work at different speeds. Today time and motion studies are conducted to find out the efficiency of individuals and even of machines. These studies have also been used to find out means by which a specific work can be done better in a shorter time. Labour and time are saved by analysing motion studies so that the essential movements can be isolated and concentrated upon. Time studies help in economizing upon the time spent in a particular operation. In modern factories, the machines, the specific places at which particular workers sit and the positions in which they sit are so arranged as to save time and to improve efficiency. All this done to eliminate all unnecessary movement and duplication of work.

10. Aid in industrial training. It is now accepted that the efficiency of a worker can be appreciably improved by the proper kind of training and that the expense involved in training is paid off double-fold. Training people can avoid accidents while the quality and quantity of their production are far higher than that of untrained people. Hence, different kinds of training programmes for different jobs are now called for. At the same time, training programmes for workers at all levels are now organised regularly. The industrialist stands to gain by all such training imparted to his employees. Such training programmes can be devised only by the psychologist, who can point out the basis of such training and methods employed in it.

11. Suggestions concerning motives. An employee must be motivated if he is to progress in his job. This motivation can be supplied through increase in wages, promotion, praise or in many other ways. In the absence of motivation or on account of disappointment, the quality and the quantity of the workers' output both suffer. The special study of motivation is the task of psychology. Only a psychologist can point out how a worker can be motivated to improve the quality and quantity of his product, how the workers' motives can be prevented from leading them to strike, how motivation can be improved even without spending money, and how wages should be paid so as to constitute a permanent motive. All these suggestions tremendously help in the working of an industry.

12. Studies of fatigue and monotony. The most important obstacle in the way of increasing production is fatigue and monotony. Psychologists have conducted extensive studies into the ways and means of eliminating them. These suggestions can be of great help in removing fatigue and monotony from industrial work.

13. Vocational guidance. Vocational guidance involves the finding out of an individual's capabilities through psychological tests and suggesting the profession for which the individual is best suited. It is the suggestion given by a psychologist, which, if acted upon by the worker, will help him to his own talent to the great extent. In most of the progressive nations, an individual is given vocational guidance about the various professions he can enter profitably, even before he has completed his education. The chief benefit of this method is that the individual can then pursue a course of studies which will train him for the right profession.

14. Advertisement and selling. In the sphere of industry, the psychologist's advice is not limited only to suggesting methods of improving production but is also concerned with suggesting methods of advertisement and selling. Advertisement is based upon the psychology of appeal. The psychologist studies those factors which are involved in appeal. It then gives suggestions about the subject matter and the layout of the advertisement so that it can attract the attention of the greatest possible number of people. One example of this is the use of neon signs for advertisement during the night. Apart from advertisement, modern industries try to make use of psychological ideas in selling so that they can convince the customer of the utility of the goods and persuade him to buy them. Psychologists have analysed the process of buying and selling things, and have given useful suggestions about selling. They not only explain how the salesmen should persuade the customer to buy his stock but also how the customer should avoid being trapped into unnecessary expenses by the salesman.

It is clear from the above explanation that psychology has great importance for industry and that this importance is increasing.

QUESTIONS FOR EXERCISE

1. What is industrial psychology? Explain its objectives.
2. What is the relationship of industrial psychology and industrial sociology.
3. Describe functions and value of industrial psychology.
4. Show the relationship of industrial psychology to general psychology.

3

METHODOLOGY

Industrial psychology, which is a branch of applied psychology, makes a study of human behaviour under industrial conditions. Hence, basically it makes use of the same methods as are used in applied psychology. In psychology, the most scientific technique is the experimental method because the conclusions gained from experiment under controlled circumstances are the most valid and reliable. Industrial psychology also makes use of the experimental method because it is the most scientific. But it also makes use of other psychological methods such as observation, interview, questionnaire, etc. A brief account of the methods used in industrial psychology are given below :

EXPERIMENT

An experiment is a question asked methodically. In this the experimenter is faced with a question which he tries to answer by conducting an experiment. This question is based on his hypothesis, which itself is based on his own experience. The results of the experiment either prove or disprove the hypothesis. If the hypothesis is proved to be valid, it is used as the basis for some scientific law which can be used as the basis for some other scientific law which can be used in other spheres. In every industry there are certain problems which are discovered through experience. Industrial psychology begins with certain hypotheses which are the various possible solutions to those problems. This can be better explained by an example. From his experience Taylor learnt of the difficulties of increasing production and in trying to overcome them he created the principle of scientific organisation, later called after him. He observed that every worker goes through certain motions in performing his functions. He came up with the hypothesis that if these motions are scientifically performed through the proper organisation of machines and training of the workers, then time can be saved and more production achieved in less time. In order to test the truth of this hypothesis, he made an experiment upon the labourers of the Bethlehem Iron Company which deal in iron. He studied their movements and conditions of work, and then explained his idea to the labourers and persuaded them to apply it. When the idea was put into practice, it was found that production increased three-to four fold. Hence, his principle of scientific organisation was proved correct. Gilbreth, a student of Taylor, made more experiments on the same principle in the brick industry and came up with the conclusions which supported Taylor's principle. Later on, many other psychologists applied Taylor's principle of scientific organisation to test its validity in many other industries. Finally, this principle was accepted as valid. It will be obvious from this example that in industrial psychology many hypotheses are tested through experiment. Those hypotheses which prove valid and correct are used as a base to make general scientific laws. These laws are valid because in an experiment, the scientist himself controls the circumstances under which the tests are conducted. For this reason, the experiment is being extensively used in industrial psychology.

SOCIAL SURVEY

Meaning of Social Survey

The term survey has two constituents : *sur* which means over and *veeir* which means to see. Accordingly the word survey means "to look over" or "to oversee" and this is precisely what we understand by survey in social context; observation is the main thing in survey. According to *Websters College Dictionary*, survey is "A critical inspection, often official, to provide exact information, often a study of an area with respect to a certain condition or its prevalence, such as a survey of the school." Social survey can be made only of a definite geographical area and that we cannot make survey if the area is unlimited. Moreover social survey deals with some definite social problems and conditions. It is a process by which quantitative facts are collected about social aspects of a community's composition and activities. It is an investigation of the structures and processes of a community, within well-defined geographical boundaries. It is a well-known fact that all social survey is undertaken with an implicit or explicit purpose of social progress and betterment. Keeping the progress and improvement of a community in view, an attempt is made to find out the conditions and causes suited to such a change. The social survey tells us both the reactionary and progressive elements in society, and this knowledge is the *sine qua non* of all social betterment. In brief, social survey is the investigation of social problems, conditions, structures, processes, etc., and the facts are collected through this means in order to bring about change for better in a social group or community occupying definite geographical limits.

The Aims of Social Survey

Following are the aims which motivate social surveys :

1. Data collection regarding social aspects of a community. The primary aim of social survey is the collection of facts about certain definite aspects of a community in order to obtain scientific and well-ordered information. For this purpose, the social surveyor makes use of various techniques to gather information from a selected group of members of a community. The information data have both qualitative and quantitative aspects. Prior to undertaking investigation, the aim and purpose of investigation are well-defined and established. In as much as there are varieties of aspects about a community, their aims and purposes are different. The land-use survey, the political or the geographical surveys are about different aspects of a community. But social survey is called social in order to distinguish it from other types and also in order to stress the fact that in it only social aspects of a community are considered. The social survey is both descriptive and statistical; besides, it aims at social amelioration.

2. The Study of social problems and the conditions of working classes. A glance at the history of social survey reveals that social survey is mainly, if not exclusively, concerned with the problems of society and the socio-economic conditions of the working classes and other depressed and underprivileged groups in the society.

The social survey aims at the study of the conditions and factors of social retardation or backwardness. It aims at the removal of reactionary forces from the society and thereby helps release of social energies into progressive channels. After making social survey and knowing the causes of backwardness, plans are formulated to remove these conditions. The socio-economic level of working classes is much lower than other groups in a society. All kinds of social problems and dysfunctions are found to abound in working classes. The problems of disease, epidemics, unemployment, juvenile delinquency, unhygienic conditions of living, moral depravity, sexual polymorphy, etc., are far more acute among industrial labour than in any other social class. Due to paucity of accommodation and low moral sense, children of workers are constantly exposed to immoral and drunken behaviour of their elders. As a consequence of this, sexual corruption and crime are rife among labour. Their moral sense is blunted. In order to improve their conditions, social surveys are a prerequisite. Most of the problems are inter-related. Unemployment and poverty, illiteracy and unhygienic conditions seem to be inter-related. Social survey studies social problems and tries to see relationship among them.

3. Practical and utilitarian viewpoint. The motivation of social survey is practical and utilitarian. All surveys are undertaken with a practical end in view. Social research is born of natural curiosity and urge to know and it aims at pure theoretical knowledge; but social survey, on the contrary, is utilitarian. It is undertaken for the purpose of social welfare and betterment. In social survey, facts relevant to problem in hand are collected and upon their basis remedial measures are recommended or suggested. As a result of social surveys, government passes various laws to protect the underprivileged against exploitation. Many other measures are taken to help in a practical way the depressed and down-trodden. The special privileges granted to Scheduled Castes and Scheduled Tribes is a case in point.

Stages of Social Survey

Now we come to the study of various stages in social survey :

1. Selecting the problem. As we have seen in the foregoing explanation of social survey, it deals with social problems. Accordingly, the first step of social survey is the selection of the problem. As long as the nature and character of the problem are not clear in the mind of the surveyors, they would not know how to make a start and will grope in dark; therefore clarity and definiteness about the problems is a *sine qua non* of any social survey. The social surveyor is not merely a spectator who can afford to dally with any and every problem he comes across in a community. His approach is practical and motivated by utilitarian considerations. Therefore, he must choose a problem which is significant and whose solution would make some practical difference to the life of the community. A social surveyor should choose his problem, keeping in view the importance of the problem for the community and the accrual of tangible benefits to the community consequent upon its removal.

2. Definition of aim. Following the choice of the problem, the aim and purpose of social survey must be well-defined and made crystal clear. Social survey will lack direction in the absence of knowledge of goals. Moreover, the efficiency of a social surveyor can be measured only in relation with the achievement of goals and if we do not know a goal, we shall have no criterion to judge the success of survey. These goals may be specialized or generic. For example, collection of census data is for general purposes. The social survey of living conditions of labourers or the statistics regarding indebtedness of labour are surveys having specific aims. At time, the aim of survey is to bring out into general notice the facts which are known by some only. Whatever may be the aim of a social survey, it may be generic or specific, but it must be well-defined.

3. Definition of problem under study. Now the nature of the problem selected should be defined. This will determine the scope of the problem and also its nature and character. For example, if we wish to study the problem of alcoholism among labour, then first of all we should define what we mean by the term alcoholism. We have to be clear in our mind as to what quantity of liquor consumed per day indicates alcoholism.

4. Analysis of problem by making a schedule. After the problem is defined, we have to analyse the various elements, constituents or factors involved in the problem so that a detailed and systematic list of these may be formulated. It is only after this step that the relevant information can be systematically gathered.

5. Constitution of a Commission for survey. The official surveys are always undertaken after constituting a commission to make survey and this commission is empowered to elicit various types of data and also has an access to classified material relevant to the study. Having constituted the commission, government defines its powers, terms, limit and scope of inquiry. It is also provided with both financial and personnel assistance. The commission also acts as processor of complaints received from surveyors or public and can redress grievances. It can and does from time to time issue instructions and determine code of conduct for surveyors. Having done fieldwork, the surveyors fill and send the data to the office of the commission where they are processed, classified and analyzed. The commission is headed by a director and has some members. The director and the members are responsible for all policy decisions. They determine the policy and oversee its execution. If need be, the commission splits itself into various committees and sub-committees to deal with specialised matters. In the event of controversy, commission members can give dissenting notes, though normally an attempt at consensus is made. In the event of dissenting notes, the majority report is considered to be the verdict of the commission.

6. Determination of scope. The scientific study of a problem implies systematic investigation into a limited and well-defined subject matter. Without setting limits, no phenomenon can be studied. Accordingly, before the beginning of a survey, it is imperative to determine the scope of the problem. In determining the scope of a problem, the following techniques are made use of :

(a) Political and administrative division, such as nation, state, town, city, locality, etc.

(b) Professional classes, rich and poor people, labourer, etc. This means limiting the problem on the basis of economic levels or considerations.

(c) Child, youth, old, etc. This involves determination of the problem on biological basis.

(d) Married, unmarried, literate, illiterate, that is, determination on the basis of social status.

(e) Hilly areas, plains, deserts, etc., *i.e.*, determination of the scope of a problem upon geographical basis.

7. Determination of time limit. Social survey requires the services of trained investigators and considerable amount of money. Accordingly, it is essential to set a time limit for it. Some problems are of topical importance and all problems undergo gradual change. In both cases, if the results of survey take too long period to be determined, the validity of results may be doubtful on account of change of conditions or the problems may no longer be quite relevant. For example, the special problems arising out of war conditions like displacement of population, etc., must be immediately tackled if the solution is to be effective. But if the government takes too long to come to conclusions about the nature and the extent of relief needed, the problem will be changed and the results of the survey will be inapplicable. Certain statistics cease to be relevant after lapse of some period. For example, if Census Commission submits its reports in 5 or 6 years, the census data collected by it will cease to be very relevant, because population of certain areas may have radically changed in number and character. While fixing the time limit, the time needed for each stage of social survey is determined and, therefore, delay in one stage will easily indicate that there would be delay in the completion of the survey.

While fixing the time limit it has to be kept in mind that time and money consumed should not be excessive; it should not also, of course, be too short. In the first event, the character of problem may be changed during the period of survey and then much money and energy would be wasted. If the time is very short, the result may lack reliability on account of insufficient care, absence of check and cross-check. At times, the time limit has to be fixed to suit the convenience of persons giving information. For example, a survey conducted among students has to be so conducted that it can be completed prior to long leaves. To a large extent, time limit depends upon the technique employed. For instance, different amount of time is taken by questionnaire, interview, biographical records, observation techniques. The well-trained and competent surveyor will take less time than the ordinary surveyor. Therefore, while fixing time limit, the above considerations should be borne in mind.

8. Examination of the means of information. After arranging survey, the next requirement is to decide about and examine the means of information. The sources of information must be accessible and free from duplicity and mischief. If the survey is being made for the first time, it is called primary survey and upon its basis there can be further advance. The data gathered through primary survey are called preliminary data. If the survey is being made a second time, it is called secondary survey and its data are called secondary data. In different types of surveys, different techniques of surveys are employed. Mostly the information is obtained through schedules, questionnaires and direct interviews of individuals. Secondary data are obtained through published or unpublished material of primary survey and also from official and non-official reports.

9. Determination of the unit of survey. Before launching survey, its unit should be determined. On account of this determination field-workers are free from doubts and can easily gather the relevant information. The unit should be definite, unambiguous, stable, harmonized, simple and capable of being surveyed. In order to formulate a representative unit, it is necessary to define and well formulate the sample. If all units are to be surveyed, there is very little difficulty in the survey; but owing to unwieldiness and vastness of the area of survey, usually only representative units can be investigated. The units have to be determined keeping in view the time and money available for the survey. Their number and form depend upon the nature of the material. The sample technique can be employed only where there is no diversity of material or incoherence of time.

10. Determination of the amount of refinement of material. Before undertaking the actual survey, it has to be made clear that to what extent refinement of the data is to be expected. In quantification, accuracy to the last percentile is considered a *sine qua non.* Accordingly, in quantitative survey, the surveyor has to obtain 100% accuracy; but in qualitative survey, the limit of accuracy and refinement is proportionate to the availability of time, funds and able personnel. However, it has to be borne in mind that in qualitative survey 100% accuracy is to use for the moon and should not be insisted upon.

11. The selection and training of researchers and data collectors. Research requires a well-trained staff of researchers and field workers. The selection of researchers and field workers should be made keeping in view the nature and the scope of social survey. Having selected them they have to be trained for the job; they must become acquainted with their respective duties and manner of performing them. In selection not only the intellectual qualities should be emphasized but the personal qualities like amiability, good humour, pleasant appearance and tactfulness have to be particularly stressed, because the fieldworkers have to deal with various types of persons, and their personal qualities and resourcefulness will be much in demand.

12. Preparedness of informers. In different types of survey, the individuals from different classes are used for collecting information. Before undertaking the survey it is essential to create responsiveness and preparedness for cooperation among individuals from whom the information is needed. For example, in the Census of 1917, government publicized through various media to make people aware of the need and importance of census, and the responsibility of public to give accurate information to fieldworkers without any fear, because all information of personal nature will be kept strictly confidential. Educated public can be informed by post or through newspaper advertisements. Uneducated persons can be approached through radio, television, cinema slides, and various leaders of the community can be entrusted to explain the uneducated persons orally the various aspects of a survey. Sometimes handbills are distributed, and, to approach uneducated, illustrated brochures are made available. If the individuals to be interviewed are persuaded to feel the importance of their cooperation, they will become responsive and give information easily.

13. Determination of survey techniques. Before starting it should be made clear as to what techniques are to be used in survey. The choice of technique depends upon the scope and the nature of the survey. The determination of techniques facilitates survey. In questionnaire technique and the schedules to be sent by post, the list of questions is prepared beforehand.

14. Field work. Having completed the above formalities, field workers go to respective individuals to gather information. In this they have to keep the convenience of persons to be interviewed in view. This work requires great resourcefulness and tact, because the cooperation of respondents can be had only if they are approached in the right manner. The fieldwork is done under the supervisor. After collecting information, the fieldworkers file it to their respective departments.

15. Organizations of material, classification and statistical analysis. The collected material is organised, classified and statistically analyzed.

16. Elucidation of conclusions. Having analyzed the data, competent and able researchers draw conclusions from them and elucidate these conclusions.

17. Presentation of graphs. Lastly, the conclusions of a survey are graphically represented. Some schedules and charts are also given to aid the understanding of these conclusions.

When the conclusions of a social survey are made definite and have been well formulated, the recommendations are made to solve or relieve the problem. These recommendations are treated with respect as they have the backing of scientific inquiry. Upon the basis of these recommendations, official and non-official agencies take the necessary steps to implement them and since these recommendations are based on realistic scientific studies, their implementation usually yields desirable results. If there are repeated surveys in a particular field, the later surveys act as verifiers of earlier surveys.

Types of Surveys

Usually social surveys are of two types : general and specialized. In the general survey the entire community is studied in a general way. A specialized survey, on the contrary, seeks to study some particular aspects of the community such as hygienic attitude, child-welfare, unemployment, etc.; of these any one is studied at one time in a single survey.

Besides the above two types, there are some other kinds of social surveys. The important ones and their basic nature are treated below :

1. Direct or indirect survey. In direct surveys quantification is possible whereas quantitative description is not possible in indirect surveys. For instance, the demographic surveys are direct; but, on the other hand, the surveys of health conditions and level of nutrition are indirect. Both types of social surveys have their own place in social study.

2. Census survey or sample survey. In the census survey all units are counted separately and then the sum of all units is computed. On the other hand, in sample survey, some representative unit is studied. Compared to total or census survey, the representative surveys are less time and energy consuming, but they are valid only if the sample selected is really representative and the entire field is harmonious. If the units are heterogeneous, sample survey is not possible.

3. Primary or secondary survey. In the primary survey, the task of survey is taken up afresh and the surveyor himself sets the goals and collects relevant facts; but if some facts are already available and there is no need to examine them afresh by a new survey, then the survey is called secondary. Primary survey is far more reliable than the secondary survey.

4. Initial or repetitive survey. If in any area the survey is being made for the first time, it is called initial but if it is being made second or third time it is called repetitive.

5. Official, semi-official or private survey. As is clear from the names, official surveys are conducted by the government, and the surveys conducted by quasi-government institutions like university, corporations, boards, etc., are semi-official. If the survey is conducted by some non-government person or agency, it is called the private Survey.

6. Widespread or limited survey. The widespread survey takes a very large area or multiple aspects for survey purposes, while a limited survey is confined to a small area and usually deals with some specific question. Obviously, limited survey has greater reliability than the widespread survey.

7. Public or confidential survey. Some surveys are of general types and their data are not of highly personal nature. Accordingly no secrecy is maintained in collection of data or publication of results. These surveys are, therefore, known as public survey. Against this if the nature of the survey is such that information collected is not to be revealed to public, the survey is confidential.

8. Postal or personal survey. If the means of collecting data are mailed questionnaires, it is called postal survey; but if the information is collection by means of direct interview of respondents, it is called personal survey.

9. Regular or *ad hoc* survey. Regular surveys are made periodically without fail. The State Bank of India makes such surveys, while *Ad hoc* surveys are conducted for a specific purpose and are not periodically revised.

Social survey in town and country areas. Herman N. Morse has enumerated ten phases of survey which are being listed hereunder for the sake of comparison :

1. Definition of the purpose of object.
2. Definition of the problem to be studied.
3. The analysis of this problem in a schedule.
4. The delimitation of area or scope.
5. Examination of all documentary source.
6. Fieldwork.
7. The arrangement, tabulation and statistical analysis of data.
8. The interpretation of results.
9. Deduction.
10. Graphic expression.

The Value and Importance of Survey Method

The various types of survey and different techniques used in survey have their respective significance and value. In a general way it may be said that surveys throw useful light on the various aspects of the social problems and help in understanding the causes of the problems and the mutual interplay of the causes. On the strength of a survey practical remedies to solve and resolve problems can be put forward and these remedies will normally be efficacious because they are the outcome of scientific study and analysis. A general or widespread survey helps us to get an overall idea of the multiple aspects of the problem ranging over a very wide field, and, this, in turn, can indicate problems for specialised survey. A specialized survey may be called depth survey because it studies threadbare a particular problem in a limited range. The conclusions of a specialized survey are much more reliable than those of general or widespread survey. Accordingly, specialized survey is more important from scientific point of view. The postal survey is less expensive than personal survey; but postal survey can be conducted only where all the respondents are literate. Moreover, in case of doubt in respondent's mind, postal survey fails whereas personal survey can take care of all such contingencies. While personal survey is undoubtedly reliable and therefore desirable, its negative features are its expensiveness and various types of lures and temptations to which a fieldworker is exposed. There is a well-known case of an American who distorted information about a poor family because the mother offered him the sexual services of her comely daughter. Public survey can be made only in situation where the information is of general type and not of personal nature. But in survey of problems of disorganization, homosexuality, lesbianism, marital discord, smuggling, crime, etc., the survey has perforce to be confidential. In regular surveys, the reliability of conclusion increases.

The value of a primary survey is directly dependent upon the technique used. Here there is a lack of comparative material and this proves a stumbling block. However, primary surveys are highly important because through them a first attempt is made to gather well-organised information on a subject and these prove to be stepping stones for repetitive surveys. The census and income data can be kept reliable only through regular surveys.

In census survey, much money, time and staff are needed. The surveys of this type are countrywide and their conclusions are reliable and precise. But, on account of being less expensive, sample surveys are widely used in social sciences. Official surveys are initiated and conducted by government to gather accurate data on some problem confronting the government. As government have large funds and large brigade of trained personnel, official surveys are quite reliable and accurate. But government is liable to suppress information unpalatable and offensive to it and which may arouse people's resentment against it. Therefore private surveys, in spite of their obvious limitations, are very useful. The direct surveys, being quantitative in character, are more reliable than the qualitative indirect surveys.

The above discussion of variety of surveys and variety of methods bring into relief the fact that the utility and importance of survey cannot be determined in abstract. It is only in relation to the nature of the problem, its scope, the aim and object of survey, the availability of funds, staff and other facilities that one can know which type of survey will be useful under the given circumstances. Each type has its pros and cons, and the choice of type of survey is very crucial in order to derive full benefits from the survey.

OBSERVATION

In industrial psychology the observation method is used wherever it is impossible to control all the conditions. For example, the aptitude of workers can be controlled only within certain limits. In the same way one cannot deliberately create tension between the worker and the management to study tension. Tension can be observed only when it is actually found existing in a particular situation. Take the examples of strikes and lockouts. The psychologist does not try to create them. He only makes a careful observation of such phenomena as and when they occur. To begin with, he makes a careful examination of the behaviour of managers and workers in a situation of strike or lockout, and then makes a record of his observations. After similar examination and recorded observation at a number of different places, the psychologist analyses the information available to discover any general patterns of behaviour that may be common to all situations of strikes and lockouts. On the basis of these general patterns, he presents some general principles. In industrial psychology the observation method cannot claim as high a degree of validity as experimental method, because observation is influenced by individual prejudices. For example, the scientist with communist leanings will find traces of capitalistic exploitation of the labour class in all examples of strikes, and he will tend by and large, to favour the working class. Some scientists, on the other hand, may be completely opposed to the workers and thus may make partial observations. But prejudices of this kind can be eliminated to a great extent by training and practice. Actually, as has been pointed out earlier, the experimental method cannot replace the observation method, because many conditions which come under the purview of industrial psychology cannot be artificially created and hence cannot be completely observed and tested.

INTERVIEW

In many spheres of industry, industrial psychology makes use of the interview method. For example, in the selection of workers from among the many applicants, workers are interviewed. Besides, sometime individual workers are separately interviewed to find out their opinions on different matters concerned with the industry or on methods adopted for improving conditions. In an interview, the interviewer and the subject sit facing each other. Success in this method depends upon the ability of the interviewer to frame suitable questions which can elicit the information he requires. The chief advantage of this method is that a personal relation between the interviewer and his subject is established, by reason of which the interviewer learns many things which he would otherwise never find out. If the subject hesitates in answering certain questions, his hesitation can be removed. As far as industry is concerned, scientists can get valuable information on different problems of industry by separately interviewing the workers, the managers and the industrialists.

QUESTIONNAIRE

Another method now being used to find out the opinion of workers, managers and industrialists is the questionnaire. As is obvious from the name itself, the questionnaire method makes use of a list of selected questions which are intended to elicit the desired information. In the closed questionnaire every question is followed by a yes and a no, one of which has to be deleted by the person answering the questionnaire. In an open questionnaire the answers have to be stated in a few words or one or two sentences. But the questionnaire method suffers from the following defects :

(i) Very often the person answering gives the wrong answer and hides the truth.

(ii) Sometimes the questions carry one meaning for the scientist and another for the person answering them.

(iii) Fairly often the answers are put down without thought with the result that the conclusions arrived at are wrong.

Despite the above difficulties, the questionnaire method is less time consuming than the interview method because thousands of questionnaires can be printed and distributed by hand or by post and the answers received can be quickly analysed. But the chief difficulty is that, in the absence of any personal relationship between the research worker and the subject, the truth cannot be easily obtained.

THE SCHEDULE

The Meaning of Schedule

There are two ways in which the response to a questionnaire may be secured. In the first, it may be sent by post to various individuals; and, in the second, the researcher may himself present the questionnaire to the individuals whose responses are desired. The first method is called the mailed questionnaire, while the second method is called schedule. A schedule is a list of questions formulated and presented with the specific purpose of testing an assumption or hypothesis. For example, a social scientist believes on the basis of his general experience that women do not enjoy good status in a joint family; he will so formulate his questions that the actual state of affairs may come to surface in responses to those questions. According to W.J. Goode and P.K. Hatt, "Schedule is the name usually applied to a set of questions which are asked and filled by an interviewer in a face to face situation with another."[1] By a schedule we cannot, however, obtain information about many things at once. It is best suited to the study of a single item thoroughly.

From the foregoing discussion, it is quite clear that in the schedule method, interview occupies a central place and plays a vital role. As a matter of fact, success in the use of schedule is largely determined by the ability and tact of the interviewer rather than on the quality of the questions posed. Because the interviewer himself poses the questions and notes down the answer all by himself, the quality of questions has not any great significance. The list of questions is merely a formal document intended to maintain uniformity in the questions asked of different persons.

Important Features of Schedule

From the above-mentioned definitions, following salient points about schedule emerge :

1. The schedule is presented by the interviewer. The questions are asked and the answers are noted down by him.

2. The list of questions is a mere formal document; it need not be attractive.

3. The schedule can be used in a very narrow sphere of social research.

---

1. Goode, W.J. and P.K. Hatt, *Methods in Social Research*, p. 133.

Aims of Schedule

P.V. Young has laid emphasis on the following aims of the schedule. According to her, a researcher makes the schedule a guide, a means of delimiting the sense of his enquiry, a memory tickler, a recording device. These may now be discussed point-wise :

1. Delimitation of the topic. A schedule is always about a definite item of inquiry; its subject is a single and isolated subject-item rather than the subject in general. The interviewer presents questions about one item and notes down answers about it. Therefore, the schedule delimits and specifies the subject of inquiry.

2. Aide-memoire. In an interview the choice of questions is left entirely to the interviewer; he may ask any question. In this there is always a chance of some important points being left. Therefore, in the schedule the list of questions is preplanned and noted down formally. The interviewer is always armed with the former document detailing the questions. Accordingly, in the schedule method, the interviewer is not dependent upon the memory.

3. Aid to classification and analysis. When the interviewer obtains replies to the questions given in the schedule, these replies are classified and analyzed. Many different tables are used in the schedule; and the questions are also of many types. Some need only yes/no answer; others require choosing one of the alternatives given or arranging them in order of preference; still others require certain amount of thinking and can be answered in small sentences. Therefore, all varieties of replies are sifted and classified under various heads. This helps in analysis of the replies.

The above aims of schedule method have been condensed by Mrs. Young in the following words : "An observation usually serves several purposes. Simultaneously :

1. it is specific memory tickler;

2. it is an objective recording device which makes possible accurate accumulation of large quantities of data;

3. it is a standardizing device and

4. it aids to delimit the scope of the study and to concentrate on the circumscribed elements essential to the analysis."[2]

---

2. Young, P.V., *Methods of Social Survey and Research*, p. 181.

Types of Schedules

Scholars have described four types of schedules. These are to be discussed now :

1. **Rating schedules.** In the fields of business guidance, psychological research and social research, the rating schedules are used to assess the attitudes, opinions, preferences, inhibitions and other like elements. As is evident from the term "rating," in these schedules, the value and trend of the above-mentioned qualities are measured.

2. **Documents schedules.** The schedules of this type are used to obtain data regarding written evidence and case histories. In these schedules, those terms are included which occur frequently in documents and are to be generally found in case-histories. For example, in the field of criminology, rating schedules are used to gather data to be found in crime studies, the different kinds of crime, their incidence, the nature of earlier crimes and the personal data on criminals like school leaving age, the age at the time of employment, the level of economic and social status and other sundry facts about crime and criminals.

3. **Institutional survey forms of evaluational schedules.** The use of these schedules, as is evident from the name, is made to gather data about specialized institutions or agencies. The form and the size of evaluational schedules are determined by the nature and the complexity of the problems of an institution; more complex the problem, bigger the size of the schedule. To study the problems of American Public Organization for Health Services, a schedule running into as many as 38 pages, was used.

4. **Observation schedules.** In these schedules, an observer records the activities and responses of an individual or a group under specific conditions. The observation schedules may need one or more research workers to be completed. The aim and purpose of an observation schedule are to verify some information.

5. **Interview schedules.** A fifth form of schedules is sometimes treated independently and at other time considered included in the fourth type. In an interview schedule, an interviewer presents the questions of the schedule to the interviewees and records their responses in blank spaces.

Of all the above-mentioned types of schedules, the observation schedule is not most frequently used.

PSYCHOLOGICAL MEASUREMENT

In industrial psychology the most important problem is the selection of the right person for a particular job. Many kinds of psychological tests are used for this. These tests reveal the capabilities of the worker, and if he is found to be fit for the particular job in question, he can then be entrusted with the responsibility. Among the main kinds of psychological tests are the following :

(a) **Intelligence tests.** The intelligence of an individual or a group of individuals is tested by getting answers to some questions or by making them perform certain tasks. Different intelligence tests are used for different age levels, and they may be verbal or non-verbal, individual or collective. They are chosen according to the situation in which they are to be used. In industry it is essential to know the intelligence quotient of the workers, as on the basis of intelligence quotient they can be graded and suitable work found for them.

(b) **Tests of special abilities.** Certain jobs require a particular set of mental abilities. Special tests are used to discover these mental abilities in individuals. One example of tests of this kind is the test battery used by the Psychological Corporation of America which includes tests concerned with verbal arguments, numerical ability, abstract arguments, internal relationships, mechanical argument, writing speed and linguistic ability. Thurston's S.R.A. tests for primary mental abilities are well-known as tests of special abilities.

(c) **Aptitude tests.** Among the aptitude tests, one of the most famous is the Minnesota mechanical adjustment test for measuring the mechanical aptitude of a person. Another famous test is the Bennet test for mechanical aptitude.

(d) **Interest tests.** According to the principles of industrial psychology, every worker should be given work which he finds interesting. Hence, tests of interest are very common in the field of industry.

(e) **Personality tests.** Certain traits of personality are essential for particular jobs in industry. Personality tests are administered to the candidate to find out whether he possesses such traits. The chief methods of testing personality are — case history method, interview method, questionnaire method, etc. By using these methods, one can find out the traits of each individual's personality.

MEASUREMENT OF APTITUDES

Studies have been conducted to find out the aptitudes of the workers, managerial staff and the industrialists — to find out their aptitudes towards the conditions of work, the conditions of wages and many kinds of reforms and improvements. Three kinds of standards are used to measure aptitudes :

(a) Opinion scale. Examples of opinion scales are — Thurston's standard, Likert's standard and Gutmann's standard. By using these measures one can find out the opinions of people and then their aptitudes can be discovered indirectly. In these methods there are differences of construction and kinds.

(b) Rating scale. In these, the evaluation of aptitudes does not depend upon the opinions or decisions of the workers themselves but upon the scientist's own decision. Rating is done on the basis of non-verbal behaviour, verbal behaviour, clinical interview, private essay, projection techniques and immediate experience, etc.

(c) Indirect scale. In these, the workers are not aware that their aptitudes are being tested. In 1938 Ash, Block and Hurzmann studied changes of opinions among industrial groups through suggestions or hints.

TIME AND MOTION STUDIES

Apart from the above methods used in industrial psychology, there are certain other methods which are used in the solution of specific problems. One important method, for example, much used in industrial psychology, is the time and motion study in which all the movements made by the worker are studied and the time consumed by him is calculated. From this one can find out those movements which can be eliminated. It is also possible to find out those motions which can help in increasing production. Many time motion studies have been conducted in industrial spheres recently.

Briefly, the methods used in Industrial psychology are growing along with the number of new problems being brought up for research. In future too, one can hope for the evolution of new methods which can provide more valid results.

QUESTIONS FOR EXERCISE

1. Give a brief description of the chief methods of Industrial Psychology.
2. Write short note on Psychological Tests in Industry.
3. Write short note on Questionnaire Method.

4

Foundations

Study of the development of modern Industrial psychology will reveal that its foundation is basically psychological, but this does not mean that the psychological basis is the only foundation of Industrial psychology. It also has economic and social foundations. But the psychological aspect should be considered more important since Industrial psychology is a branch of psychology in as much it studies human behaviour. A short description of the various bases of Industrial psychology is attempted in this chapter.

PSYCHOLOGICAL FOUNDATIONS OF INDUSTRIAL PSYCHOLOGY

In the beginning of the twentieth century, psychology came to be used in so many new branches that, based upon the practical uses to which it was put, sprang up. In the more progressive nations, as industry and the professions developed, the use of psychology in these spheres also increased. Thus a new branch of psychology called Industrial psychology came into being because it was being used to solve industrial problems. It primarily paid attention to industries and studied psychological facts which pertained directly to industry and commerce. Psychologists were appointed in many industries to give advice. In fact, these psychologists made valuable contributions in the various spheres of industry and business. It is possible to study the psychological foundations of Industrial psychology from three different angles which are as follows :

1. Psychology in industry. There are many things in the industry where the assistance of a psychologist is particularly desirable. For example, it is necessary to conduct psychological tests for the selection of properly qualified personnel for particular jobs. Similarly, the psychologist can also give valuable advice about the conditions of work, both physical and psychological. The physical conditions of work include light, temperature, ventilation, music, hours of work and rest, and other similar conditions. Psychological conditions include the security of the workers, satisfaction of their needs, inspiration in their work, their relations with other workers and senior staff, etc. Psychological research is also valuable in the sphere of promotions and the principles upon which they should be based. Suggestions given by psychologists have proved to be of immense value in improving human relations in industry and in solving industrial disputes. The use of psychology has proved valuable in the field of industry and business.

2. Individual differences. Recent psychological tests have definitely established that human beings differ from each other in respect of intelligence, interests, aptitudes, special abilities, personality, etc. These are called individual differences. If these individual differences are ignored then one cannot select the most able worker for a particular job. Industrial psychology is directly concerned with individual differences because they have to be kept in mind whenever some suggestion is given. An idea can be explained to one person in one particular way but a different method may have to be adopted to explain it to another person. Hence, from Wundt down to modern psychologists like Cattell,[1] Binet, Kraeplin and Munsterberg, all have made a special study of individual differences.

3. Personal adjustment. It is necessary for each worker that he should make his adjustment with the environment surrounding him in the factory. Without this he cannot take interest in his work and will suffer from tension. If there is adjustment, the number of accidents and industrial conflicts is much less. Fatigue, monotony and boredom are also kept in control. In this connection industrial psychologists are continuously conducting research to find out how this adjustment can be achieved and then maintained.

SOCIAL FOUNDATIONS OF INDUSTRIAL PSYCHOLOGY

Even when working in an industry, the individual is never alone because he constantly comes into contact with other workers, supervisors, managers and industrialists. In business, the worker has to deal with all kinds of people. For this reason it also becomes necessary to study the social foundations of Industrial psychology. Efforts are being made to bring industrial organisation to a scientific level. The more progressive countries try to improve the social life of the worker by organising various kinds of social programmes.

---

1. Cattell, J. Mick, *Mental Tests and Measurements*, pp. 373-80.

The following points need to be considered in a study of the social foundations of Industrial psychology :

1. Worker and social progress. The progress of the industrial workers is a part of the general social progress. Hence the movements for social progress were accompanied by movements for an improvement in the conditions of industrial workers. It was accepted as a general principle that the work of social emancipation would remain incomplete so long as nothing was done to improve the conditions of industrial workers. For this reason social workers turned their attention in this direction. Bills were passed in Parliament to this effect. Social workers directed the attention of industrialists towards the bad condition of the workers and insisted that they should be given human rights and their conditions changed so that the workers could improve their standards of living. Exploitation of workers was violently objected to and decried. Great stress was placed on providing social security to the workers. Political parties also began to pay attention to the amelioration of the lot of workers. In this manner the progressive nations linked the improvement of the industrial worker with the movements for general progress. This humanistic attitude is spreading rapidly in industry in all modern nations.

2. Workers' department and welfare schemes. As a result of this humanistic approach, most modern nations have created workers' departments which undertake the task of safeguarding the rights of workers and working for their betterment. Labour welfare is now accepted as an important element in social welfare. Labour welfare, includes the improvement in the social, economic and psychological conditions of the worker. In most large industries labour welfare officers are appointed to look after the workers and to help solve any disputes that may arise between them and the employers. The modern state is a welfare state, the object of which is to enhance the welfare of the citizens in every sphere. The worker is an important part of the population and the government which does not undertake measures for labour welfare cannot hope to achieve its ideal of social welfare. After achieving independence, India, too, has begun to pay attention to the question of labour welfare. It has, from time to time, enacted laws to secure the rights of workers in various industries. Although even now many industrialists avoid the clutches of the law by various means, the pressure exerted by the trade unions is steadily changing the situation.

3. Industrial management. Today efforts are being made to raise industrial management to the level of a science. The suggestions of Taylor and Thurston have been particularly valuable in this respect. A scientific industrial management implies the establishment of a management under which all elements of production are most efficiently employed, thus eliminating the exploitation of any one element and the exhaustive use of any other. In a scientific industrial management system, a humanistic approach is adopted to deal with the workers and efforts arc made to provide them with more facilities. The advanced countries are continuously making rapid strides in this direction.

ECONOMIC FOUNDATIONS OF INDUSTRIAL PSYCHOLOGY

Studies conducted by Industrial psychology help not only in the personal problems and social problems of the workers but also in the solution of their economic problems. For this reason economic factors have also played an important part in the evolution of Industrial psychology. It has now been established that if an industrialist wants to progress rapidly he must pay great attention to the workers employed by him and create psychological conditions in which the morale and the efficiency of the workers can be maintained. With the introduction of sophisticated machinery, the importance of the worker was reduced for sometime, but scientists quickly pointed out that this was harmful. They emphasized the fact that industrial progress is impossible if the worker is neglected. As a result, efforts were made to provide industrial management with a scientific basis. F.W. Taylor,[2] an American engineer, did pioneering work in this direction and the principles enunciated by him came to be known by the name of Taylorism. His plan was given the name of scientific organisation.

Taylor's Principles of Scientific Management

Taylor first put forward the principles of scientific management in the field of industry and thus helped the progress of Industrial psychology. Taylor's method is based on two fundamental assumptions, the first that the worker wants to get the maximum amount of money he can from the industrialist, and the second that the industrialist wants to pay the least possible amount for the highest possible production. Besides, it was also believed that there is no organisation in industry in which the relations between the employer and employee remain cordial and both cooperate

2. Taylor, F.W., *Shop Management*, New York, p. 21.

with each other for the purpose of achieving industrial progress. Taylor therefore presented a new programme of industrial management in order to achieve this objective. G.D. Babcock has explained this plan by the following four principles :[3]

1. The development of a science for every element of human work in order to remove the old fashioned methods.

2. The selection of the most capable individual for a specific job to be followed by a programme of training for that individual. This should take the place of the old practice in which the worker selected his own job and then trained himself to do it.

3. The development of a humanistic relationship between the management and the worker to promote progress, according to the principles given by the developed science.

4. Division of labour among the management and the worker in approximately equal proportions so that each department can undertake work it is best equipped to perform. This should replace the traditional conditions in which almost all the work and the responsibility fell on the shoulder of the worker.

It is evident from this that Taylor was in favour of replacing the old traditional methods by new scientific techniques. He wanted that the selection and the training should be conducted on a scientific basis. He stressed that the management and the worker should share the responsibility and the work, and cooperate in order to achieve industrial progress.

Taylor's Experiments[4]

Taylor's theory is based on certain experiments conducted by him. He used these principles first of all in solving the problems of the iron ore industry. He applied the principle of scientific management to the workers who transported iron ore, for the Bethleham Iron Company which employed nearly 75 labourers working in the traditional way. The majority of them were healthy and efficient, and were obeying the orders of the foreman. In carrying iron ore each worker bent down and lifted about 92 lbs of iron ore. He then carried it for a short distance and put it down at a particular place. In this manner he managed to transport about twelve and a half tons of iron ore in a day. The management

3. Babcock, G.D., *The Taylor System in Franklin Management, Application & Results*, New York, p. 17.

4. Taylor, F.W., *The Principles of Scientific Management*, New York, p. 42.

of the company was informed that if the workers worked according to Taylor's plan, they would be able to lift four times this weight, although the wages would not go up in the same proportion. Taylor explained that, if they worked according to his plan, each labourer would be able to lift 47 to 48 tons of iron. The management did not seem particularly enthusiastic but Taylor was not disappointed.

For his experiment Taylor selected a Dutch labourer from Pennsylvania who was well respected and had a good character. Taylor asked him whether he would like to be paid 1.85 shillings as daily wages or 1.15 shillings. The labourer naturally chose the higher rate of pay. Taylor told him that in that case he would have to work according to a new plan which would enable him to lift forty-seven and a half tons of iron. The worker had to work according to his new training and obey all the commands of the observer. This worker started to work when he was told and rested when he was instructed to rest. As a result he had lifted forty-seven and a half tons of iron by closing time and he received 1.85 shillings as wages. Using this Dutch labourer as an example Taylor tried to persuade the labourers to follow him but not everyone was prepared to work in this manner. Only one out of every eight workers was prepared to work in this way, with the result that only nine out of the original seventy-five employees of the factory were retained while the rest were turned out. The labourers unemployed as a result of this selection condemned Taylor but Taylor did not abandon his plan. Instead he tried to convince the unemployed workers that they could obtain higher wages elsewhere by following his plan of work. Actually, as a result of this plan, the workers and the management both profited. The company had to pay only a little more to obtain four times its original production because by paying 1.85 shillings instead of 1.15 shilling it got forty-seven and a half tons of iron instead of twelve and a half tons. On the other hand, the workers obtained about .70 shilling more than what they were getting. But although the labourers were working four times as much as they were working earlier they did not get a proportionate rise in wages. Consequently, the workers criticised Taylor and called him a tool of management and an enemy of the workers.

Thomson's Experiments

Another example is given to prove Taylor's principles. In this Thomson gave certain suggestions to improve the production and the quality of, the work done by ball bearing inspectors. Under this plan, provisions were made for rest within the period of work; besides, other conditions were also improved. Proper selection of workers according to the work was also introduced. Each worker was also given adequate and proper training, and allowed rest. As a result of these changes it was seen that the work previously done by 120 girls could now be done by only 35 girls. Their wages were also increased by 80 to 100 per cent. On the other hand, the hours of work were also reduced because each girl had now to work only eight and a half hours instead of ten and a half hours. On Saturdays the employees were allowed a half-holiday. Each girl began to feel that she occupied a position of some importance in the company, and as a result she began to work with greater concentration. Thus both the company and the workers were benefited by these scientific improvements.

Gilbreth's Experiments[5]

Gilbreth, a student of Taylor, also made use of Taylor's principles. He turned his attention to the mason's trade which, till then, was being followed on the traditional pattern in which no attention was paid to the location of the bricks, cement, plastering material, etc. The materials used by the mason were placed haphazardly with the result that the mason and his assistants had to make many unnecessary movements, thus wasting energy and time. Gilbreth made a study of these movements, located all the materials as near each other as possible, recruited talented masons and gave them proper training. All these reforms resulted in expected benefits. By the old method the mason could put together only 120 bricks in one hour but under the guidance of Gilbreth he began to put together 320 bricks per hour. In this way, the management was benefited by the increase in output while the mason gained through increase in his wages. Hence, both were benefited.

Elements of Scientific Management

It is evident from the above examples of the experiments conducted on Taylor's principles of scientific organisation that his main aim was to improve the conditions of work. Many means have to be adopted to improve working conditions. Taylor believed that the following methods are essential :

1. Study of the time taken in work and search for methods of increasing work in less time.

5. Gilbreth, F.W., *Bricklaying System*, New York.

2. Division of work among foremen.
3. Use of more appropriate tools for a particular function.
4. Establishment of a planning department.
5. Other rules in the organisation.
6. Using a time-saving plan and implementing simple rules and their improvements.
7. Arrangement for guidance of the worker.
8. Different scales of pay.
9. Division of work according to the construction.
10. Arrangement for guidance.
11. Determination of wages according to prevailing price levels.
12. Giving importance to outstanding work and giving incentives for it.

Taylor explained that a scientific organisation can be introduced in any industry by following these twelve principles. He also stressed that, apart from these twelve guidelines, constant efforts should be made to find new incentives and to use them to encourage the workers to increase production.

Social Aspect of Taylorism

Taylor supported the notion of social progress of the worker and made provisions for it in his system of scientific management. He pointed out that scientific management envisages the increase of wages corresponding to the increase in production and efficiency. Adoption of the scientific management system resulted in benefits for both the managers and the workers. Production and wages both increased. As a result, the conflicts between the worker and the manager decrease, both cooperate with each other and show respect to each other.

Criticism of Taylorism

Taylor's theory has been welcomed by many, but it has also come in for some severe criticism. As has been pointed out earlier, he was called the agent of the management by the workers because their salaries did not increase in proportion to the increase in production. The truth of the matter is that industrialists took advantage of Taylor's scientific plan to increase their production. In America, in particular, his plan for scientific management was enthusiastically accepted by industrialists because they benefited much more than the workers. And, there can be no denying that industrialists were chiefly responsible for propagating it. But if the worker's wages had increased in proportion to the increase in production, then Taylor's plan would have proved as godsend for the workers, although it is doubtful whether it would have been accepted by all industrialists in that case. In fact, Taylor paid more attention towards increasing production than to increasing the wages of the workers. Industrialists therefore found it a boon, and took full advantage of it. But from the scientific point of view, the importance of Taylor's plan cannot be doubted. Many of his students and followers adopted the plan to various conditions in many spheres. On the basis of his plan for scientific management, industrial psychologists conducted numerous experiments of his theories. Many industries adopted the method of selecting the most efficient workers for particular jobs, for which psychological tests were employed. In many industries attempts were made to reduce unnecessary movements and to prevent accidents and monotony. Attention was paid to the importance of periods of rest for the workers. Efforts were made to arouse the interest of the worker. Workers and foremen were given specialized training for their tasks. Studies of the necessary and proper physical conditions for health, rest and development were made. These conditions were then created in many industries. The laws concerning wages were also studied and the problems related to them were solved. In this manner Taylor's theories helped to organise the economic basis of Industrial psychology on a sound principle. Industrial psychology gained in importance because it gave suggestions for the increase of production as well as wages. The relations between the employer and the employee improved and direct exploitation was considerably reduced. Whatever exploitation remained was indirect. Industrial psychology thus helped to introduce extensive economic, social and psychological improvements in the field of industry.

QUESTIONS FOR EXERCISE

1. Give a brief introduction to the foundations of Industrial psychology.
2. Describe in detail the influence of the research of Taylor on Industrial psychology.

5
Human Relations in Industry

In the older days, the workers in factories were regarded as objects no better than the machines and tools used in it. Behaviour towards them did not qualify humane. And in many cases, the workers were no better off than slaves. In the days of British India, in the margarine blue factories of the country, many national leaders had to raise their voices in protest against the cruelty meted out to workers by the owners of the factories. In the South, too, owners of factories and mines did not treat their employees at all well. The worker was daunted into submission, and in many occupations he was often turned out without prior notice or any compensation. In cases of accident, fatal or incapacitating, the worker and his family were reduced to object of misery and impecunious poverty. When machines were invented, women and children were also added to the labour force, no concessions being made to their delicate condition and ideally exalted position of life. Even when leave was absolutely necessary for women, it was not permitted, and pregnant women were often turned out of work. The system in the factory and working conditions were almost deplorable. The owner was concerned solely with his own profit, and the conditions in which work was carried on was not his concern. It was outside the sphere of his thinking to worry about air, light, sanitation, water, etc., that were not supplied in adequate quantities. There being no legal bar to the extent of work to be forced out of the labourer, the owners forced the poor workers to work long hours on very small remuneration. Promotion was a term unheard of, in that time. Incentives to workers were not given, and equally not tendered. In this way, exploitation was the rule of the time.

Propagation of socialist and democratic principles caused people to revolt against such conditions. Labour unions were formed at most of the places. Different professions made their own organisations. In progressive countries labourers and other workers in different professions combined together to voice their desire for better working conditions, and for workers in industries to be treated as human beings. Democratic and socialist governments also turned their attention to this problem. Besides this, thinkers and scientists came forward with the suggestion that because of absence of proper human relations in industry, workers were not the only losers; the government and the owners also suffered. This led to the propagation of the thought that efforts should be made to improve working conditions and human relations in industry.

PROBLEMS OF HUMAN RELATIONS IN INDUSTRY

In industry, human relations are in evidence in two spheres, in that of administration, and that of welfare. In the field of administration it is the relations between the authority and the worker which is important. A labourer is not a machine, nor a cog in a wheel. He is repleted with such human elements as motives, emotions, feelings, hopes, desires and needs. He wants as much as any other that his good work be praised and that his efforts should bring him additional gain. Love and respect are things for which he earns. Treated like a human being by those in authority above him, his work becomes very much easier and much more pleasurable for him. Various incidents of labour strikes and lockouts were mainly of administrative origin. Administration of a factory involves proper and systematic organisation of the factory, besides humane treatment of the workers. It is desirable that a feeling of security be induced in the workers by making precise and definite rules regarding appointment, promotion, etc., within the factory. The position entrusted that the worker should be made permanent. He should be made to know that the road to progress is straight and narrow, and that honesty is very much the best policy. Absence of these conditions is reason enough for the poor worker to feel dissatisfied and to lose his concentration in the work. A worker should be praised for any extraordinary effort that he may put in. He should also be made to benefit in some manner or the other if he does something unusually good. His salaries should be increased, so should his bonus, and he should be given a higher position. Conditions of work should be improved, and the workers of a high calibre be transferred to good places. Such factors being existent, the worker's inspiration in his work continues and so does his enthusiasm. Without these incentives, no industry can achieve much good results.

Misunderstandings and differences of opinion between workers and authority are nothing to cause much worry, as they are part and parcel of life, all of them being human and capable of harbouring various kinds of emotions regarding each other. Hence, occasions of conflict are only too natural. Such problems of human relations require careful and tactful handling. If those in authority show laxity of mood, unscrupulous individuals may take undue advantages and turn in bad performances. If, on the other hand, the authorities decide to make it rough for the workers, haul them up on every little thing, interfere constantly, offend their respect and threaten them every off and on, it would be difficult for the poor workers to maintain their equanimity of mind and work enthusiastically. Actually, the attitude and nature of every worker differs from one to another, but, nevertheless, efforts must be made to maintain cordial relations between them.

WELFARE IN INDUSTRY

At an earlier stage in the development of human thought, the responsibility of an owner was supposed to end once the worker had been remunerated for his efforts on behalf of the owner. Economics, as it stands today, is more interested in welfare than in financial disposal of obligations. Governments of today are haunted with dreams of the visionary welfare state. Consequently, it is now conceded that besides paying wages to the worker, it is essential to attend to his welfare also. Human services, conveniences and pleasures should be available to the worker as to any other individual. Atmosphere at home and in the office or factory should be congenial. They should get adequate opportunities of intellectual, material, moral and economic progress. Factors in their welfare would be the provision of such conveniences as convenient housing, educational and health service facilities, good food and adequate provision for rest and recreation. For female workers it is essential to provide more holidays and rest. Creches and maternity homes should be provided near the working premises for mothers. Special help should be forthcoming to workers when they are ill. Maternity benefit programmes are essential for women workers. Educational facilities should be provided for the children of workers. The future of the workers should also be made secure so that they should be able to concentrate upon their work wholeheartedly. Provident fund benefits, pensions and life insurance schemes are some of the ways in which this can be assured. In this way, it is now believed that the owners should do their best to provide for the integral development of the workers entrusted to their care by society.

In fact, the mill-owners and industrialists get a certain percentage of returns on the money that they spend on labour welfare, as this money improves the efficiency, skill and cooperation of the worker. And if in the process of working in a factory, a worker loses his life, or his capacity to earn money, it becomes the moral duty of the owner to arrange for the upkeep of his helpless family. Actually, money spent on labour welfare is more in the nature of investment than that of expenditure since whatever is spent ultimately influences the owner favourably. Increase in the labourer's skill means an economy in raw material and increase in production. Scientific selection of workers helps to eliminate the improper exploitation at the hands of middlemen, and this improves the peace and enthusiasm of the workers who work better. In the same manner, technical training of individuals involves an initial expenditure of huge sums of money, but finally it also means considerable additions to their income and profits because a trained individual works better than his untrained counterpart and reduces overall damage. He stands to gain because the trained labourer does better both in quantity and quality of work. An employer does not have to spend much in improving light, ventilation and other facilities on the factory premises, but they have a great influence upon the health and performance of the workers, with the result absenteeism falls, workers do not complain of fatigue, and they less often fall a prey to disease. Healthy conditions of work encourage the workers to attain a peaceful frame of mind and think more kindly and favourably of their employer as they are conscious of the latter's concern for them. This improves their mutual relations, and the workers do not tend to migrate to other jobs very often. Welfare work in respect of prevention of accidents has obviously a very direct advantage for the employer, since he stands to lose just as much as the worker does. He is compelled by the law to make some compensation in case of accident, besides which such occurrences lead to unrest among the other workers. If it is a trained worker who is involved in any serious accident, the employer is quite directly hit. Prevention of fire breaking out on the premises is a form of labour welfare that should be right after the employer's own heart, and should concur with his way of thinking. But it also leads to the welfare of workers' minds. Efficiency of workers can be increased by providing means and opportunity of rest and refreshment in the factory. Organisation of canteens helps them in getting food at the right time, and they can return to work shortly.

It is in such ways as these that the employer stands to derive direct and indirect benefits from such schemes of labour welfare.

LABOUR WELFARE

Labour welfare pertains to all such works or schemes that lead to the benefit of labour, but such a general statement does not satisfy the scientific mind. It is a term whose meaning is relative to time and place; as a result it is capable of change. According to the report of the Royal Commission on Labour, "The term 'welfare', as applied to the industrial worker, is one which must necessarily be elastic, bearing a somewhat different interpretation in one country from another, according to the different social customs, the degree of industrialisation and the educational development of workers." In this manner, the meaning that the term 'labour welfare' will have in any specific country will depend upon the condition of the labourers there. Labour, in general, being uneducated in a country like India, the term will come to include their education also. As defined in the *Encyclopaedia of Social Sciences*, "Labour welfare implies the voluntary efforts of the employers to establish, within the existing industrial system, working and sometimes living conditions of the employees beyond what is required by law, the custom of the industry and the condition of the market." Hence, the term labour welfare does not comprehend those activities that are necessitated by the laws of the country, the traditions and customs of industry in that country, or by conditions of the market, instead, it means the voluntary actions on the part of the employer to improve the lot of his employees. The International Labour Organisation defines labour welfare in these words : "Workers welfare should be understood as meaning such services, facilities and amenities which may be established in, or in the vicinity of, undertaking to enable the persons employed in them to perform their work in healthy, congenial surroundings and provided with amenities conducive to good surroundings and provided with amenities conducive to good health and high morale." In this way, the term 'labour welfare' implies schemes and activities that produce conditions that improve the health of the workers as well as those circumstances that improve their morale. It may widely be taken to mean any voluntary action on the part of the employer that benefits the worker in any way. But it does not include any activity that the employer is compelled or coerced into performing, whatever be the benefit accruing to the labour class. Through the medium of labour welfare work, employers and industrialists try to achieve the integral or complete development of their employees.

LABOUR WELFARE ACTIVITY

Labour welfare work is believed to be of three kinds :

1. Statutory. Legal compulsions regarding the safety and working conditions of workers, etc.

2. Voluntary. Those works that the employer performs for the benefit of workers of his own volition, without any coercion being involved.

3. Mutual. This kind includes the welfare work done by labour unions in cooperation with each other.

Dr. Broughton's View

Dr. Broughton has divided works of labour welfare into two classes : (1) Intra-mural, and (2) Extra-mural. The main ones among intra-mural works are :

1. Scientific selection or appointment. The scientific selection of workers for the various jobs within the factory.

2. Industrial training. Training in various factories for different jobs in the factory.

3. Arrangement for light, fresh air and water. This classification comprehends arrangements in the factory for cleanliness, white washing, ventilation, drinking water, bathrooms, lavatories, urinals, light, air-conditioning, etc.

4. Prevention of accidents. This includes arrangements for the protection from dangerous machines, extreme temperatures, fire fighting, etc.

5. Other functions. Such as canteen, provision of rest rooms, refreshment, etc.

Major extra-mural labour welfare functions are the following :

1. Provision of education. This includes adult education, social education, primary education, education of men, women and children, etc.

2. Arrangement of proper housing accommodation.

3. Medical service. This includes rest, cure, paid leave, free treatment, subsidized medical aid, etc.

4. Provision of inexpensive and nourishing food.

5. Facilities of recreation. Clubs, gymnasia, cinema, radio, reading-room, libraries, etc.

In addition to the above list, the following activities are also a part of labour welfare service :

(1) Social insurance scheme, (2) provident fund benefits, (3) pension, (4) sickness and maternity benefits, (5) arrangement of maternity homes and creches, (6) provision of cooperative societies, (7) arrangement of cultural programmes, (8) schooling of children.

ADVANTAGES TO EMPLOYERS FROM INTRA-MURAL WELFARE WORK

In all modern countries, the employers do their best to introduce labour welfare programmes of various kinds because they have come to realise that the money spent upon labour welfare is not completely lost to them. A very definite percentage of the advantage accruing from it is diverted to them ultimately in the form of increased production or better quality of work rendered by the happy workers. Working in healthy and congenial surroundings, the workers feel contented and delighted in the concern that the employers evince in them. Cordial relations between employer and employee are thus precipitated, and the workers evince lesser desire to change employment at the least provocation. Prevention of an accident is a direct gain to the employer, even more so when the individual salvaged is a trained person whose training itself would have cost the establishment of a packet. Even otherwise, in case of accident, the employer owes it to his conscience to compensate the family of the sufferer in some measure. Other workers in the factory develop a feeling of insecurity if the rate of accidents is high in their establishment. Schemes and plans for prevention of fire or for fire-fighting are a direct gain to the employer, as he would not like to have his factory go up in flames. Skill and efficiency are changing things, and likely to remain in the best condition if the worker is occasionally allowed to rest and refresh himself, either by nourishing himself or by relaxing. Easy availability of good and wholesome food takes a load off the workers' minds, as it is very convenient to eat in a canteen near the premises. In this manner, the owner of a factory stands to gain directly from intra-mural efforts of the labour welfare.

Advantages to Owners from Extra-Mural Labour Welfare

An owner also gains finally from extra-mural labour welfare activity. Mainly, he is benefited in the following ways :

1. Improvement in workers' health. Ordinary arrangements like healthy residences, inexpensive and nourishing food, proper relaxation and refreshment go a long way in maintaining the health of workers. Hence, absenteeism from the factory falls to a minimum, and the per capita output improves. Dissatisfaction is a thing of the past, cordiality and fidelity permeate the very atmosphere, to the delight of the owner.

2. Improvement in workers' efficiency. When education is provided, the workers' efficiency and skill increases, and he can do better work in lesser time. His understanding improves and he is capable of avoiding the inflaming influence of vested interests.

3. Reduction in absenteeism. Prevention of disease and arrangement of medical facilities help to reduce illness or to shorten its influence as a result of which the number of absentees in the factory decreases, disease being the main cause of it. Social welfare activity helps to induce a healthy outlook in the worker and to maintain a balance in his character which guides him to honest and responsible effort and conduct.

4. Good relations between employer and worker. Provision of such facilities as social insurance, provident fund, pension, gratuity, etc., helps to remove a feeling of insecurity in the worker, as his future becomes secure, and he can rest satisfied with his employer. This improves the relations between the worker and the employer.

5. Reducing worker's dissatisfaction. Healthy recreation facilities and welcome cultural activity help to sublimate the more destructive and undesirable tendencies in the worker's satisfaction. A worker's satisfaction is further increased if his female colleague has the benefit of such facilities as maternity benefits, maternity homes, creches for their children. Being satisfied he is not inclined to strike work, as a result of which the employer gains.

6. Improvement in quantity and quality of production. When these benefits accrue to the workers in a factory, the quantity and quality of production in it improve, a direct benefit to the employer.

7. Employer's moral satisfaction. But the greatest advantage of labour welfare that goes to the employer takes the form of moral satisfaction at having served the cause of humanity. No decent minded and right-thinking employer can be happy if his employees are poor, ill-fed, badly dressed, uneducated and unpresentable. Their labour does not bring them any pleasure. Economic improvement and benefit are not the sole basis of labour welfare, even though economic benefit does result from it. Behind it is the sense of humanity, a large heart and a moral or ethical consciousness.

Absence of these things leads to the exploitation and ultimately to class-struggle.

From the above description it is evident that labour welfare activity benefits the employer no less than his employees, but such activity should be intelligently conceived and generously administered. Planning is a part of every scientific activity but generosity is an essential part of labour welfare because such plans are not based on material considerations but are instead guided by humanitarian principles and views. Finally, it can be said that intelligently conceived and generously administered labour welfare activity will ultimately benefit the employer.

VALUE OF LABOUR WELFARE IN INDIA

Compared to other countries, India has much greater need and importance for labour welfare work. Such a condition is caused by certain deficiencies in the Indian labour force, that are not to be found in its counterpart in other countries. It is these defects or deficiencies that increase the importance of labour welfare activity in the country. Briefly, then, the following are the reasons why labour welfare work in India assumes greater importance than in other countries :

1. Lack of labour unions. In India, even today the workers are not united into a class. Keeping in view the numbers, labour union movements are still in its infancy. Even in the labour unions that do exists, there is a lack of enlightened leadership, and there is no unity between these unions themselves. Welfare of labourers is a secondary concern, the primary interest being the serving of a party and vested interests. In the absence of properly organised labour unions, the workers can neither place their demands effectively before the employer, nor can they think clearly and systematically of their own interests. In other modern progressive countries, workers are strongly organised into labour unions, but as their force is lacking in India, it is essential that the welfare of labourers in the country be efficiently looked after by the employers and the government. This should be treated as a sacred trust till the workers can evolve their own efficient and reliable organisation. This will help the workers stand on their own feet, develop strong union, think properly of their interests, to progress hand in hand, and to take a definite hand in the country's development.

2. Illiteracy. As compared to other countries, the percentage of educated workers is very low, most of them being illiterate.

Consequently, they are not in a position to receive advanced industrial training, understand the problems in industries, understand their own interests and those of the nation as a whole. This can prove a source of harm not only to the workers but also to the country. Hence labour welfare is required more in India than in other countries. It will help to make the workers secure, become industrially efficient, and become responsible citizens of the country.

3. Problems of absenteeism and migration. Compared to workers in other countries the Indian labour is more restless and prone to frequent migration because life in the town does not provide for his needs, and the atmosphere in general does not suit him. Level of wages is far too low to adequately compensate for the high prices of most commodities. Hence, the labourer cannot comfortably settle down at one place. The worker's migratory tendency can be cured by providing him with adequate housing, improving the conditions in which he is required to work, and other welfare work of a similar nature. This will help the worker establish a home in the town, and he will not have to run frequently to the village for his family. Hence, the problem of absenteeism in factories will be reduced. Recreation and cultural facilities will prevent indulgence in drug addiction and alcoholism, crime and prostitution and other undesirable activity. Even more than this, the percentage of absenteeism in factories will fall.

4. Low Level of health and nutrition. The Indian worker, as compared with his counterpart in most European countries, is unhealthy and ill-fed. This has reduced his production potential, as compared to the productive capacity of Western labourers. Hence he is in very great need of inexpensive nutritive food and facility in case of hospitalization.

5. Extreme poverty. Another factor is the extreme poverty of the Indian worker. He is unable to provide a healthy living for his family and a good education for his children. Female labour in the country, as compared with female labour elsewhere, is in even a worse state of health, and adequate protection and assistance are not afforded to her in times of pregnancy and delivery. Hence labour welfare has much to do in this country. The Indian woman labourer will be as happy as other workers in the world when she is given the facilities of maternity benefits, maternity homes and creches for her children. It is essential that the education of boys and girls be provided for. Being poor, the Indian labourer is hardly in any condition to save something for the old age; hence he is in great need of provident fund, pensions and gratuity, etc.

6. Lack of training. Percentage of trained workers in India is very low. As compared to other countries, trained personnel in India are hard to come by. Hence it is necessary to have training facilities for such a vast labour force. Possibility of accident increases when the worker is untrained. Hence, there should be adequate provisions for preventing accidents.

7. Lack of healthy recreation. Healthy recreation is also at a premium in this country, with the result that the workers indulge in crime and activities of a reprehensible kind. Their efficiency is further diminished by energy being employed in all kinds of undesirable channels. Hence, it is essential that recreation and enjoyment of a healthy kind be provided.

8. Industrial backwardness of India. From the Industrial standpoint, India is far behind other countries. Industrial progress is being aimed at through the medium of the five-year plans, but Industrial progress is dependent upon the efficiency of the labour force, and labour in India is in a pitiable state. Hence, the labourers are very much in need of all kinds of labour welfare work.

It would have become evident from the above description that labour welfare work in India assumes a much greater importance, as compared with other countries due to a variety of reasons. Labour welfare activities will save the labourer from moral degeneration, reduce the number of incidents of lockouts and strikes in industries, and help to achieve success in the country's plans.

INDUSTRIAL CONFLICTS

If, in some particular profession or occupation, the workers have faith in their employer who thinks considerately of them, their mutual relations remain cordial and occasions of conflict are rare. If workers do not revolt for some reason or the other against conditions of extreme exploitation and choose to bear their lot gracefully, then also conflict does not occur. On the other hand, if the employer is tactful and chooses to use his diplomacy, there is no reason for a lockout to take place. But these things do not occur very often. What does happen very often is that employers pay no heed to the plight of their employees, even forgetting that the poor chaps are human beings with certain basic needs, the fulfilment of which is essential, and that they may revolt against extreme exploitation. In the earlier stages when labourers were not united, the unscrupulous employers could keep them suppressed by tactfully causing dissension among their ranks. But in the present day conditions in almost every country, every big industry has its organised labour unions. Some labour unions are powerful enough to spread over countries, while certain unions have political parties to support them in their struggle against exploitation. Many of their leaders are powerful enough to become members of national councils and governments. Wherever any injustice to the labour class occurs, it is brought to their attention so that they can raise a hue and cry over it in the national assemblies and take the matter up with the government concerned; and this activity and representation at the highest level create a notion of power and security in the general rank of labourers. They are in a position to take the fight into the exploiter's half, and they can resist efforts at exploitation of their energies. They organise themselves into a single body, if they need to agitate for their demands and they resort to political propaganda, to meetings, processions and ultimately to strikes. Strike is one of the major problems of modern industry.

STRIKES

Strike is an announcement of non-cooperation with the employer, the first step in it being suspension of all activity, followed by meetings, organised processions, exhibitions in order to elicit the sympathy of the population in general, public representation of their demands carried to the employer through the senior representatives of the labour force. All these activities are adjuncts of a strike. Besides all this, strike nowadays involves wide propagation of the aims of the strike in the public so that it can be persuaded to side with the labour force. Another aspect of the strike is in informing the government of its objectives and presenting it with a summary of its demands and their justifications.

Why do Strikes Occur?

Why do strikes occur at all? Basically, it stems from a distrust of the workers towards their employer. They do not strike, even when required to work in squalid surroundings, so long as they are convinced that the employer is conscious of their needs and is sincerely trying to improve their lot. But when the employer turns a deaf ear to their pleadings and entreaties, when their faith in his sincerity is undermined, they strike work. There is no necessary rule that the demands of striking workers are invariably just and proper. Some strikes take place because the workers are inflamed by some political groups that have some end of their own to achieve or are misled by some vested interests or are led to this extreme step as an expression of their disgust. They may choose this method of getting their revenge from the individual. Many workers form the idea that all that the employers possess, their magnificent mansions, their cars, their luxuries, are the outcome of exploiting workers. This leads to a feeling of jealousy which may find expression through strike even though the general behaviour of the specific employer may be good and the conditions of work normally above reproach. Occasionally, leaders of labour unions also inflame the workers and incite them to strike in order to achieve some personal objective. Most facts are twisted and distorted by the leaders and fed to the poor labourer who swallows them and prepares to strike.

Means of Ending the Strikes

In this manner, whether the strike is justified or not, whether its objectives are desirable or not, it originates in a feeling of mistrust between the labour force and the employer. This mistrust and lack of confidence are sometimes caused by the employer himself, but whoever is to blame, it is essential that conciliation should take place. Even if demands of the striking workers are unjust, they must be heard and attended to. In a strike, the workers conduct themselves in a manner similar to mob behaviour. They lose their power of reasoning. Their emotions are easily aroused and they become excited over the most insignificant thing. If in such events, the employers choose to behave in an irresponsible manner, the situation can worsen and may lead to setting fire to factories, arson and other destructive activity. But such events and damage can be averted if the workers' demands are given a patient hearing, the workers convinced of the sincerity of their employer, promises of prompt action upon them given, and the inflammatory sources disclosed.

Prevention of Strikes

But prevention is traditionally considered to be better than cure. It is for the employer to avert distrust or at least to prevent it from reaching such proportions that the worker feel to be justified in striking work. It is for him to try and win the confidence of his staff. Two things are essential for this. The first is that the behaviour towards the workers should be good and understanding, sincere and proper, and, secondly, attention should be paid to their well-being, improvements in working conditions made and their welfare considered carefully. If these things are done, the worker's trust in his employer becomes unshakable and strikes become an obsolete and an unknown activity.

LOCK OUTS

One aspect of the distrust between worker and employer is the strike, the other is lock outs. In this activity the office and working premises of the concern under conflict are locked, entry to staff and workers is prohibited. Hundreds and thousands of workers lose their source of income, and are sometimes reduced to such abject poverty that they are on the verge of death because of hunger. The workers lose, but so do the employers. While the machines lie idle, they lose their income, raw material is destroyed in many cases, trade connections are broken because of lack of supply. Secondly, a lock out can incite the workers to violent activity which may cause them to destroy the factory as their daily bread has been snatched from them. This naturally is no small blow to the employer, or his insurance company. The employer has naturally to seek the assistance and protection of the police force, which may be compelled to fire on mobs of unruly workers indulging in destructive activity. If some of them happen to die, the employer is brought into disgrace. Lock outs harm the country's economy even more than they harm the individual owner of the factory. In the modern economic structure in most countries, every industry is dependent upon some other for one or the other thing. Lock outs in one industry can lead to very serious repercussions in other industries which may follow the bad example of the first and resort to lock outs. The worker is not the only class of people dependent upon the functioning of the industry, other classes of shopkeepers and middlemen are also deeply involved. Their earnings also are greatly depleted by such subversive activity. When production of a particular commodity is stopped, its supply drops with the result that this creates such an imbalance between the forces of demand and supply in the market that the prices go up, with much adverse influence upon the poor consumers. In this way, in the modern complex that is the nation's economy, lock out in any factory has wide influence. In this manner, it can turn into a problem of national magnitude.

Causes of Lock out

A certain concatenation of circumstances may make lock out an inevitable step, but usually it is not justified. It is sometimes used by the employer as an instrument with which to suppress the helpless worker. It may even be an expression of the employer's sadistic bent of mind, as it may give him pleasure to see the worker suffering. Lock outs are sometimes thought to be essential in cases where prestige and honour become involved. It may even be used to impress the worker with an employer's power over him. In all such cases lockouts are completely and beyond doubt unjustified and improper. Its lack of justification lies in the fact that the employer is led to sacrificing the interests of the nation and those of the working force in favour of his own. It should be considered obligatory on the part of the government to intervene, because it becomes a national question. In fact, all incidents of lock outs and strikes can be effectively prevented if the government enacts laws covering labour welfare activity, improvement in their condition of work, occasional incentives being given to them, security in cases of accidents and old age being provided, and if it ensures their efficient and strict observance.

As has been pointed out earlier, lock outs and strikes are two aspects of the same problem. They stem from mutual distrust between worker and employer, prejudice, in-group feeling, selfish interests and unnecessary self assertion. All these are psychological in nature, but they do not arise without an antecedent cause. If they are present in weak conditions, they do not cause lock outs and strikes. These incidents occur only when these feelings flare up, an occurrence which can certainly be controlled and avoided. The most obvious way of doing so is by removing all causes of distrust, prejudice and assertiveness. For this, on the one hand, eye should be kept on individuals and groups that encourage them, and on the other hand, welfare work should be undertaken. But for this, cooperation between workers and employers is essential, in addition to governmental intervention. Hence, their solution should be cooperatively sought after by the government, labourers' representatives and their employers.

QUESTIONS FOR EXERCISE

1. Write a short note on industrial conflict.
2. Describe the various causes of conflict as well as areas of cooperation between labour and management.
3. Discuss some of the major labour-management problems in Indian industry. State some of the major psychological factors of conflict in Industry.

6
ORGANIZATIONAL PSYCHOLOGY

If two or more persons establish between them cooperative relations and make concerted efforts, the state of these cooperative relations and concerted effort is called as the organization. The organizations can perform simple or complex tasks. All individuals within an organization try to work for a common aim. The word organization is a derivative of the word organ. The word organ means a part or a limb of an animal or man. Thus brain, heart, liver, arms, legs, etc., are the various organs of man. The man or an animal as a whole is said to be a structure and organization. He is an organization because his various limbs, parts or organs are mutually and cooperatively related. A group of individuals working together for a definite common aim is called an organization. The mutuality and togetherness found in a group of persons engaged in industrial production is called industrial organization.

BASIC ELEMENTS OF ORGANIZATION

The organization may be industrial or formed for the attainment of some social or political aim. Every organization has some common basic elements. The basic elements constitute the structure of an organization. Generally three elements are considered basic for any organization. Firstly, an organization must have numerous components. As a living organism consists of numerous organs and millions of cells, in the same manner an industrial organization has many wings or components and hundreds of units. These components perform their respective roles. The second element basic to an organization is the adjustment also. Living organism provides best illustration. As an organism lives and functions only as long as its various organs function harmoniously, similarly an industrial organization retains its character only as long as its various components work in a complementary manner. It is true, of course, that there cannot be such ideal adjustment among the industrial components as in the case of human organism. Nonetheless without a minimum amount of adjustment there can be no industrial organization. It is not possible for workers to do any work if raw material is not supplied or supervisory staff is missing to supervise the work. The third basic element of an organization is that it should be suited to purposeful activity. This means that all elements of an industrial organization should be such as will contribute towards the aim specified for it. For the attainment of different aims, different types of organizations are required.

KINDS OF ORGANIZATIONS

Organizations are of two kinds : (i) spontaneous or informal organization and (ii) formal organization. The spontaneous organizations are natural and these are not formed for any particular purpose. The organizations in the man, animal and vegetable kingdom are the examples of spontaneous or informal organizations. A sudden voluntary get-together of human beings is an another example of informal organization.

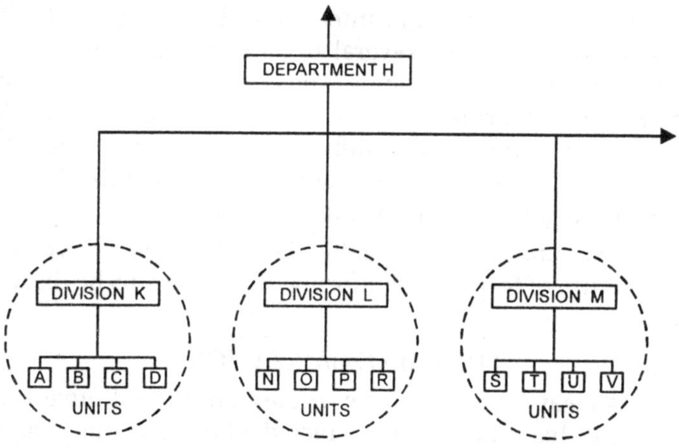

Fig. 6.1. Organizational Chart of a Typical Department

The relationship between departments, divisions, and units is indicated by the connecting solid lines, which indicate the lines of authority. Many companies have organizational charts drawn up so that positions at various levels are clearly defined. This chart is not a complete one but shows only a small department within a company. A complete organizational chart for a large company may have six or more levels. The broken lines, each enclosing a division and several units, represent potential discussion groups in which the division supervisor acts as the leader. Each unit supervisor would be the leader of groups of rank-and-file employees, not shown in the chart. All management personnel are potential participants in one grouping and leaders in another (The meanings of terms such as unit, division, and department vary from one company to another. A division may be a larger or a smaller unit than a department).

A formal organization is a result of deliberate efforts and is brought together for some specific purpose. Compared to informal organization, a formal organization is more systematic and works under specific rules. It is only within the framework of law and rules which brought it together that an organization remains an organization. In the event of violation of rules, it is liable to break down.

The industrial organizations are always the outcome of deliberate efforts and are established with a specific aim. In an industrial organization we find both kinds of organizations, that is, an industrial organization contains within it both formal and informal associations. In fact, wherever men get together both formal and informal organizations come into being. A deliberately organized structure brings together a lot of men. This togetherness, in turn, gives rise to certain formal organization which is organized to achieve certain specific aims. It has a formal character. With expansion and diversification of an industrial organization, several sub-organizations under it come into being. For example, in every huge industrial complex, several organizations of workers and managerial staff come into being. These sub-organizations can be either formal or informal. However, these sub-organizations have their role and importance within the framework of the parent organization. It is however possible that sub-organizations may be in revolt against the parent organization.

In order to understand the industrial organization, it is essential that the nature of formal and informal organizations be discussed in detail.

FORMAL ORGANIZATION

As it is clear from the above discussion, formal organization in industry is that human group which deliberately comes together for the achievement of a specific purpose or aim. Following are the chief features of a formal organization, according to C.L. Barnard :

The formal organizations are not concerned with nor do they revolve around a person or persons in particular. It is not the name or heredity or the person but his status and work that are important in a formal organization. An organization requires a man to perform according to his or her status. A formal organization has a hierarchy of status. On relinquishing of a post by one person, another person assumes his office and the work of the organization goes on. The members of a formal organization bear to each other impersonal and not personal relations. Their relations depend upon the plan of the organization. For example, if an industry X makes a component of a machinery and Y makes another component and Z fits them together, the relation between X, Y, Z is purely formal and is limited to certain processes in an industry. However, this does not mean that there are no personal relations among X, Y, Z. Indeed, in an organization, it is but natural that various members should spontaneously develop various types of relations, social, economic, religious, etc., among themselves. However, these relations are informal and are not strictly essential for the maintenance and sustenance of the industry. Within the framework of an industrial organization, the relations between members are formal but outside of its framework these are informal.

Another characteristic feature of formal industrial organization is that it is formal and functional, it is nonetheless in the background of vast social organization or system. The social atmosphere affects it much. The socio-economic-ethical conditions of a society affect the industrial organization directly or indirectly.

Another characteristic of the industrial organization is that it is scientific and systematic. Under the formal organization the role, status and importance of all the jobs is well determined. The structure of formal organization is quite explicit and this is tractable of easy investigation.

Departments of Formal Organization

Whenever an industrial organization develops and becomes vast it becomes complex and the functions within it becomes quite intricate. Under these conditions, the organization gets split up into various departments for its smooth functions. The departments are generally considered to be parts of the organization. Normally there are three such departments in an organization. These are :

1. Linear Organization.
2. Functional Organization.
3. Staff Organization.

1. Linear organization. Once an industry assumes gigantic proportions, it requires a hierarchical system which can effectively control and manage the whole organization. This hierarchy directs the entire organization towards its predetermined end. This system is known as linear organization.

2. Functional organization. The industrial organizations have variety of functions. For convenience each of these functions is entrusted to one department. This system of departmentalising of functions is known as 'Functional Organization'.

3. Staff organization. In modern industry technological changes and inventions are taking place daily. New devices and sophisticated methods of work are being discovered daily in the fields of technology, economics, law and social sciences. The discoveries in all these fields have their direct or indirect application to industry. As a result of these there is a conceptual and practical revolution in every aspect of business management, production, marketing, etc. It is not possible for everyone, to be fully posted with latest developments. Besides the scientific research is snowballing and requires special cadre to imbibe and absorb its impact. As industry requires successful application of various new techniques to maintain progress, every industry keeps a team of specialists to keep track of developments in science, technology, social research and law. Thus a successful industrial organization would have experts in engineering, sociology, science and legal studies, etc. This organization of experts is known as staff organization.

VARIOUS LEVELS OF INDUSTRIAL ORGANIZATION

Besides the classification described above, there are some other kinds of classification in an industrial organization. This classification is hierarchical and is according to status, and position. This is also known as vertical organization. According to this classification, there are different levels of posts and positions starting from labour and going up to the highest executive.

In any industrial organization, the top-wrung positions are occupied by those who are the founders of that organization. The capitalists themselves appoint the Board of Directors. The Board of Directors appointed by the capitalists elects the Chairman of the company. The chairman in turn entrusts to each director one department according to his ability and capability. There is some difference of opinion with regard to the number of top managerial posts. But generally top positions are as follows :

(1) Chairman; (2) Managing Director; (3) Executive Director; (4) General Managers; (5) Works Managers and (6) Regional Sales Managers. For example, in India; Tata Oil Mills Co. Ltd. has the above described arrangement of posts.

Next to top-wrung officials are middle-wrung officials. This set of officials comes between the topmost and the low-wrung officers and workers. The middle-wrung officials are concerned with the implementation of the policies and directions laid down or given by the topmost officials. This set of officials must have plenty of practical knowledge. These officials are usually the specialists in the fields. The staff organization described above is the organization of these officials.

The third wrung of the industrial managers is occupied by supervisory staff. They occupy a position just above the clerical staff. Their job is to supervise work and report to the higher officials from time to time.

Thus in an industrial organization we find hierarchy of status. The persons occupying different places in this hierarchy have their respective privileges and obligations.

PRINCIPLES OF INDUSTRIAL ORGANIZATION

In regard to industrial organization and business management, new principles are being continuously established. However, certain principles laid down by relatively old experts still have their own significance. Some of these experts are : E.W. Taylor, H. Fayol, C.L. Barnard, L. Uriwick and P. Sargent. The laws and principles discovered and established by them have not only historic significance but have certain validity and practicability even to-day. These principles are based on actual experience of the industrial management. Henry Fayol has laid down fourteen principles for efficient industrial management. These are :

1. Division of work
2. Authority and responsibility
3. Discipline
4. Unity of command
5. Unity of Direction
6. Subordination of individual interests to general interests
7. Remuneration of personnel
8. Centralization
9. Scales chain
10. Order
11. Equity
12. Stability of tenure of personnel
13. Initiative
14. *Esprit de corps.*

The above-mentioned principles are crucial to every industry. By following these principles, one can conveniently obtain the desired goals.

INFORMAL ORGANIZATIONS

Besides formal organization, certain informal organizations spontaneously spring up in every industry. These informal organizations are generally complementary in nature and play a supporting role in respect of the main formal organization. The informal organizations are based upon personal as against the impersonal relations of formal organizations. Wherever some persons get together there is an exchange of social and personal human relations and this forms the basis of informal organizations. Many such informal organizations are found in industries. The informal organizations are neither deliberate nor do they possess neat well-defined structure. Yet there are certain preconditions for the formation of such organizations:

1. The first type of informal organization is the totality of members of the organization bearing with each other certain relations at personal level. In the terminology of sociology, this informal group is derivative or secondary group. In the secondary group, members have interpersonal relations remaining within the primary group.

2. The second type of informal organizations are those which spring upon on account of common tastes, interests or hobbies of some persons. The members of trade unions, for example, come together on account of commonness of interest or purpose. Certain clubs or societies develop. For example, we find dramatic clubs in many industries. This is a clear example of an informal organization. We also have in industries societies based on religion and language. There are also sports clubs which again are examples of informal organization.

3. The third type of informal organizations are represented by persons doing similar jobs in an industry.

4. The fourth type of informal organizations are of very few and limited persons. There may be half a dozen poets in an industrial organization and they may form a poetry club. Again, there may be more than two persons in an industry hailing from the same family. Their association will be an example of informal organization. Besides family relations, such organizations may be based on friendship or intimacy.

It is imperative that there should be informal organizations within an industry. The informal organizations are generally complementary to formal organization. They are not contrary to it. If care is taken to nourish the informal organizations, they prove beneficial to the industry. If there is sufficient co-ordination and co-operation between industry and informal organizations within it, the chances of strikes and lock-outs are minimized. Any work connected with industry can be done easily through the heads of informal organizations. The efficient managers try to maintain rapport with these heads.

Now the questions is, why is an informal organization necessary and how it comes to be established. The answer lies in human nature. Basically, man is gregarious and has an instinct for establishing informal relations with his fellow beings. It is on account of this instinct that informal organizations come into being. Secondly, industrial workers are in the habit to avoid work. They need some or other thing to fill their empty hours. The informal organizations fill this void. The habits of gossiping, smoking, etc. are symbolic of this. Another reason for coming into being of informal organizations is that every worker knows well that he can be shunted from work, therefore he feels comparatively secure. Besides, informal organizations give emotional security.

INDUSTRIALIZATION IN INDIA

Though industrialization in India is making rapid strides, it is still far behind the industrial growth in Western countries. After India became independent in 1947, the Government of India paid particular attention to industrial growth. It helped the local industry to grow rapidly. In order to put India on industrial map fast, the government decided to enter the field of heavy industry which demanded huge investments. The government set up many heavy industrial complexes all over India in order to promote a balanced growth and also to help the ancillary industry to expand fast.

As a result of fast industrialization, the process of urbanization too, is growing fast and this is having deep impact upon the society. The industrialization is not only pushing up the urban population but is also affecting the social conditions in nearby villages.

The Social Impact of Industrialization

The important consequences of industrialization, in India are as follows :

1. Urbanization. As a consequence of industrialization, the population in the cities has gone up. This will be clearly seen in the following table :

Year	*Urban Population (% of Total)*	*Increase*
1872	8.8	—
1881	9.3	0.6
1891	9.4	0.6
1901	10.0	0.3
1911	10.3	1.0
1921	11.3	1.9
1931	12.1	0.8
1941	13.9	1.8
1951	17.3	3.4
1961	18.0	0.7
1971	19.0	1.0
1981	23.0	4.0
1991	25.7	2.7
2001	27.8	—

2. Impact of Urbanization. The process of industrialization increases the urban population. It is on account of industrialization that there is progressive rise in the population of cities in India. Whatever social impact is due to, the urbanization is indirectly due to industrialization. Therefore, the impact of industrialization and the impact of urbanization are in fact the facets of the same underlying process, namely, industrialization. The following are some of the important social influences of urbanization :

(i) ***Decline in the feeling of Sociality*** : The first and foremost impact of urbanization in India is the increase in the population of the cities, and this, in turn, has resulted in the progressive decline in the feeling of sociality. In villages, the feeling of sociality is stronger than in the cities. Therefore, the loss of village, population and increase of city population results in the decline of feeling of sociality.

In cities, the activities of almost everyone are self-centred and governed by the calculus of self-interest and personal gain. Therefore, no one really bothers about other people except insofar as their association is helpful in promoting one's self-interest.

Thus people in cities prove to be calculating and display little altruism.

(ii) ***Decline in social control*** : With the decline in the feeling of sociality there is consequent decline in social control. Due to lack of community feeling and the fear of social disapproval, people are bound to become increasingly individualistic and even arbitrary in their conduct. Thus we find in towns to-day a glaring neglect of tradition and contempt for social approval. Everybody wants to do whatever pleases him.

(iii) ***Decline in family control*** : As the population of cities has grown, the cities have expanded. This has resulted in there being great distances between the places of work and places of residence, between educational institutions and homes. This has meant that people stay away from home environment for the best part of the day. Small wonder, then, that under these circumstances, there is progressive decline in the control of family over its members. The modern education, the excitement of cinema, fashion, clubs and societies have contributed greatly to this trend.

(iv) ***Decline in the influence of religion*** : The increase in the population of the cities leads not only to the decline of social and family control but also to decline in the influence of religion. In metropolitan towns, the life is highly materialistic and individualistic. This in turn promotes atheism. This means that people in cities are not guided by tradition and are indifferent to religious beliefs. Their conduct is governed by rational or personal considerations. Thus the life in cities is relatively devoid of the influence of religion.

(v) ***Change in the institution of marriage*** : The increase in urban population has resulted in certain changes in the institution of marriage. Generally, care is taken to take into confidence the spouses before marriage. Whereas, in villages, marriage is an affair between families rather than individuals, in cities to-day no marriage can be solemnized if any of the spouse is opposed to it. Even the incidence of love marriages is growing.

(vi) ***Changes in the institution of family*** : Another impact of urbanization is the gradual extinction of the joint family system and its replacement by nuclear family. Nowadays, most families consist of husband, wife and their progeny.

(vii) ***Changes in the condition of women*** : With the changes in the institution of family, there are also changes in the position of women. Women are becoming increasingly independent and education among them is also spreading. They are becoming increasingly conscious of their rights and privileges but along with it there is also a tendency of arbitrary and wilful conduct. The incidences of illicit sexual relations, divorce, etc., are also on increase. The ostentation and intense fashion have also become the order of the day.

(viii) *Increase of male ratio* : A significant impact of urbanization on the population is that the ratio of male population is increasing. The main reason for this phenomenon is that, due to shortage of housing, millions of people are forced to live single in cities. The evil of this phenomenon is that this gives rise to sexual corruption.

(ix) *Commercialized entertainment* : On account of industrialization there has been widespread growth of commercialized entertainment. The cinemas are becoming tremendously popular, prostitutes roaring business. Indeed there is a change on every kind of entertainment in the cities.

(x) *Housing shortage* : The growth in population in cities is so fast that it is not possible to provide people with adequate residential accommodation. Indeed pressure on space in cities is so tremendous that most people are forced to live on roads or in shabby accommodation in cities like Bombay. The shortage of residential accommodation compels people to stay without families. The persons coming from villages are unable to bring their families with them. This phenomenon, as observed earlier, leads to inevitable sexual corruption.

(xi) *Growth of slums* : Industrialization has resulted in shortage of accommodation and this, in turn, has given rise to slums, overcrowded shabby living quarters. These slums are populated by workers and other indigent people. The persons living in these slums are constantly exposed to all kinds of diseases, are liable to become social deviates and criminals; and loss of morals is an inevitable consequence of living in slums. The *ahatas* of Kanpur, *bastis* of Delhi, *chawls* of Bombay and *cheris* of Madras are stigmas on the face of India. These shabby quarters are worse than stables of horses and pens of cattle. There is no ventilation, no drainage, no drinking water. A besmirched, ragged piece of jute hanging in front of homes is an eloquent testimony of their pitiable condition. The glaring contrasts in the palatial lives of industrialists and the dirt-laden existence of workers testify to the hollowness of our socialism and democratic life J.L. Nehru was so moved emotionally on seeing slums that he wanted them to be burnt down and the persons responsible for them to be hanged. They symbolize extreme moral and physical decline — the nadir of all that is bad in life. According to Dr. Radhakamal Mukherjee, "In the thousand slums of India's industrial centres manhood is, unquestionably, brutalized, women dishonoured and childhood is poisoned at its very source."

THE ECONOMIC CONSEQUENCES OF INDUSTRIALIZATION

The following are the important consequences in the economic field of industrialization in India.

1. Growth of capitalism. As a result of industrialization there is tremendous concentration of wealth in few hands. Due to industrialization, one man can control a business of crores of rupees and go on amassing wealth unabated. Thus like other countries, industrialization in India has also given tremendous fillip to the growth of capitalism.

2. Vast production. As a result of industrialization, there is production on a large scale. In India steel, cement, sugar, jute, fertilizers, electrical equipments, rail material are being produced on massive scale. India with its vast population is near self-sufficient in these commodities and, today, it exports many of these.

3. Growth of trade. On account of vast production there is unparalleled growth in trade and commerce. The development of fast means of communication has contributed a lot towards this end. The foreign trade has also shown tremendous rise.

4. Division of labour and specialization. An economic impact of industrialization is the division of labour and specialization. Gradually, the number of technocrats and highly skilled personnel is growing.

5. Rise in the standard of living. As a result of industrialization, there is a certain rise in the living standard. To-day electric fans, gas, radio and iron are common household goods.

6. Economic crisis and unemployment. But whereas means of comfort and luxury are now easily available, there is, on the other hand, grave economic crisis. The mechanization of all production has thrown millions of people out of work. Due to industrialization there is a glut of many commodities. This leads to grave economic crisis.

7. Industrial disputes and accidents. The industrial disputes and accidents are inevitable accompaniments of industrialization. Wherever there is industry, there are thousands of workers. It is a natural tendency of workers to expect more and more out of their work; on the other hand, the industrialists want more production for less wages. Under these circumstances there are bound to be clashes of interests resulting in industrial disputes. The working conditions in Indian industry are not of high standard and accidents are very likely.

8. Problems of workers. Besides strikes and lockouts, workers have some other problems. An important problem in this connection is that of rest and relaxation. Firstly, they have to work for long hours so that they get little rest. Secondly, whatever rest they get, there are not adequate sources of healthy entertainment available.

9. Spread of socialism and individualism. The industrialization has promoted both socialism and individualism. As a result of it, capitalism grew and with it spread the ideas of individualism and *laissez-faire.* On the other hand, the ideology of socialism also spread as a result of industrialization. The industrial workers organized themselves into trade unions and political parties in order to gain their support to professed socialism.

10. Class conflict. Like other countries industrialization in India has given rise to class conflicts and class war. There is a continuous tension among the poor and rich. However, the class war in India is as yet not very intense.

11. Decline of rural industry. As a result of industrialization, the goods of daily use are produced on mass scale. The quality of machine-made goods is standardized and they are cheap. This results in larger inflow of goods into villages and has ruined the cottage industry of the villages.

INDUSTRIALIZATION AND SOCIAL DISORGANIZATION

Industrialization gives rise to many such processes which lead to social disorganization. The industrialization produces many problems at family, individual and community level. Industrialization induces individual and family disorganization. Industrialization gives rise to such facts as are responsible for social disorganization. Following are such facts :

1. Facts of individual disorganization. The industrialization gives rise to facts which cause disorganization in the individual. Millions of workers migrate from villages to towns for jobs. As there is acute shortage of accommodation in towns and the life is otherwise costly too, they are unable to bring their families to cities. Therefore, after a day's hard work they can get neither any healthy entertainment nor the peace of home. Lacking all suitable alternatives they take to drinking and prostitution, etc. This leads to their moral degeneration. The gaudy and exciting urban environment and materialistic outlook of life also contribute to moral degeneration. This produces disorganization not only among workers but in other persons, too.

2. Unemployment. While industrialization has created employment opportunities for millions, it has also led to unemployment. The mechanization of production greatly reduced the need for workers. Whenever a new sophisticated machine is installed in any factory, hundreds of workers are thrown out of job. Many rural women come to cities in search for job, but, unable to find one, are forced into prostitution. The unemployment in turn leads to social disorganization.

3. Crime and immorality. The process of industrialization has also led to rise in the incidence of crime and immorality. As referred to earlier, thousands of workers in the town are unable to find suitable accommodation or are unable to cope up with high expenses of urban life. They are forced to lead secluded existence. Being not highly morally trained, they succumb to the twin lure of wine and women. They drink country liquor and visit lowly prostitutes. The industrialization has also given rise to factionalism, materialism and mechanical character of life. All these things have encouraged crime. As a result of industrialization, small boys and girls take to work and they are easily spoiled.

4. Factionalism and heterogeneity. The industrialization has contributed to factionalism and given rise to economic disparities. This is proving highly subversive of social cohesion and unity. The difference between rich and poor keeps growing and both classes tend to develop anti-social tendencies. Whereas industrialists live in fully air-conditioned palatial mansions, the poor are constrained to sleep on footpath and whereas the former live a luxurious life, the latter are unable to make their both ends meet. This economic disparity is productive of social disorganization.

5. Cultural lag. The process of industrialization resulted in cultural lag. This is due to the fact that industrialization leads to fast progress in materialistic things. The manner and mode of life outwardly changes very rapidly but there is little progress of inward culture. Thus inward change does not keep pace with outward changes and this contradiction results in cultural lag.

6. Changes in values. Industrialization has resulted in changes in values. On account of industrializations jobs are now available to women and children. This has resulted in changes in relations of husband and wife and children. Women are no longer chattel pieces of men. They enjoy now relative economic independence and their outlook on life has changed. The relations between various people are no longer based on tradition but are guided by the calculus of self-interest.

7. Family disorganization. Industrialization has resulted in disorganization of family life also. The husband and wife go to their respective places of work and there is no one back at home to take care and look after the children. Where children also do jobs there can be no proper provision of education. Due to changes in values and consequent change in the attitudes, the cohesion of family life is severely disturbed. If husband and wife both stay out of home, chances of disharmony among them increase. If women and girls go out of home for job, the chances of illicit sexual relations increase. On account of all these factors, family disorganization results.

8. Urbanization. An inevitable consequence of industrialization is the increase in urbanization. Due to urbanization, big cities spring up with population far in excess of their capacity. As a result a large number of persons have to live in one or two-room quarters. In this situation there is disaffection among married couples and unmarried persons get frequent opportunities to peep upon sexual activities of married persons. This has evil effect on impressionable young persons and they indulge in premature sex. Many a time queer sexual intimacy among family members is the outcome of this hopeless and helpless situation. The relations among individuals in cities are of impersonal character. The urbanization results in loosening of social control. The community life is disrupted. The gaudy and exciting life of cities produces imbalance in social and personal relations. The freedom of contact between sexes also disturbs family life. The life in clubs and society is a life of rebellion against social traditions and restrictions. The slums, the epidemics, immoral outlook have all combined to knock the bottom out of harmonious and peaceful life in cities.

Steps to Check Effects of Industrialization

From the above discussion of social and economic effects of industrialization, it is quite clear that industrialization has been rising due to a number of evil effects. These include housing shortage, labour problems, unnatural life, increase in crime and exploitation, ruin of rural industry, etc.

Following measures should be taken to counteract the evil influences of industrialization :

1. Town planning. The industries should be at a reasonable distance from the residential colonies and the main centres of the city. The slums should be cleared and replaced by good hygienic houses.

2. Planning of factories. The factories should be well planned. They must be well-ventilated and must have all amenities. They should be so structured and equipped that the chances of accidents are minimal.

3. Enactment of labour laws. There must be well laid down rules for the workers. Their wages, bonus, working hours, gratuity, pensions, leaves, etc., should be governed by laws enacted by the government and these should be strictly enforced.

4. Promotion of rural industries. The government should encourage rural industries. It must give liberal loans for their development.

5. Decentralization. Many an evil effect of industrialization is due to the fact that there is usually concentration of industry at one place. This should be avoided and there should be diversification of industries.

6. Development of cottage industry. A number of evil effects of industrialization are due to mechanization and specialization. This lop-sided development can be greatly averted by promotion and encouragement of cottage industries.

7. Housing. As a result of industrialization there is acute housing shortage in industrial towns. Numerous evil effects flow from the shortage of housing. These can be avoided by giving building of houses top priority.

8. Healthy entertainment. The increase in the incidence of crime, juvenile delinquency and prostitution in industrial towns is due to lack of healthy entertainment. If we know the cause of a phenomenon, it is easy to control it. Thus by providing healthy entertainment we can counteract the above-mentioned evils.

All the above-mentioned suggestions for the improvement of urban areas and for counteracting the ills of industrialization have been in one form or the other accepted, at least in principle by the Government of India. Fortunately, industrialization in India is still not so intense and concentrated as to produce alarming problems. If some advance steps can be taken at this stage, it is possible to mitigate the more severe types of ills consequent upon industrialization. The acute problems of industrialization are in India confined to few metropolises like Calcutta, Bombay, Kanpur, etc. Of course, the efforts being made at these centres to mitigate the evil effects of industrialization leave much to be desired. The existence of slums is a glaring fact of all industrial centres. It is an indelible blot on our society. The working conditions of labour are neither healthy nor hygienic. There is no provision of wholesome entertainment. The government needs to pay special attention to this aspect. The closing down of red-light areas is no solution of the problem. The government alone does not have resources to solve the monumental problems posed by industrialization. It needs the cooperation of local-self government and also the efforts of the industrialists.

QUESTIONS OF EXERCISE

1. Describe formal organization in an industry.
2. Explain informal organization in an industry.
3. Describe the relationship of industrialization and social disorganization.

7
Industrial Bureaucracy

In the industrial system the most important factor is that of industrial bureaucracy. The industrial bureaucracy is a hierarchical arrangement of authority in the industry. The first systematic study of industrial bureaucracy was made by the eminent sociologist Max Weber. In the times of Max Weber bureaucracy was establishing itself as a result of great strides being made in the field of industrialization. According to Weber bureaucracy is a hierarchical arrangement which helps to control and regulate the industrial management.

MEANING OF INDUSTRIAL BUREAUCRACY

The literal meaning of the term bureaucracy is hierarchical arrangement of authority in the field of industry. The term bureaucracy is derived from the French word "Bureau" which means desk. Therefore, quite appropriately, Finer has termed bureaucracy as Desk Government. The word bureau also means tier or step and therefore it signifies hierarchical arrangement of officialdom or management in the field of industry. In modern world the states are so big in size that it is not possible to run their administration; it has to be done indirectly through a large paraphernalia of officers and subordinates. The modern scientific technology has transformed the entire complexion of industry. The industries of the world today are nothing but king-sized. Some of them are indeed big giants and empires. No single person or even a set of persons can afford to control them directly. We shall now examine some of the definitions of industrial bureaucracy given by eminent authorities :

1. According to Max Weber, "Bureaucracy is a system of administration characterized by expertness, impartiality and absence of humanity." In this definition industrialized systems are taken to be akin to a type of administrative system whose chief characteristics are efficiency in work performance, an objective and impartial outlook and most important of all lack of human touch, that is, it

operates mechanically. The absence of human touch and sensibility in the bureaucracy is due to the fact that bureaucracy functions under the framework of rules and regulations though this may militate against human sensibility. Bureaucracy, as a rule, is riddled with formalism and red-tapism. Bureaucracy has come under trenchant criticism on account of these features. Besides above features, there are some other characteristics of bureaucracy, according to Max Weber. These include tier-wise arrangement of officialdom, predominance of files and written work and dependence upon written formalized rules and regulations. Bureaucratic functioning requires technical training.

2. According to Professor Laski, "A system, the control of which is so completely in the hands of officials that their power jeopardizes the liberties of ordinary citizens." Professor Laski's definition of bureaucracy is more in the nature of critique than an explanation of the bureaucracy. Laski considers the freedom of citizen to be crucially important and is opposed to any restriction of their essential freedom. However, this cannot be said to be the chief characteristic of bureaucracy, Admittedly, there is a constant threat to freedom from bureaucracy.

3. According to Robert K. Merton, "Bureaucracy is a secondary group structure designed to carry on certain activities which cannot be performed on the basis of primary group criteria." This definition emphasizes the fact that bureaucracy is based on secondary group structure. The characteristic features of secondary group structure, namely formalism, social differentiation and indirect relations are based upon its sociologic peculiarity and the same are found duplicated in the realm of bureaucracy. The dependence of bureaucracy upon secondary group structure implies, Merton clearly emphasizes, that the tasks assigned to bureaucracy are such as cannot be performed by the primary group. As it has been stressed earlier as long as the industries were on the level of cottage or small scale, the need for bureaucracy was not felt. The need for bureaucratic set-up is felt only when the number of persons engaged in a particular unit exceeds the limit in which direct and face-to-face relations are not feasible.

4. According to Louis Coser and Rosenberg, "Bureaucracy may be defined as that type of hierarchical organization which is designed rationally to co-ordinate the work of many individuals in the pursuit of large scale administrative tasks." In this definition the bureaucratic set-up is likened to hierarchical structure which is used to co-

ordinate the works in large scale organizations. Thus as a matter of fact, bureaucracy is indispensable in large scale organizations and there is indeed nothing wrong as long as it is free from corruption and other malpractices. In conclusion we must admit that for running the modern large-scale industries, the bureaucratic set-up is unavoidable.

CHARACTERISTICS OF THE INDUSTRIAL BUREAUCRACY

The bureaucracy displays the following characteristics :

1. Particular system. The bureaucracy is a special type of system needed to run the organized industry.

2. Hierarchy. The bureaucracy is arranged in a system of lower to higher order. In a hierarchical arrangement, papers move from below to top and the policies are laid down at top and implemented by the lower cadres. There are various levels or rungs in a hierarchical system and it is the peculiarity of this system that under it no level can be side-tracked or circumvented. The papers must move through all the levels intervening between the level initiating them and the apex.

3. Definition of duties of officers. In bureaucracy the rights and duties of all the concerned officers are well-defined. Anyone acting beyond his jurisdiction is taken to task. It is violative of the code of conduct to attempt a task which does not explicitly belong to the person concerned.

4. Specialization. In bureaucracy the officers at different levels possess various types of qualities and have specialized in different areas. When an industry needs officers at a particular level, it advertises for the post and also mentions the minimum requirements, special qualifications and abilities needed for the proper performance of jobs.

5. System of fulfilment of duties. In as much as the various officers at different levels have particular qualifications and possess specific specializations, each man in the bureaucratic set-up has specialized duties. As long as each man performs functions and duties proper to him, there is harmony and smooth working in bureaucracy and the bureaucratic system proves fruitful.

6. Based on documents and files. The majority of bureaucratic functions are performed through the medium of files and documents. A detailed record of the appointment of workers, their grade, cadre, salary, increment and promotion is kept by all industrial organizations. Besides a written balance sheet of expenditures and receipts is also maintained. The record of old files is also maintained for certain specified periods. The files are maintained in a serial order and subject-wise. The efficiency of bureaucracy rests in the quick disposal of files. A clumsy and inefficient handling of files is known as red-tapism.

7. Promotion on seniority and ability. In an industrial organization there are two bases for promotion : seniority and ability. The dual criterion of promotion is essential for the healthy functioning of bureaucratic set-up. Both seniority and ability must be given weightage in deciding upon promotions. This is so because if seniority alone is adopted as criterion of promotion, the able will suffer because persons of lower abilities will occupy senior positions. Moreover, the men of ability may leave the organization to join some other industrial organization which gives more consideration to ability.

8. Service for career. In bureaucracy every person tries to do his job earnestly and honestly in order to gain a better place in the organization. The able, efficient and hard-working individuals are rewarded by better situations and successes in career. Thus, ability and efficiency of a person in bureaucracy can be safely gauged from his career. But when people take to corrupt practices in order to advance their careers, the results are deleterious.

9. Difference in theory and practice. Generally we find a gap between theory and practice in bureaucracy. This has given rise to the view that bureaucracy is an inhuman system. But inhumanity is not an invariable concomitant of bureaucracy. It can be removed.

10. Secrecy of functions. In bureaucracy each official maintains secrecy of his functions.

11. Training. As a matter of fact, in bureaucracy each official gets intensive training prior to his joining the post. But, in order to increase proficiency, these officials are allowed to undertake special training.

12. Bureaucrat personality. An important feature of bureaucracy is that there is usually a gap or chasm between the official and non-official personalities of the bureaucrats. At times there is conflict and tension between the two. Though such instances are common, yet this cannot be considered to be an essential feature of bureaucracy. Indeed a successful bureaucrat is one who can keep his personal and official interests separated. If he completely identifies with his official work himself there is no conflict. But an ambivalence between official and personal interests is dangerous.

TYPES OF BUREAUCRACY

The types of bureaucracy are determined by the criteria adopted for the recruitment of bureaucrats. For example, if officers are recruited on the basis of merit, the resultant hierarchy of officers will be called Merit Bureaucracy. And if this recruitment is made on the basis of caste, the Caste Bureaucracy results. Besides the classification of bureaucracy is made on the basis of the conduct of officers. For examples, if the conduct of officers is guided by the principles of justice and fair play and is directed to general welfare of the masses, the system is know as Guardian Bureaucracy. And if the conduct of officers displays favouritism and is directed to protect the interests of a particular section, this system is called Patronage Bureaucracy. It must, of course, be obvious that compared to Caste Bureaucracy, the Merit Bureaucracy is to be preferred and that compared to Patronage Bureaucracy, the Guardian Bureaucracy is to be preferred.

ADVANTAGES OF BUREAUCRACY

The foregoing description of the features and types of bureaucracy brings to relief the following advantages of bureaucracy :

1. Systematic administration. As is evident from the various definitions of bureaucracy, its system is devised to make administration systematic and scientific.

2. Administration by able persons. In a bureaucratic set-up the work of industry is divided into various levels and departments and the persons having suitable qualifications for each type of work are recruited. This ensures that only capable persons are allowed to handle each type of work.

3. Effective control. The bureaucracy functions on principles, and, under it no room is allowed for personal likes and dislikes. At times this feature may render it seemingly inhuman, but this ensures effective control and minimizes arbitrariness.

4. Possibility of large scale industry. Above all, the greatest advantage of bureaucracy is that with the help of this system, huge industrial empires can be built up and run efficiently. Whatever may be the defects of bureaucracy all these are overruled and set aside by the fact that, without bureaucracy, no big industry can be conceived of.

DISADVANTAGES OF BUREAUCRACY

The above advantages of bureaucracy notwithstanding, various eminent thinkers have bitterly criticized bureaucracy. According to

Laski, it is an attack on the freedom of common man. Bernard Shaw calls it the feudalism of high dignitaries lusting for power. Ramsay Muir has likened bureaucracy to fire, which, as a servant, is indifferent to humanitarian considerations. Briefly, following are the demerits of bureaucracy :

1. Red-tapism. Red-tapism is the biggest defect of bureaucracy. In a bureaucratic set-up, the files and papers move at a snail's pace and it takes inordinately long time to reach any decision on any matter. Usually, so much time is consumed in the disposal of files that by the time a decision is taken it loses relevance. Of course, the red-tapism is more serious in public and government-run industries, whereas in private managements the defect of red-tapism is not so serious.

2. Authoritative tendency. In a bureaucratic set-up the officers occupying top ranks are liable to make an arbitrary use of their authority. They tend to act with scant consideration for the harmful effects of their decision upon the persons concerned. Therefore, bureaucracy tends to become non-human.

3. Superiority complex. In bureaucracy the top ranking officers are afflicted to egoism; they bluff and bluster. Drunk with power, they treat their subordinates with little respect. Therefore, the subordinates feel slighted and demoralized.

4. Emphasis on impersonal relation. It is a common observation that even those personnel who are very polite and courteous in their behaviour turn rude and indifferent upon assuming the position of authority. As a rule, impersonality of relations is an essential characteristic of bureaucracy and within limits this is rather good, but, when this tendency is carried to extreme, it becomes an evil and creates an unbridgeable gulf between the officers and subordinates.

5. Circumlocution. In bureaucracy the officers tend to abide by a too literal interpretation of rules and give credence to statistics available in their books even when a reasonable doubt can occur in this matter. All this leads to unrealistic solution of problems.

6. Conservative. Bureaucracy is conservative and is opposed to any idea of equality. The officers wish to have strict control over their subordinates, and, in the name of discipline, determinedly crush any innovative thinking among the subordinates.

7. Class consciousness. In bureaucracy, the officers consider themselves as an upper caste and look down upon the subordinates.

8. Emphasis on routine. In bureaucracy, innovativeness is sacrificed and routine encouraged.

SUGGESTIONS FOR REFORMS

As we have had an occasion to refer to earlier, the above-mentioned defects of bureaucracy are characteristic more of giant industrial houses or public companies than of small industries. In giant complexes, bureaucratic structure itself becomes so vast, that it gets out of control. As a matter of fact, if strict control is maintained on bureaucracy as is done in private managements, many of the above-mentioned defects can be removed. Following constructive suggestions can be offered :

1. The bureaucracy should be kept under strict supervision of the industrialists or governmental authority. As and when the actions of the bureaucrats are inimical to general welfare, they should be suitably reprimanded.

2. The bureaucrats should not act as patrons but guardians of their subordinates. They should not overlord them but try to work for their welfare.

3. A number of defects in bureaucracy creep in due to faulty recruitment. If ability alone is kept as the criterion of recruitment, most of the defects are avoided, but when patronage or caste is the criterion of recruitment, the above-mentioned defects are bound to creep in.

4. There should be an independent tribunal to adjudicate the complaints of subordinates against the officers high-handedness.

5. A research should be made into ways and means of improving the bureaucratic set-up.

QUESTIONS FOR EXERCISE

1. What is Industrial Bureaucracy? Describe its characteristics.
2. Give types of Bureaucracy. What are their disadvantages? Suggest reforms.

8

INDUSTRIAL LEADERSHIP

At various levels or stages of work in industry, the senior officers supervise, guide and control the functioning of their subordinates. The supervisory function is not merely one of overseeing but also involves guidance and control. In one word, the supervisory function includes the function of leadership. The supervisor is not a mere observer who passively watches what others are doing; but, on the other hand, it is his business to guide and control the overall direction of work. He is therefore required to co-ordinate the work of subordinates under him. Thus supervision is a complex activity and includes co-ordination, guidance and direction. In the words of M.S. Viteles, "Supervision refers to the direct, immediate guidance and control of subordinates in the performance of their tasks." While guidance is a positive aspect of supervision, control is its negative aspect. In industrial supervision both aspects are of equal importance. The value of supervision in industry cannot be exaggerated. Its importance is realized by all and is clear from the fact that everywhere in industry we have supervisors. The supervisors perform various kinds of functions. They not only supervise but also critically evaluate and redirect the works of their subordinates. They also try to remove chances of friction and conflict in the course of work. Besides they train the workers as how to do the task efficiently and well. Above all, the supervisor has in him the quality of leadership which inspires the men under him.

LEADERSHIP IN INDUSTRY

The study of leadership comes into the province of Social Psychology. In all walks of life there are leaders. The leaders co-ordinate, direct and guide the behaviour of their followers. The industrial psychology dwells on the psychological aspects in industry. The field of psychology is the field of human behaviour and conduct. The terms behaviour and conduct include both personal and social behaviour. The leadership in human affairs plays the role of setting standards and guidelines of human behaviour and conduct. Thus in modern industry there is great value and importance of leadership. In some industries certain persons are specifically appointed leaders; but even in those establishments where there are no such specific appointments, certain individuals automatically emerge as leaders. We can thus see leaders anywhere. Wherever there is a group of human beings working together, the emergence of leadership is automatic and natural. However, the leaders who are superimposed, that is those who have been appointed by the management, do not enjoy an unqualified support from the workers and are unable to play as effective and salutary a role as those who are elected by the workers themselves. The reason for this state of affairs is obvious. Only on the basis of personal qualities can one be a true leader. These qualities can by no means be endowed on any one by the management or government. Besides one can voluntarily follow only that person whom he has elected or willingly accepted. On the contrary, a person externally imposed, no matter how hard he may try, cannot evoke and receive voluntarily allegiance of workers. This is the reason why labour leaders are far more powerful than the leaders appointed by the management. The management can ill afford to ignore the labour leader. The popularity of a worker can be gauged from the sociogram of the group of which the worker is a member.

LEVELS OF LEADERSHIP

In accordance with the object of leadership we find three levels of leadership. These are :

1. Senior managerial level. At this apex level are those senior executives by whose order a mill or a factory runs. If this top executive maintains a rapport with the workers, the workers carry out his orders. But, however, in the absence of such a rapport, the labour leaders may prove to be more powerful than senior executive.

2. Intermediate managerial level. At this level we find middle range executives like foremen, supervisors, etc. They have intimate contact with the workers and are capable of providing effective leadership.

3. Labour leaders. These leaders, as is apparent from the name, are the representatives of workers and are usually elected by the workers. Each group of workers selects a leader. There may be conflict among the leaders of the workers. However, if there is a single trade union in a mill or a factory, then there is one leader in the whole of the factory. The labour leaders are quite powerful.

They can organize strikes at a short notice. They act as go-between among management and workers. Sometimes labour leaders are more anxious to find out their own political interests than to work for the real welfare of the workers. As a result of this duplicity of labour leaders, no real benefit accrues from strikes, etc. It is essential that workers should beware of these leaders and keep them at a distance.

TYPES OF LEADERSHIP

Psychologists have classified the types of leadership and supervision in identical terms. In other words, the types of leadership and supervision are similar or parallel or that the supervisory role in industry is the same as that of leadership. The present study of leadership, however, has nothing to do with the problem of political leadership. The industrial leadership and political leadership are quite distinct affairs. The study of leadership in this chapter concerns only the first two types of leadership described above. It is not concerned with labour leaders, who, according to psychologists, are not industrial leaders. An industrial leader *ex hypothesi* must be a supervisor, too. Thus we find the following types of industrial leaders :

(I) Authoritative supervisor. An authoritative supervisor exercises control and direction over his subordinates by virtue of the authority vested in him. In authoritative leadership we have the two following types of supervisors :

1. The hard-boiled autocrat. An autocrat, as is explicit from the term, believes in unflagging discipline and firm control over the workers. He would rarely appreciate the role or work of his subordinates. Rather he looks upon them with slight and mild contempt. He keeps himself aloof from the workers and does not give them a chance to get near him. An autocrat wants automatic obedience of his orders and can brook no criticism of his directions and orders. Though workers obey such autocrats, but, from the core of their heart, they oppose him. Whenever possible they ruin the work and shift the responsibility to someone else. Such autocrats are apt to give credence to backbiting and this leads to tension and conflicts in industry. In as much as autocrats show no respect for the feelings of their subordinates, the subordinates also harbour a spirit of vindictiveness against such persons. At times this flares up and finds expression in violence against supervisors. As a matter of fact, a hard-boiled autocrat does not deserve to be called a leader. He lacks all the qualities of leadership. The obedience of

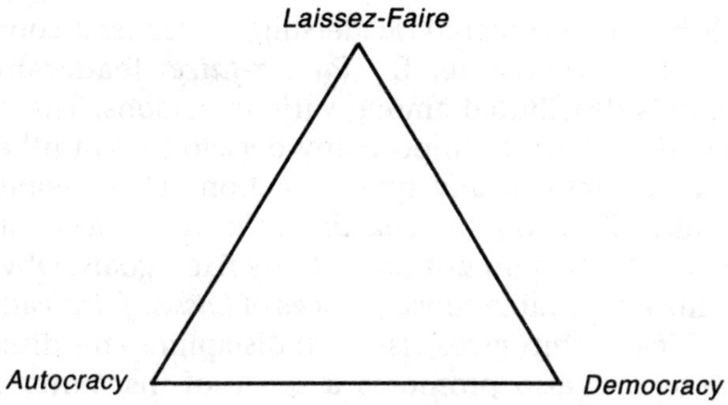

Fig. 8.1. Relations among Autocracy, Democracy and *Laissez-faire*

Democracy is not the opposite of autocracy; rather, both are deviations from individual freedom or *laissez-faire*. In group effort, complete individual freedom leads to chaos. Both autocracy and democracy limit freedom, but, in one case, the limitation is imposed on the group while, in the other, it is assumed by the group.

which he is able to claim is not due to any personal quality in him but is due purely to the authority vested in him.

2. The benevolent autocrat. The benevolent autocrat gives guidance and direction in all matters. He wants to maintain discipline and is annoyed by any infringement of the discipline. But unlike the hard-boiled autocrat, the benevolent autocrat is not averse to saying a word of praise to the workers who perform their duties well. The workers carry out the orders of such supervisors though they do not really feel inspired by them.

In modern times an extensive research has been done to evaluate the authoritative leadership, to discover its *pros and cons*. It is true that authoritative leaders are capable of giving express orders and have them carried out. In certain cases these leaders come to symbolize the father and this helps to bring forth easy and free allegiance of workers. This helps smooth functioning of the factory or a mill. The authoritative leader is impressed by the quality of his decision but his decision cannot become an effective instrument, unless and until it is accepted by all workers, and they feel agreeable to it. There is a little difficulty in its successful implementation.

(II) *Laissez-faire* leadership. In *laissez-faire* leadership the freedom of workers is of greatest value. This type of leadership is exact reverse of the autocratic leadership. While in autocratic leadership there is no place for the personal freedom of workers, in *laissez-faire* leadership the personal freedom of workers is respected. Whereas in autocratic leadership, the leader is considered responsible for everything, in *laissez-faire* leadership the responsibility is distributed among various persons. The *laissez-faire* leaders do not try to impose any decision upon others nor do they coerce them to any type of action. These leaders act democratically. They try to seek the voluntary cooperation of workers. These leaders do not project any fixed goals. Obviously, there are some undesirable consequences of *laissez-faire* leadership. This type of leadership gives rise to indiscipline and discontent among workers. It also promotes a sense of insecurity among them. There is loss in production also. That is why we rarely find such type of leadership in industry.

(III) Democratic supervision. Today the most prevalent form of leadership and supervision in industry is democratic supervision. According to Bradford, democratic leader believes in the following things :

1. Problems should not be allowed to crop up.
2. For the sake of collective action and thinking, assemblies and conferences are a must.
3. There should be fixed collective ideals.
4. The criteria of action should be fixed.
5. The reasons for decisions should be known.
6. With progress, freedom and responsibility increase.

As we have referred earlier, the above-mentioned characteristics of democratic supervision are corresponding to and congruent with modern democratic ideals. In democracies this is the most appropriate form of supervision. However, everyone cannot be led democratically. Some workers misunderstand the democratic attitude of the supervisor and take it to be a symptom of weakness. They try to exploit this weakness and shirk work. This results in loss of production.

Democratic leadership is not opposed to autocratic leadership. Indeed both are deviant forms of *laissez-faire* leadership.

The complete and unfettered freedom degenerates into license. The licentious freedom is obviously fraught with great dangers. It easily results into anarchical conditions. The licentious freedom is possible only in *laissez-faire* leadership. Under democratic leadership everyone gets a chance to participate in supervision. This increases the mutual confidence among workers. The workers feel that whatever they are doing is a result of their own free will.

The supervisor merely proffers technical advice and he is accepted by workers as one of them. Briefly, democratic leadership or supervision is a collective leadership and it is best suited to industry.

THE CONDITIONS OF EFFECTIVE LEADERSHIP

The quality of leadership determines the nature of relationship between senior officers and his subordinates. Thus by effective leadership we mean an effective control and deep impression of the leader upon his followers. Following are conditions essential for effective leadership :

1. Favourable social environs. An essential condition of an effective leadership is the creation of an atmosphere of mutual trust and confidence. It must be able to associate workers in decision making and feeling of responsibility. Under such an atmosphere, the directives of the leader are easily accepted and carried out by the workers.

2. Knowledge of company's policy. Another condition of effective leadership is the knowledge of policy and philosophy of the company. The leader must know the fundamental tenets which govern the functioning of the company. Without possessing such

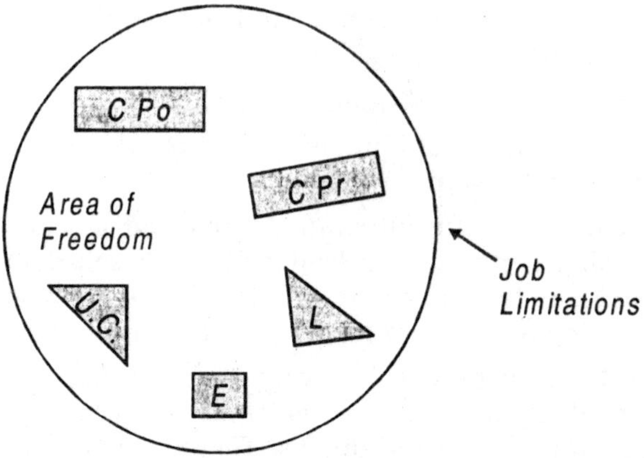

Fig. 8.2. The Area of Freedom for the Practice of Democratic leadership.

The circle represents the limitations which the job situation imposes upon activity; C. Po. and C. Pr. represent the limitations imposed by company policies and company practices, respectively; U.C. and L represent activity areas removed by union contracts and legislation, respectively; and E represents problem areas solved by experts. The remaining area falls within the authority of a given level of supervision, and problems in this area may be solved by group techniques. (From N.R.F. Maier, "A Human Relations Program for Supervision," *In dust and Labour Rel.*, Rev., 1948, 1, 442-64).

knowledge, no leader can be successful. The leader must acquaint the workers with the policy and the rules of the company. He must further explain in clear and frank terms his status and role in the company. This would enable him to feel secure because he knows what he has to do and what he must avoid doing.

3. Gaining confidence of workers. A good leader should win the confidence of workers. Before effecting any change in the technique of production, a good leader will consult the workers even if the change has been finally decided upon. This will help to induce a sense of well-being and confidence among the workers and they will highly appreciate the fact that workers are considered worthy for consultation by authorities.

4. Strict discipline. Whatever rules and regulations are framed once, these should be strictly adhered to. If a worker violates them and deserves to be penalized, he should be penalized without fail and without any let or hindrance; similarly the good works must be rewarded. Therefore, if the performance of a worker is noteworthy and deserves reward, he must be rewarded ungrudgingly.

5. Participation in decision-making. Finally, it is very necessary for good leadership that workers should be given a chance to participate in the decision and policy making of the company. This will enthuse workers to toil hard and work with grit and determination.

General Principles of Good Leadership

The psychologist Blum has suggested the following principles for good leadership :

1. Don't be an autocrat. As referred to earlier, autocratic leadership is not a good leadership. It is self-defeating because the workers feel alienated and do not obey the leader willingly. Therefore autocracy in leadership should be eschewed.

2. Listen carefully. It is very essential that the leader should be a good listener. The supervisor must listen carefully to everything told to him by his subordinates. He must accord full opportunity to the worker to present his case. Only when the worker has presented his case should the leader express his opinion.

3. Don't decide hurriedly. It is rash to form an opinion about some person hurriedly after a casual glance or brief hearing. Some persons deny their subordinates the opportunity to speak out of their mind and pay no attention to their complaints. While it is true that most of the complaints are not genuine, some are certainly so and if these are not removed, the morale in the company would suffer.

4. Don't argue with subordinates. A supervisor should under no circumstances indulge in arguments with his subordinate, because if he fails to be persuaded or convinced by his subordinate, or his arguments, he is liable to issue orders to vindicate his point of view. This creates frustration and sense of insecurity among the workers. The good leader does not argue but listens carefully. Only after careful listening he issues orders.

5. Don't criticize publicly. Nobody likes to be told off or reprimanded in the presence of others. If a worker is rebuked publicly he feels insulted. The workers are usually rash and they tend to retaliate if they are wounded emotionally. Therefore, a good leader avoids discussing the faults of workers in public. He points them out in private and in a direct manner.

Some more facts can be pointed out with regard to successful supervision. However, it is not possible to describe and classify all laws about supervision. The supervision is an art rather than a science; and it is not possible to describe all facts about art. Some persons are very persuasive in their reasoning. They have the gift of leadership and they are easily accepted by others as leaders. The persons who have the natural qualities of leadership are the best supervisors.

QUALITIES OF LEADERSHIP

1. Physical qualities. (i) Sound health, (ii) Vitality, (iii) Endurance.

2. Psychological qualities. (i) Personal Magnetism, (ii) Enthusiasm, (iii) Co-operation, (iv) Ability to inspire, (v) Forcefulness, (vi) Tact.

3. Intellectual Traits. (i) A high degree of intelligence, (ii) An open mind, (iii) A capacity for sound judgement, (iv) An ability to teach, (v) Scientific Approach.

4. Qualities of Character. (i) Integrity, (ii) Self-discipline, (iii) Fair play, (iv) Willingness to accept responsibility, (v) Physical and moral courage, (vi) Humanism.

TRAITS COMMON TO ALL LEADERS

The traits approach to leadership study was especially popular during 1930-50. As traits have no direct relation with the leadership, therefore, common traits are hardly found in two leaders. Each leader has different traits. Therefore, analysis of traits in different leaders made the list of traits longer and longer but there was very little consensus over common traits among researchers. Though very significant in determining a successful leader but personal traits and leadership have no relations. The studies of past leaders' life indicate that certain useful traits which they had really made them leaders such as 'strength of character' or 'power' or 'dominance' but it was the environment which made the traits active.

IMPORTANCE OF LEADERSHIP

1. Directing group activities. In an organization leadership is mainly concerned with the group. Its main responsibility is to get the work done effectively by fruitfully engaging the workers or subordinates. For this purpose, the leader promotes the sincerity of purpose among the workers and directs them rightly towards the accomplishment of organisational goals. By his personal conduct and behaviour, the leader-infuses confidence in his subordinates and induces them to work hard. To quote George R. Terry, "A leader shows the way by his example. He is not a pusher, he pulls rather than pushes."

A group cannot work efficiently without leadership because a leader alone can consolidate the efforts of the group and divert those efforts towards the goal. He interprets the goal and plans of the group to the followers and takes the lead in all activities. So, directing the group activities towards a common goal is the main function of the leadership.

2. Better utilisation of manpower. The leader is important as he makes plans, policies and programmes and carries them out. As plans, policies and programmes cannot work themselves, he mobilises the workforce to engage them to get higher performance. He co-ordinates their efforts to utilise the available manpower effectively so as to get highest production with minimum human cost. Achieving best performance from workers is the key to successful and effective leadership.

3. Source of motivation. Leadership is a source of motivation to the subordinates. It does not mean simply the existence of leadership traits in a person. It is to utilise those traits in motivating the people at work towards the desired goal by applying a leadership style most suited to the situation. Motivation is an element of dynamic leadership in whose absence the success is doubtful.

4. Developing good human relations. Human relations represent the relations between the leader and the subordinates. An efficient leadership develops the talents of the individuals, promotes self-confidence in them and provides them an opportunity to demonstrate their ability apart from the motivation towards the accomplishment of goal. Thus, the leader emphasises the co-operative attitude of workers. It creates an environment of good human relationship which increases the productivity of the organisation.

5. Promoting the spirit of co-ordination. The activities of members of a group and those of different groups must be co-ordinated in order to achieve the desired goal. A leader promotes the spirit of co-ordination among workers.

6. Fulfilling social responsibilities. Only an effective leadership may get the work done effectively. A well satisfied worker will help serving the organisation's interest under a good leadership. Good leadership is always concerned with the need and satisfaction of its workforce which provides higher standard of living to workers, higher productivity and production to the organisation, lower price to consumers, increased revenue to the nation, and a fair return to the investors. Thus, only under the guidance of dynamic leadership, an organisation can fulfil its social responsibilities towards different sections of the society : consumers, workers, investors, government, etc.

FUNCTIONS OF LEADERSHIP

1. Integration. Leadership integrates the efforts of its followers and directs them towards organising goals. The leader integrates the efforts of the group. Common objectives cannot be achieved and co-ordination is not possible without that. In this age of specialisation, each individual does a part of the whole work. The integration of the parts of the whole is the leadership function.

2. Communication. Communication of organisational policies, procedures and programmes is necessary in order to integrate the efforts of the members of the group. A leader communicates authority and responsibility to each individual so that he may come to know what he is to do and what not. He knows the way as to how he can attain the goals and discharge his responsibilities.

3. Production. A leader should follow the production-oriented supervisory style of leadership; he should do utmost to increase the production and productivity of the organisation though not at the cost of human relations.

4. Representation. A leader represents the organisation and its objectives before those who work for it and those who are outsiders. He represents workers before the higher management and outsiders. He represents management before the workers. Thus, he provides link between his management and subordinates.

5. Fraternity. Leadership should promote fraternity among the subordinates. Its approach and style play an important role in developing industrial harmony. He should develop a climate of co-operation among workers in the organisation to achieve the success.

6. Organisation. Organising capacity of a leader is an important trait. He is to decide who will do what and how? He provides necessary inputs to get the work done effectively. Failing in organising functions, he loses his confidence among the workers and also the organisation.

7. Evaluation of Performance. A leader evaluates the performance of his subordinates. If a worker does well, he is adequately rewarded and if he fails in discharging his responsibility, he is punished. Both reward and punishment aim at motivating people to improve the situation. In the words of Stogdill, "Leadership is concerned with problems of human performance and interaction."

8. Initiation. A leader must lead. He should take initiative to introduce changes in the organisation and the group's efforts wherever necessary. He should communicate the changes and reasons behind them to convince the workers about their rationality.

9. Domination. A leader dominates his followers. He holds authority and some organisational power to use his power constructively or destructively. He may ignore his follower's wishes but he should not do that. He should be participator. He must use his power in the interest of group of which he is a leader.

DIFFERENT APPROACHES TO LEADERSHIP

Broadly, there are five main theories of leadership : (1) Traitist theory, (2) Situationalist theory, (3) Behavioural theory, (4) Followers theory, (5) System theory or Path-Goal Theory.

1. Traitist Approach or Theory

According to this classical theory, leadership behaviour is produced by certain traits (qualities) inherent in a person. In other words, leadership behaviour is sum total of the traits. A leader behaves according to his traits. Studies have focused the traits of past and present leaders in terms of their family background, education, career, events, character, etc. They have made a list of traits or attributes which a leader should possess. A number of traits have been identified by various researchers to distinguish successful leaders from unsuccessful ones or followers. The one way to identify the traits is to enquire from the leader himself, how he considers himself different from others.

A successful leader is supposed to have the following traits :

(i) Good personality, (ii) Tirelessness, (iii) Ability to quick decision, (iv) Courage, (v) Persuasion (vi) Intelligence, (vii) Reliability, (viii) Imagination, (ix) Physically fit, (x) Intellectually sound, etc. Psychologists have grouped these traits of a leader into four categories: (a) Physical, (b) Psychological (c) Intellectual and (d) Qualities of character.

Earlier, traits theories maintained that leadership qualities are inherited. Later theorists conceded that many of these traits could be acquired and developed by experience and training. Thus, traits are not only inborn but acquired as well. It has now been well established that leader is not only born but also made.

Weaknesses of Traits Theory

Though widely accepted for a pretty long time during 1930s-1950s, trait theory suffers from the following weaknesses :

1. No exhaustive list. Various thinkers have supplied different list of qualities of a successful leadership. No two lists agree on the essential characteristics of the effective leader. None of the thinkers have listed the traits; in order of importance, lists of traits sometimes confuse the readers.

2. No common or universal traits. Neither leadership traits are common nor universal. Therefore it is very difficult to indicate what traits are necessary to make an effective leader. Measurement of traits is problematic.

3. No room for future leaders. Traits theory stresses the inborn qualities of an individual which cannot be developed or acquired. Earlier it was assumed that leaders are born and, therefore, it left no scope for development of future leaders. It was later accepted that such inborn traits can be developed or acquired through experience or training.

4. No Consideration of situational factors. Trait theorists do not consider the situational factor for leadership which influence the leaders more than their inner traits. Traits come to light when a situation arises. They are helpful in facing a particular situation but traits are useless without a situation.

5. Different roles require different traits. This is so even in the same organisation. At lower managerial level, where there is a direct contact between a worker and the supervisor, technical knowledge is of paramount importance. Human relations and skills are of prime importance at middle management level, where policies are elaborated and interpreted. Conceptual skill gains prominent position at higher management level, where policies are framed and planning is undertaken. In a larger organisation, leadership has a limited role. In a small organisation it demands multiplicity of roles. Thus different combinations of traits are required in different organisations or at different organisational levels.

6. Negligence of other variables of leadership. These include acts of leader, followers and their acts, situation and their effects on the leader.

7. Traits of an individual cannot be known unless situation arises. When an individual faces a problem, then only the presence or absence of the traits is known otherwise traits remain unknown.

2. Behavioural Approach or Theory

When it was apparent from the critical evaluation of traitist theory that traits fail to explain the leadership phenomenon, the theorists diverted their attention to the study of leadership behaviour.

Under classical management approach, a man or worker was regarded as a commodity or just an appendage to a machine. Hence the management coerced, directed and motivated workers through the offer of economic rewards. It attempted to increase efficiency or productivity by reducing waste of time and material. No consideration was given to men as an asset. The basic assumption under classical theory was that the people, by nature, were lazy, uncreative and irresponsible and therefore the leader should be directive. However, scientific management approach in management by Taylor and Hawthorne experiments by Elton Mayo and his associates discovered that human behaviour of workers is the sole concern for the leadership.

This approach demarcated various leadership styles such as autocratic, democratic or supervisory style which produce different and conflicting results, since the behaviours of leader and followers differ in different situations. Behaviour theory explained the leadership phenomenon in terms of behaviour of the leader. What the leader does was the main concern. Hence the investigators examined the styles followed by the leader, *i.e.*, authoritarian or democratic. It may be a mix of the two.

The main limitation of behavioural approach is the questionnaire which has its own limitations. Scientific tests cannot be applied in studies which are likely to be affected by perceptual differences and a variety of interpretations of questions. As no measurement methodology, *i.e.*, questionnaire, observation or interviews has been universally accepted by behavioural researchers, this is an unavoidable limitation.

3. Situationalist Approach or Theory

While the trait approach explained some of the desirable characteristics that a leader should have, it could not suggest that one who possesses particular set traits shall be a leader. On the other hand, the behavioural approach explained the various practices or styles available to a leader to discharge his leadership function but failed to indicate the best style of leadership which may be universally appropriate. Both these theories — Traits and Behavioural Theories — initiated further researches. During 1970s it was established that it were not the traits or behaviour of a leader that mattered but it was particular situation in which a particular trait or behaviour (style) was effective or ineffective. Thus both Trait and Behavioural approaches accepted the situation as an important element.

Situationalist theory advocates that a leader is strongly affected by the situation in which he works. It is a situation that helps developing leadership and from which leaders emerge, while traits or behaviour may be supportive elements. A person may be a good leader in a particular situation or set of circumstances, but he may be quite ineffective in a different situation. Situationalist theory further believes that there exists an interaction between a group of workers and its leader. The people tend to follow the leader who is capable of fulfilling their aspirations. The leader is to recognize the needs of situation and the aspirations of the followers and to act accordingly. Thus, it is a situation that produces the leadership.

Situational theory suffers from the following weaknesses :

(i) ***Overemphasis on the situational aspect of leadership :*** Situations may affect the decision of a leader in a particular time but it is not everything. Hence it should not be overemphasized.

(ii) ***Neglect of the traits and behaviour :*** The theory neglects the traits and behaviour of a leader which play an important role in the emergence of a particular leader. The head and heart of a leader play a decisive role in every situation.

4. Followers Theory or Acceptance Theory

Followers theory asserts that the followers are important in deciding whether a person is a leader or not. If they accept a person as their leader, he is a leader irrespective of his traits or behaviour. This theory cannot be applied without a group of followers. It is based on the assumption that groups have certain basic needs which they want to be fulfilled through their leader. A person is assumed to be their leader who is successful in satisfying their basic needs. If he does not succeed in getting their needs satisfied, he may neither be said to be a good leader nor will he be allowed to function as such. Thus need of the followers is the most crucial and guiding factor in the leadership event.

Followers theory ignores the quality aspect of leadership. However, modern managers are of the opinion that it is the followers theory that is now playing a significant role in managing the people today. This theory is playing a dominant role in business, industrial and political leadership in India.

5. System Approach or Path-Goal Theory

According to this theory, leadership is governed by a person's acts rather than by his traits. Leadership co-ordinates the efforts of the people and stimulates them towards the achievement of their goal in a particular situation. This approach is called system approach because it considers all the variables present at the same time, *i.e.*, leader, followers, situation, goals, leadership traits, environment, and group's nature, characteristics and needs, role, behaviour of the leader and his co-ordinating efforts. This theory is recognised as the modern theory of leadership.

LEADERSHIP STYLES

Styles describe how a leader behaves with his group or how leadership is applied in practice.

1. Motivational Styles : Positive and Negative Leadership

Motivation of followers or workers in a business enterprise is the main function of a leader. Motivational styles cover two main approaches, which are generally followed by a leader : (i) Positive approach and (ii) Negative approach.

(i) ***Positive approach to leadership*** : Leadership is said to be positive when a leader motivates the people to work hard by offering them various rewards, monetary or otherwise. The more is the reward, the higher is the efficiency. Positive leadership promotes industrial peace. For example, encashment of leave will certainly reduce the absenteeism in the organisation because it increases 'workers' real wages.

(ii) ***Negative approach to leadership*** : It is said to be a negative approach or negative leadership where the leader induces the followers to work hard and threatens them to penalise if work is not up to the mark. Thus, in a negative leadership, emphasis is laid on penalties for the shortcomings. The stronger is the penalty, then more negative it is. For example, if a manager imposes a salary cut for the absence from duty it is a negative approach to improve absenteeism.

Though negative leadership gets acceptable performance in many situations, it has high human costs. Negative leaders are domineering. They impose the penalties like loss of job, reprimand before others, leave without pay, etc. In order to get the work done, they display their authority with the false assumption that it frightens everyone into productivity. They are more bosses than leaders.

In negative leadership, followers work only to protect themselves. They always try to shift their responsibility to others.

Almost every manager uses both the styles off and on but the predominant style sets the tone within the group. It depends on the situation of the case, and the organisation behaviour model as to which of the two styles is the best. A manager may follow the positive approach but he may be a supporter of negative approach next time in similar case due to a situation. Thus a modern manager uses both styles according to the circumstances of the case.

The organisational behaviour model also sets the tone. The autocratic model tends to cause a negative style. The custodial model follows somewhat positive or somewhat negative or a mix of both the styles and the supportive model is clearly positive. Positive leadership achieves higher productivity to the organisation and higher job satisfaction to subordinates.

2. Power Styles — Autocratic, Democratic and Free-rein Leaders

Style of use of power also establishes a type of style. Power styles may be of three types : (a) Autocratic Leadership,

(b) Democratic Participative Leadership and (c) Free-reign Leadership.

(a) ***Autocratic or authoritarian leadership*** : Under this style, power or authority and decision making are centralized to the leaders. They create work-situations and environment for their subordinates. The subordinates, in turn, do whatever they are told, nothing less and nothing more. The leaders enjoy full authority and assume full responsibility. They are power-loving and never like to be devoid of power. Subordinates or followers are not aware of the organisational goals; they feel insecure and afraid of the leader's authority. This leadership is negative. However, leadership may be positive under this style if the leader uses his power in the best interest of the group and disburses rewards to motivate them. Autocratic leader having positive motivational style is known as benevolent autocrat. The benevolent autocrat gets productivity and full satisfaction as followers are habituated to culture of authorities in the society such as teachers, parents, government bureaucrats, etc. They feel satisfied and secure under autocratic leader. They respond well to action. Sometimes, benevolent autocrat leaders are more successful than the democrat leaders.

Advantages of Autocratic leadership

(i) It provides strong motivation and reward for the leader.

(ii) As a single person decides for the whole group, quick decision-making is guaranteed.

(iii) Less competent sub-managers are not involved in decision-making process. They may be used to carry out the orders of the boss.

(iv) Decision making, planning or organising need no initiative.

Disadvantages of Autocratic Leadership

(i) It is disliked if it is extreme and the motivational style is negative.

(ii) Frustration, low morale and conflict develop easily because subordinates dislike the work they have to do. They work half-heartedly due to lack of any motivation.

(iii) Managers are poor motivators.

(iv) Full potential of subordinates and their creative ideas is not used for the benefit of the organisation.

(v) In the absence of the leader, organisational continuity is threatened because subordinates gets no opportunity for the development.

If subordinates are uneducated, unskilled and submissive, autocratic leadership is appropriate, because subordinates in such cases cannot take decisions. It may also be desirable when the organisation endorses fear and punishment as accepted disciplinary techniques.

(b) ***Participative or democratic leadership*** : As opposed to autocratic leadership, under this style, power and authority are decentralised and thus decisions are not unilateral. Subordinates are consulted before taking any decision, and thus they are fully aware of the path and goal of the organisation. The leader and group work together as a social unit. While autocratic leaders control through authority vested in themselves, participative leaders exercise control mostly by using force within the group.

Democratic leader delegates his authority to his subordinates to get the work accomplished towards goals of the organisation. The present trend is towards wider use of the participative practices. Workers' participation in management is gradually getting popular.

Advantages of Participative Leadership

(i) Workers or subordinates are consulted. They participate in the decision-making process and hence they feel satisfied.

(ii) Workers are aware of what is happening in the organisation. Hence they take interest in producing more and more.

(iii) Subordinates get full opportunity to utilise their capabilities because it cultivates decision-making ability of subordinates.

(iv) The leader adds to his abilities through the contribution of his followers.

Disadvantages of Participative Leadership

(i) Power is not centralised to the leader. He may use it only in consultation with his subordinates.

(ii) Decision-making and implementation are delayed as compared to autocratic leadership because under this style, more than one person is involved in decision-making process.

(iii) As authority is decentralised, less competent executives cannot be used.

(iv) It cannot yield positive results when subordinates prefer minimum interaction with the leader.

(v) It may be used as a means of passing the buck to others and of abdicating responsibility.

(vi) It requires considerable persuasive and communicating skill on the part of the leader.

(c) *Free-rein leadership* : Under free-rein style, leaders enjoy no power. They delegate their authority to the subordinates themselves who take decision. The leadership is employee-centred. The group of employees is free to establish its own goals and work-out its own problems. The members of the group train themselves and provide their own motivation.

The leader keeps contact with outsiders to bring to the group the information and resources, the group needs to fulfil its job. Leadership ignores the leader's contribution in the same way as autocratic leadership ignores the group. It fails to provide the benefits of leader's inspired motivation to the group. Sometimes it creates chaos.

Advantages

(i) Job satisfaction and morale of subordinates increases.

(ii) There is a maximum possible scope for the development of subordinates.

(iii) Potential of subordinates is fully utilised.

Disadvantages

(i) Subordinates do not get the guidance and

(ii) Leader's contribution is ignored.

3. Orientation Style or Supervisory Style

(i) *Employee-oriented leadership* : Employee-oriented leaders are concerned about the needs of their employees and pay attention to their subordinates' attitudes, interests and necessities, etc. They try to get increased productivity by improving the working conditions and environment and solving the problems, if any, faced by them during the course of their action at the job.

(ii) *Production or task-oriented leadership* : Production or task-oriented leaders believe that they are concerned mainly with the production while employees are not of much concern. They believe that they can attain results by planning better methods, keeping people constantly busy and using them to produce. They do not consider human aspect of the workers.

Employee-oriented and production-oriented leadership styles are both related and independent. They are not opposed to each other. A manager who is more employee-oriented, is not necessarily against production-oriented or *vice-versa*. Each orientation is somewhat independent. A manager must combine these two orientations. He must think in terms of higher production and not at the cost of human values. He must honour the initiative and abilities of employees and try to satisfy their needs.

Suitability of the Different Styles

Modern research findings about leadership style suggest that a universally accepted 'best' style is very difficult rather impossible due to the complexities of the modern organisation. Those who consider a single style of leadership to be best for every kind of organisation at every level and with any kind of subordinates, ignore important influences of factors like subordinate characteristics, level of education, and standard of living. As a leader's style does not operate in vacuum and influences the others' behaviour, these situational factors cannot be ignored. It is highly unrealistic to talk of a single best or normative style of leadership. A leader should not be rigid to any one style of leadership. He should get the work done as the situation warrants. He may be autocratic at one time and democratic at the other. Sometimes he motivates people through positive rewards and sometimes he is forced to get results through democratic methods involving the people at large in the decision-making process, satisfy human needs not at the cost of human values, by following positive motivational measures. But he cannot always abstain from attempting negative autocratic style, if a situation so warrants.

FIEDER'S CONTINGENCY MODEL

Application of Contingency Model

Fieder and his associates have classified the relationship between consideration and structure, and presented 'Contingency Model of Leadership'.

This theory specifies that the effectiveness of a group is contingent upon the motivational system of a leader and the degree to which the leader has control and influence in a particular situation. The leader's effectiveness may be measured with the leader-member relations, task structure and leader's position and power. The situation is regarded to be highly favourable to leadership effectiveness. If leader-member relations are good, task is structured and leader position power gets strong. On the contrary, if leader-member relations are not good, task is unstructured and leader's position and power get weak, and the situation may be regarded as highly unfavourable to the leader's effectiveness. Favourableness or unfavourableness determines the effectiveness of the leadership. As a leader operates in a particular situation, it is an important question to decide what type of leadership style is needed in a particular type of a situation. Contingency theory suggests that a particular leadership style is effective only in a particular situation. In other words, the effectiveness of a leader is contingent upon the relationship among all these variables.

Types of Variables

1. Leader-member relations. The leader-member relations are determined by the manner in which the leader is accepted or rejected by the group. For example, if in an organisation there is a group friction, orders are generally flouted, the leader-member relations are said to be poor. If there is co-operation between leader and members, orders are carried out in proper manner and according to leader's desire, and the relations may be regarded as good.

2. Task structure. A task is said to be highly structured. It is highly specific, if it can be done only in one way and rules and procedures are well defined, and there is no scope for different interpretations. The task is regarded as highly unstructured if it is completely non-routine, there are many routes to reach the goal or rules and procedures are not clear. In a highly structured task, leader's ability to influence the group is restricted because the task dilutes the leader's potential influence. In case of unstructured task, the leader has great potential for influencing the group as he has more knowledge than his followers.

3. Leader position power. Leader's positional power indicates the power provided to him by the position in an organisation such as power to hire and fire, status symbols, power to give promotion and pay raise, punishment, rewards, etc. In most business organisations, the leaders possess high position power while in social organisations, leaders have very low positional power.

In addition to leader's employee-orientation ranging from a highly favourable position to a highly unfavourable position for a leader, Fieldler has considered eight combinations of three variables. In the middle of these two extremes is the intermediate position of favourableness for the leader.

(i) ***In highly favourable situation*** : The task-oriented leader performs better. The least preferred worker is also motivated by task accomplishment.

(ii) ***In favourable situation*** : The workers support him when task is structured and leader-member relations are good, even if the task-oriented behaviour of the leader may be considered friendly.

(iii) ***In unfavourable situations*** : When task is unstructured, the relations between the two are not good, and the power position of the leader is poor. He is more concerned with the performance and his efforts are to remove the ambiguity and anxiety. If the leader possesses more knowledge than his subordinates, the followers are willing to accept the task-oriented structure.

(iv) *Intermediate favourableness* : A leader obtains better group performance in moderate conditions. (i) The task is structured and leader is disliked, therefore, he demonstrates that he cares for the emotions of the subordinates, or (ii) the leader is liked and the task is unstructured and the leader depends upon the willingness and creativity of the group's members to accomplish the goals.

Leader Match Training

On the basis of his contingency model of leadership, Fielder developed the 'leader match' training programme to improve leadership's effectiveness. The programme was based on the assumption that as it is much easier to change the situation rather than to change the fundamental style, therefore, the job should be fitted to the manager.

Thus, the contingency model of Fiedler has helped to resolve confusion about optimum conditions for a considerate, people-oriented leader, compared with a more structured, task-oriented leader.

Criticism of Contingency Model

1. **Undimensional.** While the model suggests that the leader can be either task-oriented or relationship-oriented, in reality, leader is multidimensional. It is not necessary that a leader, who is high on one side may be low on the other side. He is rather a combination of the two.

2. **Confusion of combinations and style.** Fiedler suggested a measuring rod of style, putting eight possible combinations on the LPC (Least Preferred Co-owners) which is quite confusing and unreliable. Different researchers reveal that there is no direct relationship between the combinations and style.

3. Changing appropriateness. Fiedler's model fails to explain why the same style is appropriate in both — most favourable and most unfavourable situations.

4. Negligence of many variables. The model does not consider many situational variables such as subordinates' expectations of leader's behaviour, ability of the leader to influence his superior and the congruence of leadership styles among organisational levels.

5. Complex. The model is very complex and based on small samples. It does not explain how the situational variables affect the leadership style.

Advantages

In spite of the above limitations, Fiedler's model of leadership has proved advantageous because it operationalises the set of actions that may be used to improve leadership effectiveness. It considers both personal and situational variables. It has intuitive appeal. It is based on commonsense reasoning. A leader can enforce accountability, if his power is strong, but when his power is weak he has to cultivate relationship to get things done.

QUESTIONS FOR EXERCISE

1. What is industrial leadership? Explain condition of effective leadership.
2. Explain the themes industrial leadership.
3. Describe styles of industrial leadership.

9
Industrial and Personnel Management

MEANING OF MANAGEMENT

A review of the following definitions of management will help to make clear the meaning of the term management :

1. **Encyclopaedia of Social Sciences.** "Management may be defined as the process by which the execution of a given purpose is put into operation and supervised. The combined output of various types and grades of human effort by which the process is effected is known as management in the human sense."

2. **F.C. Hooper.** "Management is the driving force that inspires an undertaking to knit itself into an entity and creates the conditions and relationships which bring about a full use of all its powers and resources."

3. **J.L. Lundy.** "Management is principally a task of planning, co-ordinating, motivating and controlling the efforts of others towards a specific objective."

4. **F.F.L. Brech.** "Management is the responsibility for the effective planning and regulation of the operation of an enterprise; such responsibility involving (i) the installation and maintenance of proper procedure to ensure adherence to plans; and (ii) the guidance, integration and supervision of the personnel comprising and carrying out operations."

5. **Kimbal and Kimbal.** "Management may be broadly defined as the art of applying the economic principles that underlie the control of men and materials in the enterprise under consideration."

6. **Wilson.** "Management is the development of people and not the direction of things."

7. **E.H. Peterson.** "Management is the ordering and co-ordinating of functions and of the men fulfilling their functions in order to achieve a given purpose."

CHARACTERISTICS OF MANAGEMENT

From the above definitions, the characteristics of management become quite plain. These are :

1. Science. As management is based upon certain scientific principles, it can be considered to be a science.

2. Art. There are quite a few aspects of managerial skill for which no scientific principles can be laid. These depend upon sound judgement and fact. Hence, management can be said to be an art.

3. Procedure. The management in an industry or a factory is based upon certain procedures. A manager tries to achieve his objective of working within the limits laid down by the procedures.

4. Definite aim. Management is always goal-directed and has a definite aim in view.

5. Direction of efforts. If the workers are allowed arbitrary choice of action, this will lead to chaos. It is necessary, therefore, that actions of various workers should be properly concatenated so as to give definite results.

6. Co-ordination. In an industry work is divided into many sections. This needs co-ordination.

7. Control. Besides direction, instruction and issuing guidelines, it is also essential to exercise control on the activity of workers.

8. Standard. The work in the industry must conform to a specified standard.

9. Co-operation. Above all, co-operation between managers and workers is necessary for successful management.

CONCEPT OF INDUSTRIAL MANAGEMENT

According to *Encyclopaedia of Social Sciences*, a group of persons who cooperate to work for some project are engaged in the industrial management. Thus industrial management involves direction, planning, adjustment, control and co-operation for realizing industrial projects. In an industrial project, a number of elements are involved such as materials for production, workers, managers, capital investment, etc. The materials for production include land, raw material and machinery. According to J.R. Tarry, industrial management consists of realizing the industrial aim with the help of wherewithal of industrial production. There are various types of management. The important ones are as follows :

1. Production management. In the production management are included the following elements, (i) job analysis; (ii) determination of the system or production; (iii) standardization; and (iv) study of time, speed and fatigue.

2. Development management. In this we study the kind and quality of raw material, techniques of production and also the consumer needs.

3. Financial management. Under this, budgeting is done and also data regarding market conditions are collected.

4. Distribution management. Under this are included advertising, market research, export and sale, etc.

5. Sales management. Under this are included inviting tenders, organizing sales and making provisions for stock and storage.

6. Maintenance management. Under this are included maintenance of building, etc.

7. Transport management. Under this are included arrangement for packing, transportation, warehousing, etc.

8. Office management. Under this, data regarding production and distribution are collected and their record maintained.

9. Personnel management. Under this are included the recruitment and training of workers and managers. Also the pay scales are determined and rules for promotion arid increment laid down.

FUNCTIONS OF INDUSTRIAL MANAGEMENT

The industrial management is a complex process and it involves a number of functions. In brief, following are the main functions of the industrial management :

1. Forecasting. First and foremost function of the industrial management is to make industrial projection, that is, to assess before hand the demand for goods. Besides, when a new venture is undertaken, forecasting consists of making assessment of the needs for labour and equipment.

2. Planning. By dividing the complex industrial processes into their constituents, planning is done. In words of L. Urwik, planning is a mental process, a decision to do the work in a proper manner.

3. Organization. According to Brech organization is to divide the responsibility and entrust it to various departments. To organize means to entrust each worker in an industry with jobs for which he is suited.

4. Direction. According to G.R. Terry, direction consists of the following steps to speed up the work, to inspire the group and to create in each worker an aptitude and liking for the work.

5. Leadership. The business of leadership is to guide and inspire the workers in such a way that optimum production is achieved.

6. Staffing. The most important element of any industry is workers. The quality of workers makes or mars the industry. Therefore, appointment of workers is the most important factor in the industry. The appointment, training, etc. of workers come under this head.

7. Motivation. In an industry production is done by various machines but these machines are operated by men. Men need to be motivated if satisfactory results have to be achieved.

8. Co-ordination. Defining co-ordination, Brech writes that coordination in an industry means distribution of work in such a way that cordiality of relations is maintained. Mary Parker Follet has enumerated four principles of co-ordination. These are :

(i) To effect co-ordination in various processes from very beginning.

(ii) In order to remove the defects of bureaucracy to maintain direct contact with the workers.

(iii) Co-ordination of production, sale and labour.

(iv) To maintain and sustain co-ordination.

9. Control. Defining control, Brech calls it to achieve maximum production by determined effort. The control is of four types : budgetary control, control over cost of production, control over management and lastly financial control.

10. Communication. To maintain contact and rapport between workers, consumers, shareholders and suppliers is called communication.

PERSONNEL MANAGEMENT

By personnel management we mean the recruitment, supervision and control of the labour force. Personnel management also deals with the efficiency of labour force and increase of production and general welfare of the workers. It is the aim of personnel management to maximize the utility of workers for industrial production.

Definition

The following definitions of personnel management will help to make clear the meaning of this term :

1. **E.F.L. Brech.** "Personnel management may be conveniently described as part of the management process which is primarily concerned with the human constituents of an organization. Its object is the maintenance of human relationships on a basis which by consideration of the well-being of the individual enables all those engaged in the undertaking to make their maximum personal contribution to the effective working of the undertaking."

2. **T.G. Spates.** "Personnel administration is a code of the ways of organising and treating individuals at work so that they will get the greatest possible realisation of their intrinsic abilities, thus attaining a maximum efficiency for themselves and their group and thereby giving to the enterprise which they are a part, its determining competitive advantage and its optimum results."

3. **M.W. Comeng.** "Personnel management is concerned with obtaining the best possible staff for an organization, and having got them, looking after them so that they want to stay and give their best to their respective jobs."

Characteristics

From the above definitions of personnel management we learn its following characteristics :

1. **Branch of industrial management.** P.G. Hastings has aptly observed that the personnel management is the aspect of management having it's goal to the effective utilization of the labour resources of an organization.

2. **Art of maintaining workforce.** According to American Society for Personnel Administration, "Personnel administration is the art of acquiring, developing and maintaining a competent workforce in such a manner as to accomplish with maximum efficiency and economy, the functions and objectives of the organisation."

3. **Cultivation of workers' qualities.** From the definitions given above it becomes plain that personnel management helps to cultivate among the workers qualities like zest, education, responsibility and *esprit de corps*.

4. **Job satisfaction.** In personnel management, the work is so organised as to afford maximum satisfaction to the workers. According to G.P. Fillipo, "Personnel management is the planning, organizing,

directing and controlling of the performance of those operative functions."

5. Good relations among workers and managers. It is the paramount task of the personnel management that cordial relations are obtained between the workers and managers.

6. Reform management. In personnel management adequate attention is paid to the conditions of work, pay-scales, technical education and recreation of the workers.

7. Maximum worker capacity. Lastly, it is the endeavour of the personnel management to maximize the efficiency and the work capacity of the worker. For this purpose there should be a unanimity of objectives among the labour, management and employers. Only co-operation and mutual understanding between the three can bring about maximization in production.

Aims

The aims of personnel management are divided into two sections : general and specific.

(A) General Aims. According to learned authorities L.P. Alfred and H.R. Britt, the general aim of personnel management is the reform and improvement of the services with the help of technical advisors and to inspire confidence in workers. Briefly, following are the general aims of personnel management :

1. Maximum use of human resources.
2. To promote active co-operation among workers.
3. Maximum utilization of the services of each worker.

(B) Specific Aims. Besides general aims there are certain specific aims of personnel management. These are :

1. Recruitment of workers.
2. Training and guidance of workers.
3. Effective means for the adequate remuneration of workers.
4. Promotion of the morale of workers.
5. To secure adequate allowances and other economic benefits besides adequate wages. Included among the facilities are medical aid, provident fund, paid holidays, technical training, recreation, etc. Above all, the retirement benefits like pensions, etc. must be ensured.
6. Another specific aim of the personnel management is to sort

out the complaints of workers and to ensure adequate promotion facilities.

7. To ensure cordial relations between workers and management.

8. To promote research.

Principles

1. **Learned authorities.** The specialists have enumerated following principles of personnel management :

(i) ***Justice*** : In an industrial management, the most important principle is that of justice. In securing justice, six things must be taken care of. First of all there must be adequate wages and remuneration of work. For this purpose minimum wages for each kind of job should be fixed. The payment of wages must be done on fixed days. The skilled workers must be paid according to their proficiencies and workers must also get adequate share out of gains on the capital. Secondly, there must be proper avenues for promotion, increment, etc. Thirdly, workers should be inspired to make progress and for this purpose it is necessary that the promotion should be non-partisan. Fourthly, workers should be allowed to determine the conditions of their work. Fifthly, deficiency of management must be removed and the conditions for full employment must be created. Sixthly, penalties for faults and misconduct must be just and opportunity of appeals must be there.

(ii) ***Personality*** : It is an important principle of personnel management that all-round development of the personality of workers should be encouraged.

(iii) ***Co-operation*** : The third principle is that there should be cordial relations and cooperation among the workers and management.

(iv) ***Democratic basis*** : The management must be democratic. Each person should have the right to put across his viewpoint and he must get the opportunity.

2. **George D. Helse** has enumerated following principles necessary for successful personnel management :

(i) Proper and intelligent selection of workers.

(ii) Providing suitable jobs to workers.

(iii) Ridding the workers of the feeling of uncertainty and insecurity.

(iv) To inculcate a feeling of pride and glory for the company in which a worker works.

(v) To ensure healthy and congenial work environs.

(vi) To create an organisation in which the duties and obligations are clearly understood.

(vii) Objective assessment of the work performance.

(viii) Participation of workers in management.

(ix) Upright conduct and appropriate policy.

3. Institute of Labour Management of Great Britain has enumerated the following principles of personnel management :

(i) Determination of appropriate principles of personnel management.

(ii) All workers should have a right to approach the management overtly or covertly.

(iii) The job should be secure; there should be open policy of recruitment; ability should get precedence over all other considerations; the recruitment should be made on scientific principles; there should be realistic assessment of work performance; there must exist adequate facilities for training and nobody should be dismissed without adequate grounds.

(iv) The policy of adequate wages should be followed.

(v) To create an atmosphere and conditions congenial to discipline.

(vi) To raise the standards of work.

(vii) Promotion of harmonious relationships between labour and management.

(viii) Freedom to become members of the trade unions for the workers.

(ix) To provide for the recreation and other facilities for overall development of the personalities of the workers.

Functions

The personnel management functions are of four kinds : (1) Advisory Functions; (2) Managerial Functions; (3) Administrative Functions and (4) Workers' Welfare Functions. Each of these will be discussed below:

1. Advisory Functions. Under this function an attempt is made to establish a rapport between the workers and managers. This is done to establish a rapport between the workers and managers. This is also done to establish a cordial and congenial atmosphere so as to boost production and avoid friction in industry.

2. Managerial Functions. Indeed these are the main functions of personnel management. These include :

(i) ***Recruitment and employment*** : Under the recruitment and employment are included finding suitable means of filling up the vacancies; to scrutinize the background, antecedents and other particulars of the employees; to acquaint the new entrants with the policy of management and to collect data about wages, etc.

(ii) ***Training*** : Training is an important constituent of the managerial function. The method and rules for training are laid down and arrangement for the training is made.

(iii) ***Promotion, transfer and retirement*** : Under this, rules and guidelines are determined regarding promotion, transfer and retirement.

(iv) ***Functions concerning service*** : In this, schemes for labour welfare, education and recreation of workers are made.

(v) ***Remuneration and incentives*** : Under this, rules regarding pension, bonus, insurance, loan etc., are made.

(vi) ***Collective bargaining of workers' representation*** : Under this, attempts are made to associate workers with management.

(vii) ***Remuneration scheme*** : As is clear from the heading under this an effort is made to evolve a pragmatic management.

(viii) ***Unification of organizational and worker's interest*** : In this an attempt is made to boost the morale of the workers.

3. Administrative functions. Lastly, in personnel management the management of the welfare of workers is of crucial importance. By welfare is meant the promotion of physical and mental health of the workers and an improvement in their social and economic status. Much thought is being accorded these days to this aspect and new ways and means to improve the welfare of workers are being suggested.

DEPARTMENTS OF PERSONNEL MANAGEMENT

The work of personnel management has become so intricate and complex as to require it's division into various departments. These are :

1. Employment department. The function of this department is to provide the necessary labour force. It keeps statistics of vacancies and also maintains contact with sources from where workers might be available. Besides it also determines the pay-scales and lays down guidelines for transfer etc.

2. Training and education department. In order to increase the efficiency of the workers, there is need to give them training and education in the suitable skills. These functions are looked after by the training and education department.

3. Welfare department. This department looks after the physical, mental and cultural welfare of the workers. It sets up clubs where workers can play, read and amuse themselves.

4. Security department. For the protection of men and materials and goods in the industry, a posse of security force is employed.

5. Medical and health department. This department takes care of the health of the workers and gives them medical aid when a worker is ill or hurt.

6. Industrial relations department. This department determines the policy regarding relations between workers and management.

7. Wages and salary department. This department is concerned with the assessment of the work performance and determines the wages and salary of the workers.

8. Research and data department. This department collects statistics and carries on scientific research.

9. Women labourers' department. An industry employing a sizable portion of women labour force maintains this department.

PERSONNEL POLICY

The personnel policy should specifically take care of the following points :

1. Clear. The policy should be brief, lucid and clear.

2. Just. The policy should be just toward workers.

3. Personal. Policy should be such as to give workers a sense of belonging.

4. Security. The policy should increase security among the workers.

5. Cordiality. The policy should be such as to promote cordial relations among the workers.

6. Recognition of work. The policy should allow adequate room for the recognition of the work done by the workers.

7. Flexibility. The policy should be such as to adjust itself with the changing circumstances.

QUESTIONS FOR EXERCISE

1. Explain the concept of individual management.
2. What is Personnel Management? How is it carried on?

10

PROFESSIONAL INDUSTRIAL MANAGEMENT IN INDIA

India experienced industrialization in 19th century under British rule. In the initial stages enterprise was owned and managed by a single individual owner or along with his kinship members. Later on Britishers introduced joint stock companies. This paved the way for the emergence of large scale industries. These industries needed huge capital investments. Therefore, a group of persons with their joint capital started big industries. The increasing complex organization of these large scale industries led to the need of a specialized person, other than proprietor or director, to manage. With this need, management has passed from family hands to outside personnel, the managers.

Earlier manager was considered responsible to carry out only the daily routine jobs. He was concerned with the implementation of the decisions and policies stated by the managing directors. After Independence, India stepped on planned industrialization. Now the importance of managerial role increased further. Some of the factors which provided for the take-off stage of management in India are : increasing size of industries, huge capital investments, keener competition within the country and outside, wide scientific researches, mechanization of production operations, need for better quality, scarcity of resources and energy, increasing number of labourers and their unionization, bureaucratization of industrial organizations, complex legislations, the governing idea of business as public service, etc.

More and more calculation, market research, technical know-how, planning, budgeting, costing, etc., require formally trained personnel to perform these tasks effectively. Obviously, owners on their own could not afford to acquire all these managerial skills. Hence, the importance of management, training and trained managers in the industries of 20th century. Today managers hold the key position in the industrial organization. Management has developed as a new profession. Professional managerial class is emerging as a new social stratum. Managerial role is not limited to the industry. Manager is expected to play a constructive role in the overall development of the nation. This increasing importance of the role of managers has led to many unresolved issues.

REVIEW OF LITERATURE

Due to the stronghold of a few families over the industries, there was little scope for professional management. Sen (1974) called this situation as 'the jagirdari system among Indian managers'. After independence India exhibited a slight movement towards managerial revolution. In a survey of 1958 (Myers, 1959) 24 managers per one thousand employees were calculated in the factory sector. It was expected that industry will need 3,084 managers additionally per year. The once 'closed shop' family-owned industries are now admitting qualified non-family members who are receiving managerial education. Managers are developing as a distinct class of professionals (Agrawala, A.N., 1970; Sethi, 1978).

Few studies have analysed the factors contributing to the development of professional management in India (Dutt, 1965; Basu, 1967). Increasing size of industries, operation, development of industries for social welfare have led to the development of management. The factors impeding the emergence of management as a profession have also been identified (Trivedi, 1969). Concentration of economic power in few hands, tendency of employers to give jobs to their own kith and kin, are the two factors which inhibited the development of professional management. Regionalism, religion and casteism also played a negative role.

One of the most debated issues which the divorce of owner and manager has led is that who is the main decision-maker between the two? Scholars have responded differently. While some argue that now manager is the main decision-maker than owner, the others argue that he is only the implementer and the decisions are made by the owner. The votaries of managerial revolution (Sengupta, 1974) argue that even though managers have very small or no shareholding in the capital, they enjoy the power to control due to increasing technical complexities of business operations. The diffusion of ownership and management led to the emergence of the latter as a free floating centre of power. The old picture of a ruthless and self-oriented company director has given place to the picture of a modern, non-propertied manager responsible to society at large. They call managers as 'The New Maharajas'.

The advocates of pluralist model (Subramaniam, 1971; Poulantsas, 1975; Kumar, M., 1982) strongly disagree with the proponents of managerial revolution approach. In the bureaucratic organization, the real economic power lies in the hands of owners and the managerial class is more in a sense of faithful servants of ruling class of owners. Managers in this sense become magnified clerks. Only those managers have powers who have large shareholdings. Further, managers at the middle and lower levels have least powers and only the managers at the top enjoy certain amount of power.

After the separation of owners from management, it was expected that the industrial organization has democratised, and the exploitation of workers has reduced. But scholars like Karl Marx (1959) and C. Wright Mills (1959) disagree with this. Managers belong to the elite class and serve the purpose of the owners. They are tools for extracting the surplus value in a much systematic way. Managers are loyal to the owners and to the community.

The increasing need of trained managers and the increasing specialization in the knowledge of management have paved the way for the professionalization of management. It has been assumed that the management training makes the manager professional. But the management training alone does not make a manager professional. The trained managers do give emphasis to the careerism (Rudrabasavaraj, 1978; Rao, 1978). K.L. Sharma (1982) maintains that the number of managers holding degrees in management is not the only requirement but conformity to the professional techniques and values is the index of professionalization of management. He further explains that this conformity may depend upon the extent of authority and autonomy enjoyed by managers. The empirical studies on Indian managers' ethic conclude that managers are more influenced by egoistic concerns like prestige, honour, dignity, power. In administration they practise bureaucratic and not professional authoritarianism. They are more concerned with high profit, high production, efficiency and stable growth of organisation (Aggrawal, K.C., 1978; Rao, 1978; Dhingra and Pathak, 1982). For managers, what is good for business is good ethic. Therefore, they exploit by bribes, personal, favours, gifts, etc. (Monappa, 1977). These studies show that Indian managers do not have professional values. There is a need to frame managerial philosophy according to Indian values. Keeping in view the changing scene of industries, the managerial ethic is to be redefined. Every manager should have a set of professional values necessary for effective functioning (Mehta, 1961; Dayar, 1964). Indian manager is still in search of style (Roy, 1967; Vatsal, 1970). Hence, managers have no style, no specific professional ethic. Sharma (1980) concluded : "The Indian manager is anything but professional as his ethical values are not clearly defined, the young managers made no contribution to the profession; their ethical standards are more identified with organizations rather than the profession. Managers do not have a client or community orientation which they must have as professionals. They do not have collective authority, autonomy and monopoly."

The change-over from hereditary to professional management is a challenge to management organizations in India. Management has to develop a professional ethic, a unique style, a philosophy of its own. This is not an impossible task but only needs a systematic attempt (Mafat Lal, 1964; Saraogi, 1976; Dias, 1976).

Professionally trained managers are perceived as more efficient for industrial organization than those who are not (Haga, 1976). The need of a trained manager is felt with the increasing mechanization of industries. At the same time it has been noticed that it makes no difference whether a manager is professionally trained or not (Lorant, 1980). In industrial organization many situations come where common sense, guess-work and dynamism are required and not only training. It has been noticed that the professionally trained managers expand the organization size beyond expectations thus leading to the increasing consumption of organizational resources.

Numerous roles, other than organizational are expected to be played by the professional manager. On the one hand he has one responsibility that is to contribute to the economic performance of the industry. On the other hand, management is supposed to perform major social responsibilities in addition to economic ones. Manager is responsible towards the employees and towards the public. He should not restrict himself to micro issues. He needs to extend his vision beyond the problems of his daily routine job. He is a social worker and, therefore, has to look after the interests of the community. He is a responsible citizen and should contribute constructively in solving the problems of the nation. Private sector managers should observe the interest of the people as the public sector managers do (Randeria, 1963; Wood, 1964; Aggarwal, S.C., 1976).

Scholars have compared Indian managers with their counterparts in other countries (Haire and Porter, 1963 and 1964; Sethi, 1969). In such studies it has been stated that the style of working of the former is different from that of latter due to the socio-cultural and industrial environment of the country.

Professional manager has to function in a bureaucratic organization. The relationship between the professions and bureaucratic organizations has been debated a lot. One finds two streams of thought on this issue : firstly, professionalization is positively associated with bureaucracy (Wilensky, 1964; Weber, 1966; Ritzer, 1972; Montagna, 1977). Secondly, from the point of view of free profession, a professional will always face unavoidable conflict situations in bureaucratic organisation (Etzioni, 1959; Scott, 1966; Gouldner and Ritt, 1967; Richard Hall, 1967 and 1968).

The proponents of inherent conflict approach argue that the conflict between the two is necessary and unavoidable. Professional autonomy is one of the basic characteristics of the professions which provide the support to this argument. Professionals require a kind of autonomy, that is antithetical to Weber's model of rational legal bureaucracy. The ideology of professionalism implies a trade-off between professional's autonomy and power in the organization. In a bureaucratic industrial organization, manager will come in conflict with the bureaucratic hierarchy, between the service to the organization and the service to the community, between loyalty to the professional community and to the organization, between the ethics of the organization and of the profession, etc.

Scott (1966) while summing up professionals' position in a bureaucratic organization argues that on the one hand, professionals will be able to operate in organizations more effectively by applying greater expertise with respect to task knowledge. On the other hand, professionals are increasingly likely to resist or reject various bureaucratic rules, standards and supervision. They may reflect only conditional loyalty to the bureaucracy. He maintains that the professionals are likely to reject bureaucratic rules because they perceive themselves as capable of establishing a more functional set of rules. Their expertise entitles them to operate professionally without the constraining regulations or interference from others. They resist standards of bureaucratic organizations, because they adhere to the standards of the profession. They are increasingly discontented with bureaucratic supervision in many instances, as the authorities over them are not qualified in their own field of specialization. However, the loyalty of professionals towards their employing organizations cannot be predicted absolutely. Professionals follow the norms and behavioural expectations of their profession rather than those of the employing organization.

These arguments, given in reference to professionals' functioning in a bureaucratic organization are fully applicable in regard to manager's position in industrial bureaucratic organization. Professional manager is a salaried employee, performing his activities within the structural framework of bureaucratic organization of an industry. Jenkin's (1970) while summing up the position of the professional manager in a bureaucratic organization, maintains that he participates in two distinct irreconcilable systems. The professional manager is a member of two institutions — the profession and the organization. Each of these attempts to control his occupational activities, and the manner in which the former establishes standards and norms for the conduct of professional activities, contrasts with the way in which the latter specifies task objectives.

This assumption of an inherent conflict has been questioned by many scholars. Bureaucracy is not a necessary bar to professional commitments. It has been argued that all the components of Weberian ideal typical of bureaucracy are not negatively related to the professions *e.g.*, rationality is the common characteristic of the two. Further, there are different types of bureaucratic organizations far and near to the ideal of typical construct and with this it depends on the nature of the organization concerned. No generalization in this case is possible. Professionalization and bureaucratization are interdependent. Weber (1966) himself has noticed a two-way relationship between the two that is each contributing to the other.

Management is not a full-fledged free profession. It has to function in a bureaucratic industrial organization. Etzioni (1969) mentions that there is a continuum of professionalism upon which the fully-fledged and semi-professions can be identified. Semi-professions are employed largely in bureaucratic organizations. They have a shorter period of training than the fully-fledged professions, a less legitimated status, a less specialized body of knowledge. Thus, management is a semi-profession. The arguments made by the advocates of inherent conflict approach become of less importance as they perceive management from the viewpoint of a free profession which it is not.

The role of professional managers has been compared with the role played by the dynamic entrepreneur-owner. It is argued that the success of an industry depends more on entrepreneur rather than on the professional management. Aiyar (1983) argues that the professional manager is an invaluable instrument for preventing industries from being spoiled by incompetent generation of owners. If we look at the big industries of the world we will notice that the credit of success goes to the entrepreneur and not to professional manager. However, there are a number of cases where professional management has failed. In Indian public sector, professional management has failed to give any good results. Multinational subsidiaries in India have always been run by professionals. These industries used to look down with contempt at the Indian business families trying to compete with them. He gives the example of Firestone which was one of the best known multinationals in the world. When Modi group wanted to enter the tyre business, Firestone, Dunlop and Goodyear, the three multinational firms with professional managements were already there. Today Modi group has defeated all the tyre companies in competition. Firestone has been sold out to Modis. After the Modi family took charge from the professional management, the production of this went up by 50 per cent. The success of Tata and Birla is due to dynamic entrepreneurship and not due to professional managers.

Aiyar has not been justified in neglecting the role of professional management. He maintains that the professional management only helps in maintaining an industry established by the entrepreneur. There are examples where professional management is successful *viz.*, Hindustan Lever Limited, Brook Bond, Lipton, Bata, etc., multinationals. On the other hand, there are examples where family managed industries are decaying *viz.*, Modi Industries, Swadeshi Cotton Mills, Dalmia Cement etc. However, one cannot neglect the role of professional management in the success of an industry. Flory (1983) maintains that if a new industry is to be successful, its management must complement and enhance the personality of entrepreneur. Thus, managers are the vehicles for entrepreneurial excursions.

One may find many reasons for the poor performance of professional managers. One reason may be the conflict between the owner's ethic of self-interest and the professional manager's ethic centred on the community interest (Sharma, K.L., 1975). The other reasons may be the limited autonomy, and the structural constraints. Further studies in this area are required.

The managers have been studied in both the sectors public and private. Banik (1965) and Hanson (1962) both studied the role of managers in public enterprises. They have also discussed the managerial control and autonomy subsequently. On the other hand, Murthy (1964) has discussed the functions performed by managers in a private sector industrial organization. Little attention has been given to the comparative studies of public and private sectors. Some of the studies indicate that as far as the functions performed by the managers are concerned, no significant difference has been noticed between the managers of two sectors (Mathai, 1965; Lau and Pavett, 1980). The main difference lies in terms of the emphasis given to the profit orientation, which is of less importance in public sector management in the two sectors. It has been, therefore, suggested that the managers of both the sectors should look into a total perspective, that is, managers in public sector giving due importance to profit orientation and vice versa the managers in private sector should take into consideration the community interest.

The young generation of professional managers is perceived as more mobile. The mobility depends on two factors, *i.e.*, manager's own motivations and the opportunities available to him. The first may be perceived as subjective and the second as objective. Manager's educational qualifications play an important role in his movement. If he has technical qualification or professional training in management, he will get more chances for movement. Manager's career also counts for his movement. Laggatta, T. (1978) has identified the following factors influencing manager's mobility, *i.e.*, age, level of education, nature of education, organizational size, career and length of service.

Manager's mobility is perceived in two ways. Firstly, intra-organizational movement and secondly, inter-organizational movement. In big industrial organizations, the chances for intra-organizational movement are more than in small or medium size organizations. Srinivas (1965) studied managerial mobility in an organizational perspective. In his view managers should be exposed to the new situations in order to make them more dynamic and functional for organizational effectiveness.

Few studies are focused on manager-workers relations probing into the workers' expectations from managers (Singh, 1962; Desai,

1969). Few scholars have studied managers from the leadership perspective identifying the leadership characteristics of managers as ability to undertake the challenging tasks, ability to organize, ability to inspire confidence among the subordinates (Kapur, 1963; Singh; 1963). Managers are yet to be studied adequately from the perspective of a profession.

STATEMENT OF THE PROBLEM

It is argued that after the separation of ownership and management, it is the manager who holds the key position in the industrial organization. Now the question arises what authority has been given to managers and how much autonomy do they enjoy in a bureaucratic industrial organization. It is argued that professionals will certainly face unavoidable conflicts in a bureaucratic organization, since there is a conflict between the ideology of business and profession. Business is centred on the pursuit of self-interest in contrast to the profession which is concerned with service to the community regardless of one's own interests. Business is based on egoistic motives while profession maintains altruistic motives. All these arguments indicate the structural constraints a manager will face in a bureaucratic industrial organization.

From the review of literature it is noticed that managers have not been adequately studied from the perspective of professional authority and autonomy. The structural constraints managers face in the areas of authority and autonomy, are yet to be studied systematically.

Objectives of the Study

In view of the above discussion, the research objectives for the present study may be specified as below :

1. To identify the nature and extent of manager's authority.

2. To examine the amount of autonomy managers enjoy in the area of their authority.

3. To elucidate the structural constraints that managers face in the area of authority and autonomy.

4. To explicate the sources of these structural constraints.

5. To analyse the reactions of managers to these structural constraints.

UNIVERSE AND SAMPLE

The rationale for selecting Meerut city for the present study was the fact that the industries of this city have not been studied, since industries emerged here much later than in other cities of Uttar Pradesh such as Kanpur and Ghaziabad. No statistical principle was applied for drawing specific sample. Since it is an exploratory study and no list of managers in the industries of Meerut was available, no statistical method could be followed in drawing the sample. Fifty managers were interviewed, *i.e.*, 26 from public limited industries and 24 from private limited industries. The size of sample was arbitrary.

METHOD OF DATA COLLECTION AND ANALYSIS

An interview schedule was constructed in order to obtain the data. Data thus collected were codified and classified into meaningful categories. Some questions received multiple answers which were minimized into meaningful categories without losing the objectivity of the data.

CHARACTERISTICS OF MANAGERS

Managers have been portrayed as a new class in a loose sense of the term. The professional managerial class comprises salaried mental workers, not owning the means of production, who tackle the common problems and situations (Enrenreich and Enrenreich, 1977). It has been argued that a growing centralized surplus and increased struggle between the bourgeoisie and the proletariat were the necessary conditions fostering the expansion of managerial class. Pal (1966) maintains that this growing managerial class is emerging as an elite social group. They are the main decision-makers in the industries of today.

Laggatt (1978) does not agree with the advocates of professional managerial class. On the basis of his study of the British managers, he submits that the managers do not make a homogenous group. They are heterogeneous and do not form a class. There are disparities in their economic statuses. This criticism of Leggatt, however, does not seem to be logical one. The advocates of professional managerial class do not have an economic perspective in defining it. They define it from the perspective of profession. The professional managerial class is a social category. They belong to the same profession, sharing common values and ethical standards, thus forming a class.

The entry in the professional managerial class is open. There is no restriction as we find in the entry in other professions. Managers are coming from different educational spheres, *viz.*, law, social sciences, natural sciences, engineering besides management courses. Professional management training is not a necessary prerequisite for becoming a manager. Professionally trained managers are considered to be more efficient, but untrained managers are also recruited because of their managerial qualities, *viz.*, dynamism, achievement motivation, enterprising aptitude, etc. On the other hand in other professions *viz.*, legal and medical, entry is restricted. Minimum educational qualification for entering the profession is clearly stated. Without having that minimum education one cannot become a member of that profession. For entering in legal and medical professions, one must have a graduate degree in the respective disciplines. Thus professional managerial class is an open class. This is one reason why there is educational heterogeneity in managerial class. This heterogenous educational background subsequently leads to other heterogeneities *viz.*, in ethical values, aptitudes, motivations, etc.

For analysing the class backgrounds of professional managers in India, an attempt has been made in the study of S.C. Jain (1971). He maintains that managers generally come from families with high educational and occupational background. They are mainly urbanities and belong to enterprising communities *viz.*, Jain, Marwari, etc. They come largely from families engaged in elite occupations. Their fathers are business executives, government officials and professional men. The majority of managers have come from the most industrialized or urbanised states. Managers are found to be a highly educated group, nine out of ten managers having had a college degree or professional diploma. He studied the influence of the social background factors on the mobility of managers. He maintains that at the initial stages, regional origin does not have a significant influence on the career of a manager. But at an advanced level, it does *i.e.* managers coming from the native state of their employers, move faster than others. Subramaniam (1983) has also found more or less similar background characteristics. According to him, the large majority comes from the professional middle class and more than half from the upper middle class. Majority attended a public or convent school. They are heavily drawn from urban areas. Majority is drawn from states such as Maharashtra, Gujarat, Tamil Nadu, Kerala and Punjab. In most of the cases they are domiciled in states other than their states of birth. Caste-wise, majority comes from the literate Brahmin and high caste non-Brahmin communities. Marginally they are from the commercial castes. B.R. Sharma (1976) studied the social background of candidates who applied for admission in management courses. He found that candidates from higher income groups had a much better chance of getting admitted. Those who had their early education in English-medium public or missionary schools and colleges had an edge over those who came from a non-English school. Further, urban domiciled had a better chance of selection than rural domiciled. These findings reflect on the managers' social background.

Significant changes have taken place in the Indian management scene in the past two decades, says a study made by Director of Foundation of Organizational Research, Mr. N.K. Singh (1984). He does not find any notable change in the religion and caste profiles of managers. He maintains that a large majority of managers continue to be drawn from amongst Hindus. One-third of the total managers are drawn from among Brahmins. However, there has been considerable change in the rural-urban distribution of managers. While in 1971 people of urban origin dominated (80 per cent), in 1983 only 60 per cent were drawn from urban areas. The study says, elitism seems to be on the downward trend if family occupation is the criterion. In 1971 one-third of the manager's jobs were held by occupation groups such as business, profession and management. In 1983 majority (60 per cent) of the managers were from salaried people. The educational level of Indian managers seems to be on the increase as the study revealed that 84 per cent of managerial jobs in 1983 were occupied by graduates and post-graduates against 65 per cent in 1971. The managerial world is becoming more broad-based in terms of regional distribution. While in 1971 the majority of managers came from Gujarat, Punjab, Maharashtra, Tamil Nadu and Kerala, in 1983 Delhi, Andhra Pradesh and Uttar Pradesh also started making significant contribution, Findings of the study on the personal background of managers show that 60 per cent of managers belong to cities or large towns and only 13.4 per cent are from villages. In terms of income groups, 76.8 per cent have come from upper middle income families.

There are very few studies comparing the background characteristics of Indian managers with the managers of other countries. Every country has its own peculiar social structure which plays a significant role in the supply of managers, *e.g.*, in India caste and religion play an important role. Kassem (1971) did an attempt in this direction. He compared the background characteristics of managers in India, Egypt and the U.S.A. He maintains that the socio-cultural milieu of a country has a unique influence on the native managers.

PROFESSIONAL AUTHORITY

Professional authority has been considered as one of the most important characteristics of professionals (Carr Saunders, 1933; Goode, 1957; Ritmer, 1975). The professions and occupations form a continuum. For an occupation to move towards the professional end of the continuum, the attainment of professional authority through formalised education and technical competence is a basic prerequisite (Hughes, 1971). It is expected that the specialised knowledge will be used for safeguarding the interests of the clients. This belief became the basis for providing the professional authority to the professionals.

Authority is an institutionally recognized right to influence the actions of others, regardless of their immediate personal attitudes to the direction of influence. It is exercised by the incumbent of an office or other socially defined status (Parsons, 1949). Authority in this sense is an institutionalized power which has the legitimation of coercive sanctions. Professional authority gets its legitimacy from the community sanction which is based on the technical competence of the professional. Parsons maintains that the professional authority is based on the superior 'technical competence' of the professional man. The area of professional authority is limited to a particular technically defined sphere. It is characterized by specification of functions. The technical competence is always limited to a specific field of knowledge and skill. A professional has authority only in his own field of knowledge. Other scholars have also accepted that the specialised and technical competence is the basis for legitimacy to the professional authority (Millorson, 1964; Wilensky, 1964; Halsey, 1970). The professional can decide what is good or bad for his client who accepts his authority with the belief that his knowledge will benefit him. The client's ignorance in the field of the profession's competence reinforces the authority. The community gives the professional a right to make decisions in the area of his specialised knowledge.

Managers are perceived as forming an elite class on the basis of the high amount of authority they enjoy in an industrial set-up. It is argued that the managerial revolution consisted of a drive for the attainment of power and the position of a ruling class. The fusion of knowledge and authority has created a new kind of professional technocrat occupying the elite position (Burnham, 1945; Mills, 1956).

In the present study it is noted that the managers claim professional authority on the basis of their managerial skills. Specialized knowledge and technical competence do not provide the basis of authority. One of the reasons for this may be the slow space of the professionalization of management in India. In the present sample, only very few managers (6 per cent) were having specialized knowledge or training in management. The managers who are professionally trained in management are perceived as professional managers. In view of this fact it can be stated that the managers do not have professional authority based on specialized knowledge and technical competence. The legitimacy of their authority is based on the rules and regulations of industrial organization which are usually stated by the managing directors. Thus, the source of manager's authority is the managing director, who has the final decision-making authority in an industry. Despite the high claims of democratic functioning, most organizations have rigid authoritarian structures and scant scope for participation of managers in decision-making. This sometimes reduces the managers to nullity. Managing directors can withdraw, increase or decrease their authority.

Manager's authority can be perceived in two forms, *i.e.*, ascribed and achieved authority. Ascribed authority is inherent in the job itself by virtue of its responsibilities. The sphere of this authority has been clearly specified in the rules of the industry. This authority is conferred to the office of the manager irrespective of the person who occupies it. In Weberian paradigm it is called legitimate authority, legitimacy of which is drawn from the rules laid down by the managing directors. On the other hand, achieved authority is one which the manager, due to his personality traits, skills, etc., acquires from his subordinate incumbents and managing directors. This is the traditional type of authority, legitimacy of which lies in the obedience to the particular person concerned.

Manager's authority is often limited. The job description, the union involvement, revision of authority, special executive orders, etc., constrain his authority. Moreover, authority can also be resisted by subordinates through group inaction and informal organization. Subordinates may function in direct confrontation by subtle or other means when the authority is felt to be unwarned, excessive or threatening. The limitations on authority are sometimes formalized by providing different degrees of authority which may be pending, subject to review, shared with other departments, exercised only as granted, delegated and granted for a limited duration and for a particular purpose.

PROFESSIONAL AUTONOMY IN THE AREA OF PROFESSIONAL AUTHORITY

Professional autonomy signifies the freedom from control by an outside agency, *i.e.*, a profession is self-controlled. Professional autonomy has two aspects, *i.e.*, structural and attitudinal. Structural autonomy is maintained with the help of professional associations. These associations control the entry into the profession and provide the right to practise profession with autonomy and control the member of professionals. A professional can make judgement with relative confidence which can be questioned only by the professional peers. Attitudinal autonomy is the feeling in the professional that he is free to make decisions in the area of his specialised knowledge. He is free from the external pressures of clients and of those who are not the members of the profession.

The degree of autonomy enjoyed by a profession depends on the extent to which professional practice is based upon theoretical knowledge and the degree of observation of the ideal of altruistic service (Carr Saunders, 1933). Goode (1960) maintains that the profession is a powerful force in the society and over the individual. Most of the legislations concerning the profession are generated by the professional peers. Society's legal control is weaker because public and legislators do not know much about the work of professionals. This mechanism allows the profession to maintain its autonomy.

The autonomy of the professional in the work setting is the freedom from the control over one's work. To maintain the autonomy of a profession, its body of knowledge must remain secret, a mystique must be built around its practices. To ensure autonomy, professionals will often attempt to strengthen the mysticism of the profession by introducing new and complex ideas and practices (Hughes, 1971; Johnson, 1972). Freidson and Rhea (1965) have provided a more exclusive definition of professional autonomy. They perceive it as control over the technical content of work. They call it 'autonomy of technique'. The professionals have the special privilege of freedom from the control of outsiders. This privilege is justified by three claims : first, their work requires such a high degree of skill and knowledge that only fellow professionals can make accurate assessment of professional's performance. Secondly, a high degree of selflessness and responsibility characterises professionals, so they can be trusted to work conscientiously. Thirdly, in those rare instances in which industrial professionals do not perform with skill, their colleagues may be trusted to take the proper regulator action. A similar definition has been given by Larson (1977). She maintains that professional autonomy signifies the self-control, *i.e.*, they can become almost immune to external regulations. It allows the professionals to select, according to their will, the inputs which they will receive from the laity. They live within ideologies of their own creation.

Professional autonomy is based on the monopoly over the specialized knowledge. The professional is able to attain and maintain his position because the masses do not have the prerequisite knowledge to replace him. Further, professional autonomy has the sanction of the community. It is believed that the professional will use his knowledge in the interest of the society. He is expected to give first preference to community interest sacrificing his own interests.

The client needs the services of the professionals since he is unable to solve his problems himself. The professional is expected to have that knowledge with the help of which the client's problems can be solved. It is expected that the professional uses this knowledge in the best interest of the client. In this client — professional relationship lies the autonomy of the professional. Professional is given full autonomy in the sphere of his specialized knowledge because the client has a trust over him.

Professional autonomy is determined by the amount of authority a profession has been able to attain. Authority is an institutionally recognized right to influence the actions of others. On the other hand, autonomy signifies the freedom from external influences. To explain it further, it can be stated that on the basis of the professional authority, a professional can influence the actions of his clients while on the basis of his autonomy he cannot be influenced by anyone who is not the member of his profession. Those professions which have more authority are comparatively more autonomous. Further, if the profession is well organized and has its own controlling body or association, it attains more autonomy. Hence, the more organized the professions, the more the autonomy.

Management is not a free profession. The managers have to function in the bureaucratic organization of the industry. Thus, managers' autonomy cannot be thought of in terms of the autonomy enjoyed by the professions like law, medicine, etc. The goals, policies and rules of an industrial organization limit managers' autonomy. Though his autonomy is defined by the rules of the industry yet on the basis of his personality traits and expertise, he may be able to extract more autonomy. The conflict between manager's professional ethic based on the primacy to community interests and in the business ethic based on primacy to self-interest, may limit his professional autonomy. Manager's autonomy also depends on his position in the management hierarchy. Those at the top may have more autonomy than those who are at comparatively low positions. Further, there are so many other organizations within the industry which may limit manager's autonomy *viz.*, the labour union, union of white-collar employees, etc.

STRUCTURAL CONSTRAINTS IN THE AREA OF PROFESSIONAL AUTHORITY AND AUTONOMY

Management is not a free profession. Managers perform their activities in a bureaucratic industrial organization where they are to face unavoidable conflict situations. On the one hand it is argued that the bureaucratic organization enhances the efficiency of a manager. On the other hand, a difference between the ethics, goals of professional managers and industrial bureaucratic organization is noticed, which reduces the efficiency of the managers.

Scholars have identified various sources of these strains. Seller (1963) has classified these various sources into two categories *viz.*, traditional and modern. Traditional causes of conflict include personality differences, personal ambitions and whims, competition with the colleagues for more power, etc. Modern causes are hidden in the industrial organization itself *viz.*, distribution of authority in various departments and shifting of responsibilities when the task is shared by two or more departments.

Various causes of strains which are observed in the field situations can be classified into two broad categories *viz.*, subjective and objective. Subjective causes include personal values, ambitions and way of thinking. Objective causes include communication gap, union involvement, misunderstanding with subordinates, colleagues, senior personnel, etc.

Parsons (1949), contrasting the business and profession, maintains that the former is based on self-interest and the latter on disinterestedness. The businessman was thought of as pursuing egoistically his own self-interest, while the professional was altruistically serving the interests of others. He further maintains that in spite of the differences in the nature and interests, the two have three features in common *viz.*, rationality, specificity of function and universalistic value orientation. MacIver (1955) has also differentiated the business from profession on the basis of ethics. The business has not attained a specific code of ethic, resting on considerations broader than the sense of self-interest. Hans Nagpal (1971) also, just like Parsons and MacIver, found a contrast between the unselfish preoccupation of the professional who serves his fellow-men without much consideration of monetary rewards and the selfish preoccupation of business, *i.e.*, to accumulate personal profit at the expense of others. Thus, a fundamental contradiction of the ethics of business and professionals has been considered as the major cause of strains between the two.

There are very few studies focused on conflict analyses in an industrial bureaucratic organization (Choudhary, 1969; Dayal and Adhikari, 1969; Prabhakar, 1979; Sheth and Patel, 1979). Choudhary in his study found a generational conflict between the younger and senior managers created by the differences in their ideas. Dayal and Adhikari noticed that the stresses and strains are caused by the authority relationships among the managers. Sheth and Patel maintain that the differences between the goals and aspirations of an organization and of managers cause strains in their relationships. Prabhakar in his empirical study studied the conflict between the production and purchase departments of selected industries. It was pointed out that the cause of conflict was the clash of authority. This may be due to the diffused distribution or overlapping of authority. The difference in personal values was also a cause for such conflict. Thus, various causes, subjective as well as objective, have been identified by different scholars.

While discussing conception of bureaucracy, Sharma (1983) maintains that in Weber's view bureaucratic organization is characterised by harmonious relations and absence of extraneous pressures which generate higher efficiency among the members. But he argues that this conclusion is based on invalid assumptions. The incoherence of the interests of the members causes tension, conflict and minimizes the harmony of relations. This argument holds true in reference to industrial bureaucratic organizations also. It is noticed that many times the interests of the owners and managers do not coincide which leads to strains. Not only this, the managers at many occasions come in conflict with colleagues and subordinates as well.

Thus, in view of the above discussion it can be said that the main source of conflict between the manager and managing directors or owners is the difference of their ethic. Here two specific issues crop up. First, will the manager be completely dominated by the organization, *i.e.*, will be rationalized and ignore his personal values when these come in conflict with the impersonal, efficiency-dominated and profit-oriented values of organization? Second, will he maintain his altruistic values when these come in conflict with the profit oriented values of the organization? These two propositions are yet to be tested.

In a family controlled industry, the main source of strain lies in manager's relations with the managing director. Manager is dependent on him for his job, salary, promotion, career and thus, becomes obedient. But the obedience to the owner may sometimes hurt his professional sentiments. In order to maintain his professional ethics, sometimes, the manager will have to deviate from this obedience. It cannot be expected from a professional manager to be a blind follower to the authority of the managing director. However, this deviance will lead to the strains in their relations. Secondly, unnecessary interference of the managing director, in the day-to-day functions of managers, may lead to strains in their relations. Thirdly, managers have to get their major decisions sanctioned by the managing director, who can modify these decisions and can also completely change these. This undue interference in managers' decisions leads to strains in their relations. Fourthly, the manager recommends for the appointment, transfer, promotion, demotion, reward and penalization of his subordinates. Managing director may or may not accept these recommendations. His negative response to manager's recommendations leads to strains in their relations. Fifthly, in big industries the manager's career within the organization depends on managing director. Sometimes, a manager's promotion is made on the basis of his relations with the managing director and not on his skills. Thus, the more deserving manager may suffer if he does not have very cordial relations with the managing director. Lastly, managing director's way of dealing with the managers determines the nature of relations between them. Sometimes managing director is not well behaved. He may scold or even abuse the manager. This misbehaviour leads to the strains in their relations. These are some of the basic factors causing strains in manager's relations with the managing director.

Every manager has his own network of relations within the organization. This network of relations can be classified in three categories *viz.*, relationship network with seniors, colleagues and subordinates. A manager may have strains in all the three categories of networks. In big industries where the number of senior managers is large, he may have strains with them which may be due to various reasons *viz.*, misunderstandings, communication gap, etc. Sometimes senior managers exploit junior managers by virtue of their seniority, which leads to strains. Manager may have strains in his relations with his colleagues due to many reasons *viz.*, diffused distribution and overlapping of authority. Every manager has to maintain harmonious relations within his department. He has to resolve all the conflicts emerging among his subordinates. In doing so he may have strains in his relations with them because in such situations he cannot always satisfy both the parties equally. Thus, it will lead to strains in his relations with the dissatisfied party.

INDUSTRIAL MANAGEMENT IN INDIA

After Independence India exhibited a slow movement towards professionalization of management. Some of the factors which provided for the take-off stage of management in India are : increasing size of industries, huge capital investments, competition within the country and abroad, mechanization of production operations, scarcity of resources and energy, increasing number of labourers and their unionization, bureaucratization of industrial organizations, the governing idea of business as public service, etc. To tackle these problems efficiently, a need for trained manager with the specialized knowledge of management has paved the way for the professionalization of management.

From the review of literature it is found that managers have not been studied adequately from the perspective of a profession. The professionalization of management has led to many unresolved issues. Two of the most debated issues are : first, what authority managers have been given after their separation from owners? Second, while functioning in a bureaucratic organization a professional has to face many unavoidable conflict situations. Thus, the amount of autonomy managers enjoy while functioning in the bureaucratic organization of an industry is significant.

The present endeavour has been made to study five interrelated research objectives : first, to identify the nature and extent of managers' authority. Second, to examine the amount of autonomy managers enjoy in the area of their authority. Third, to elucidate the structural constraints that managers face in the area of authority and autonomy. Fourth, to explicate the sources of these structural constraints. Fifth, to analyse the reaction of managers to these structural constraints.

This study has been conducted in the Meerut city of Uttar Pradesh. The rationale for selecting this city was the fact that the industries of this city have not been studied. The industries emerged here much later than in other cities of Uttar Pradesh. Fifty managers were interviewed from both the sectors — public limited and private limited. Data were obtained with the help of an interview schedule.

By the study of the background characteristics of managers, it is found that the majority of the managers are below forty years. Religion-wise, most of the managers are Hindu and few others are Jain, Sikh, Parsi and Muslim. In terms of the level of education, the majority is highly educated. So far as the nature of education is concerned, the majority has general education. The role of engineer-managers and professionally trained managers in management is increasing. Most of the managers are from Uttar Pradesh with few from Punjab, Maharashtra and Delhi. All the managers are married and the majority have planned family *i.e.*, three or less than three children. Highly educated young managers perceive planned family as an ideal. Service; class families dominate the supply of managers. The remaining few are from business families, professionals' families and the farming families. Majority of the managers are drawing a salary of less than Rs. thirty-five hundred per month. Age-wise senior managers are drawing high salary. Level of education has no significant association with salary. More or less similar background characteristics have been found by Jain (1971), Subramaniam (1983) and Singh (1984).

Majority of the non-Hindus and immigrants are in public industries. This can be explained by the fact that such industries are large size and in most of the cases are multinationals. The criteria for the selection of managers are more universalistic specified by the rules which are strictly maintained. The salary scale of managers is high in public limited industries than in private limited industries. This may be due to their large size and huge capital investments. In private limited industries, engineer-managers are in great number. Such industries cannot afford to have engineers and managers separately due to their small size and small capital investment. The engineer-manager is more economical.

The first objective of this study was to identify the nature and extent of authority managers have been given in the industrial bureaucratic organization. Managers do not have professional authority in the true sense of the term. Professional authority gets its legitimacy from the community sanction which is based on the technical competence of the professional. Managers' authority lies in their office. The legitimacy of their authority is based on the rules and regulations of the industrial organization which are usually stated by the managing director who may withdraw, increase or decrease it. Authority in this sense is an institutionalized power which has the legitimation of coercive sanction.

Managers' authority is scored in two ways. First, their overall authority and secondly in different areas of their functioning, *i.e.* decision-making, directing, coordination, staffing, planning, reporting and budgeting. The mean score is calculated, and it is perceived that those scoring below it, have low authority and those above, high. Most of the managers perceive that they have sufficient amount of authority. Very few managers were not satisfied. While scoring overall authority of managers it is found that 50 per cent of the managers have high authority and the remaining have low authority. Their authority in decision-making is very limited. All the major decisions taken by them are to be sanctioned by the top management which may change them, reject them or accept them. To carry out these decisions, the managers give general and specific instructions to their subordinates directly or indirectly depending on the person for whom they are made. Majority of the managers have low authority in the sphere of directing. Now the question emerges : how much flexibility managers give to their subordinates in carrying out these instructions? Majority of the managers want their instructions to be followed strictly. Few sometimes allow flexibility and few give sufficient flexibility to the subordinates. Further, it is reported that before giving instructions, every manager seeks the opinion of the concerned person.

Managers recommend for the awards and punishments for their subordinates. Further, appointments, terminations, promotions, demotions and transfers of the subordinates excluding senior personnel, like assistant manager, engineers, etc., are recommended by the manager. All these recommendations are to be approved by the top management. Managers have low authority in such matters.

Managers have very little authority in the area of planning. Their plans are put before the managing directors for approval. In most of the cases they are changed. Further, every manager sends the progress report of his department, sometimes weekly, monthly, biannually or annually depending on the rules of the concerned industry. The top management may call for explanation on this report. Managers do not have much authority in budgeting. One-third of the managers do not have any participation in budgeting. Very few managers participate directly and about 50 per cent participate indirectly. All the final decisions in such matters are to be taken by the top management.

Senior and high salaried managers have more authority. Level of education has no significant association with the amount of authority. Those who are at high positions in the organizational hierarchy have more authority.

In all the areas of their functioning, managers in the private limited industries have more authority than their counterparts in public limited industries. Various reasons may be adduced to explain this variation. First, managers in such industries are more committed due to their personal involvement in the interests of the organization on account of which they are given more authority. Secondly, managers in such industries have a direct and frequent access to the managing director due to which they are able to extract more authority by way of influencing him. Thus, it seems that the size of the organization has a bearing on managers' authority. The small size of private limited industries is the basic factor which facilitates the managers to have high authority. In public limited industries, due to their large size and more division of labour, authority is shared, and it also overlaps. Further, due to a distance in the relations with managing directors, they do not get much opportunity to manipulate more authority. Hence, less authority to managers in public limited industries.

The second objective of this study was to examine the amount of autonomy managers enjoy in the area of their authority. This objective has been examined in view of the obtained empirical data. While professional authority signifies the institutionalized power to act in a certain way, the professional autonomy is the freedom of action and the absence of external interference. On the basis of his professional authority, a manager can influence the actions of his clients while on the basis of his professional autonomy he cannot be influenced by anyone who is not the member of his profession. Professional autonomy is based on the monopoly over the specialized knowledge. Managers' autonomy is not much based on this monopoly over the specialized knowledge in the true sense of the term. Their autonomy has two sources, first, from the rules of the industrial organization and secondly, their own personality traits and to a very little extent the specialized knowledge they have.

Managers' autonomy is scored in two ways. First, their overall autonomy and secondly in different areas of their functioning similar to those of authority. The mean score is calculated and those below it are perceived having low autonomy and those above it high autonomy. It is found that the majority of the managers have low overall autonomy. In decision-making they do not have much autonomy but in giving instructions to carry out these they are quite autonomous. The recommendations they make for the awards and penalization for their subordinates are normally accepted. Managers do not have much autonomy in recommending for the appointments, terminations, promotions, demotions and transfers of their subordinates. In planning, majority of the managers have high autonomy particularly those who have high authority in planning. In budgeting all the final decisions are taken by the top management and managers do not have much autonomy. Those managers who have direct active participation in budgeting have high autonomy.

Senior, highly educated and high salaried managers have comparatively more autonomy. The managers who have high overall authority have high overall autonomy. The managers who are at the higher position in the organizational hierarchy have high autonomy.

Most of the managers have moderate autonomy and they are satisfied with it. Few, who have little autonomy are just satisfied or dissatisfied. On being asked how much autonomy managers should be given, majority favoured moderate autonomy.

Managers in the private limited industries have more autonomy than their counterparts in public limited industries. This variation may be explained in various ways. First, in private limited industries, the number of senior and peer managers is less. Therefore, the check over managers' autonomy is very limited. Secondly, in such industries managers make every decision after consulting the colleagues, senior managers and managing directors and thus are able to extract more autonomy. Thirdly, managers in such industries are more autonomous. On the other hand, in public limited industries, due to their large organizational hierarchy, managers have little autonomy particularly those who are at the middle and low positions. Further, involvement of the unions also limit their autonomy particularly in dealing with subordinates.

Structural constraints managers face in the area of their professional authority and autonomy, their sources and managers' reaction to these have been analysed in this study. Managers face strains in all directions of their network of relations, *i.e.*, with managing directors, seniors and peer managers and subordinates. The main source of strains lies in their relations with the managing directors particularly in a family-controlled industry. The main reason being the difference in their ethics *i.e.*, egoistic ethics of the managing directors and altruistic ethics of professional managers. Other sources of strains are unnecessary interference in managers' authority and autonomy, undue response to his recommendations, etc. At many occasions senior managers exploit juniors on the basis of their authority. The overlapping and diffuse distribution of authority among peer managers leads to strains in their relations. Communication gap and involvement of the union lead to strains in managers' relations with subordinates.

The various problems which the managers face in the industrial organization become the sources of strains. Managers were asked to point out some of the most common problems causing strains. Most of the managers reported communication gap as a major problem leading to strains. The other problems causing strains are misunderstanding, misbehaviour, involvement of the union, laziness of workers, low morality, no sincerity, etc. Managers try their best to tackle these problems. Sometimes they feel helpless in spite of their urge to tackle them, may be due to their limited authority.

The strains become very severe when any decision is imposed on managers or they are stopped from doing according to their own will. Managers may respond to such situations in many ways. Majority of the managers discuss with the top management before following the imposed decision. Few keep quiet and follow such decisions while others show reluctance. Senior, high salaried managers respond more boldly in such situations. Level of education has no significant association with managers' response.

The size of the organization has a bearing on the extent of strains faced by the managers. In large size organizations of public limited industries, the strains are from varied sources and are more severe. Such industries, have a large hierarchy of managers who have competition with each other which becomes a cause of strains. Further, there are more chances of communication gap, overlapping and diffuse distribution of authority leading to strains. In private limited industries due to their small size, these problems remain within control. Managers in such industries work with more mutual understanding and cooperation with managing directors, senior and peer managers and subordinates. Such industries almost do not have the problems caused by the unions which is very severe in case of public limited industries.

In a nutshell it can be maintained that the majority of the managers are satisfied with the amount of authority and autonomy they have been given. On the other hand, few are not satisfied or just satisfied and they want more authority and autonomy. A good number of managers are not satisfied with the amount of autonomy. Managers favoured for moderate autonomy. In private limited industries, managers have more authority and autonomy than in public limited industries. Various reasons have been adduced for this variation. The strains managers face are part of the game. They try their best to overcome these and usually get success. The strains in large size organizations of public limited industries are more severe and from varied sources. Two issues crop up here which need further probing. First, how much authority and autonomy managers should be given so that they may function efficiently? Secondly, in what ways the strains managers face can be minimized and a conducive, healthy industrial environment developed?

QUESTIONS FOR EXERCISE

1. Write an essay on professionalism in Industrial management.
2. Explain the problem of industrial management in India.

11

Industrial Supervision

MEANING OF SUPERVISION

1. Literal meaning. Supervision is a Latin word in which 'super' denotes 'from the above' and 'vision' 'to see'. In ordinary sense, the term supervision is called 'overseeing activity'. But 'overseeing' alone does not convey anything worth taking note of. In management supervision means 'overseeing the subordinates at work with authority and with an aim to correct the employee if he is going to be wrong.' The real purpose of supervision is to oversee the employees at work.

2. Vitales. "Supervision refers to the direct and immediate guidance and control of subordinates in performance to their task."

3. Davis. "Supervision is the function of assuring that the work is being done in accordance with the plan and instruction."

4. G.R. Terry. "Supervision is the task of achieving the desired results by means of intelligent utilisation of human talents and utilising resources in a manner that provides a challenge to human talent. It is concerned with initiating action, putting into effect the plan and decisions by stimulation of the human resources of the enterprise."

To conclude, supervision is the direction, guidance and control of working force with a view :

(i) to see that they are working according to the plan, policy, programme, instruction and keeping up the time schedule and

(ii) to help them in their working if they are in need of help of any kind to accomplish their assigned tasks.

Who is a Supervisor?

America's Fort Hartley Labour Act of 1947 defines supervisors as "those having authority to exercise independent judgment in hiring, discharging, disciplining, recording and taking other actions of a similar nature with respect to employees." Therefore, supervisors are those persons in authority who have direct control over their working force. According to Allen, a supervisor is an authority who is responsible to get the work done. He is to see that directions are being followed, instructions and orders are being carried out, the plans, policies and programmes are being executed and deviations, if any, are being corrected and reported to the authority to whom one is answerable.

ESSENTIAL QUALITIES OF A SUPERVISOR

1. Knowledge of techniques of supervision. A supervisor should have knowledge of different techniques of supervision. This will enable him to know his men and he can make use of them according to the requirements.

Supervisory techniques are usually divided into the following three categories :

(i) ***Autocratic technique*** : In it there is a concentration of power in the hands of the supervisor. He uses 'rules of thumb' as weapon discriminately. He is a hard taskmaster. He imposes his will upon the workers who are to carry it out without 'if's and but's'. Workers have nothing to say about in the management decisions. The, supervisor commands fear and has full control over his men.

(ii) ***Democratic technique*** : In it the democratic principles are followed. Workers have full say in the management decisions. They are taken into confidence by the management. They are allowed to participate in the decision-making process. Debates precede the decision. Supervisor is also responsible for getting the work done. He is not allowed to function by rule of thumb; he has to rule by consent. He seeks co-operation. He motivates their skill, knowledge, training, working capacity and wisdom and helps them in increasing their abilities and efficiency.

(iii) ***Free-reign technique*** : In it the policies, programmes, the time schedule and objectives, etc. are fully explained to the workers. The workers are left free to work as satisfactorily as possible for them within the framework of the instructions, methodology and other allied things already explained to them. They have to follow the explained path and procedure and are responsible and answerable for deviations. The supervisor only guides the workers. He leaves the supervision part of his functions to the sound judgement of the workers themselves.

It is the individual trait, the working force, the work and the requirement which decide as to which of the three techniques are best for an organisation or in a given situation. It may differ from one situation to another, one individual to another, one group to another and one organisation to another.

2. Leadership qualities. The supervisor leads a group of personnel who look at him for guidance and direction. Unless he possesses the leader's qualities he will lack the rhythm of supervision and thus desired discipline, loyalty and efficiency in the group cannot be expected.

3. Managerial skill. The supervisor is a part of the management. He must therefore possess the knowledge of managerial skill. The management functions require him to encourage team spirit in his men and solicit all types of co-operation. He must command respect and unquestioned loyalty to him by the use of managerial skill and technique.

4. Unbiased and fair. The supervisor should behave in an unbiased manner. He should be fair to all. He should not be prejudiced to any-one of his men. Bias leads to troubles and vitiates the atmosphere. Therefore, it should be avoided at all costs.

5. Know and let know. The supervisor's duty is to know all his men, their work, conduct, skill, training, knowledge, wisdom, success, failures, habits, temperament, likings and dislikings, social status, domestic problems, and all which that could possibly be known. He should understand the spirit of his men. And his behaviour should be adjusted accordingly. On the other hand, he should let his men know about him. This will remove suspicion, develop friendly attitude and create oneness.

Thus, a supervisor is required to play a very significant role in an industrial organisation. He is in constant and direct touch with the operating staff, that is, the real working force. He is responsible for getting the work done from the work force of which he is the supervisor, and, who, are under his direct control. Because of his peculiar but significant position in the organisational structure the supervisor :

(i) influences the work environment,

(ii) influences the support of workers and

(iii) influences (a) the attitude, (b) the behaviour, (c) the conduct and even (d) co-operative efforts of the workers under his charge.

He is a morale booster. He influences the wholesome attitude of the whole lot. To quote Peter F. Drucker, "Even the best supervisor is not a substitute for poor principles and practices in managing workers."

TYPES OF SUPERVISION

Scholars have classified the types of leadership and supervision in identical terms. The types of leadership and supervision are similar or parallel. The supervisory role in industry is the same as that of leadership. The industrial leadership and political leadership are quite distinct affairs. An industrial leader *ex hypothesis* must be a supervisor. There are the following types of industrial leaders :

1. Authoritative supervisor. An authoritative supervisor exercises control and direction over his subordinates by virtue of the authority vested in him. In authoritative leadership there are the two following types of supervisors :

(i) ***The hard-boiled autocrat*** : An autocrat believes in unflagging discipline and firm control over the workers. He rarely appreciates the role of work of his subordinates. Rather he looks upon them with slight and mild contempt. He keeps himself aloof from the workers and does not give them a chance to get near to him. He wants automatic obedience of his orders and can brook no criticism of his directions and orders. Such autocrats are apt to give credence to backbiting and this leads to tension and conflicts in an industry. As the autocrats show no respect for the feelings of their subordinates, the subordinates also harbour a spirit of vindictiveness against such persons. At times this flares up and finds expression in violence against supervisors. In fact, a hard-boiled autocrat does not deserve to be called as a leader. He lacks all the qualities of leadership. The obedience which he is able to claim is due purely to the authority vested in him.

(ii) ***The benevolent autocrat*** : The benevolent autocrat gives guidance and direction in all matters. He seeks to maintain discipline. He is annoyed by any infringement of discipline. But unlike the hard-boiled autocrat, he is not averse to saying a word of praise to the workers who perform their duties well. The workers carry out the orders of such supervisors, though they do not really feel inspired by them. In certain cases, such a leader comes to symbolize smooth functioning of the factory or mill. The authoritarian leader is impressed by the quality of his decision but his decision cannot become an effective instrument, unless it is accepted by the whole group.

2. *Laissez-faire* supervisorship. The *laissez-faire* is exact reverse of the autocratic supervisorship :

(i) *Freedom of workers* : While in autocratic leadership there is no place for the personal freedom of workers, in *laissez-faire* leadership the personal freedom of workers is respected.

(ii) *Responsibility* : Whereas in autocratic supervisorship, the leader is considered responsible for everything, in *laissez-faire* supervisorship the responsibility is distributed among various persons.

(iii) *Autocracy of democracy* : The *laissez-faire* supervisors do not try to impose any decision nor do they coerce the workers to any type of action. These supervisors act democratically. They try to seek the voluntary co-operation of workers. These supervisors do not project any fixed goals. The *laissez-faire* supervisorship gives rise to indiscipline and discontent among the workers. It also promotes a sense of insecurity among them. There is a loss in production also. That is why one rarely finds such type of supervisorship countenanced in an industry.

3. Democratic supervision. The most prevalent form of leadership and supervision in an industry is democratic supervision. According to Bradford, a democratic leader believes in the following things :

1. Problems should not be allowed to crop up.
2. For the sake of collective action and thinking, assemblies and conferences are a must.
3. There should be fixed collective ideals.
4. The criteria of action should be fixed.
5. The reasons for decisions should be known.
6. With progress, freedom and responsibility increase.

The above-mentioned characteristics of democratic supervision are corresponding to and congruent with modern democratic ideals. However, everyone cannot be led democratically. Some workers misunderstand the democratic attitude of the supervisor and take it to be a symptom of weakness. They try to exploit this weakness and shirk work. This results in the loss of production.

CONDITIONS OF EFFECTIVE SUPERVISION

1. Favourable social environs. Creation of an atmosphere of mutual trust and confidence is an essential condition of an effective leadership. It must be able to associate workers in decision making and feeling of responsibility. The directives of the leader are easily accepted and carried out by the workers under such an atmosphere.

2. Knowledge of company's policy. The leader must know the fundamental tenets which govern the functioning of the company. He must acquaint the workers with the policy and the rules of the company. He must explain his status and role in the company in clear and frank terms. This would enable him to feel secure because he knows what he has to do and what he must avoid doing.

3. Gaining confidence of workers. A good leader should win the confidence of workers. Before effecting any change in the technique of production, he should consult the workers even if the change has been finally decided upon. This helps to induce a sense of well-being and confidence among the workers and they highly appreciate the fact that workers have been considered worthy for consultation by respective authorities.

4. Strict Discipline. Whatever rules and regulations are framed once, these should be strictly adhered to. If a worker violates them he should be penalized without let or hindrance. Similarly, if the performance of a worker is noteworthy and deserves reward, he must be rewarded ungrudgingly.

5. Participation in decision-making. Finally, it is very necessary for good supervisorship that workers should be given a chance to participate in the decision-and policy-making of the company. This will enthuse them to toil hard and work with grit and determination.

PRINCIPLES OF EFFECTIVE SUPERVISION

The psychologist Blum has suggested the following principles for good supervisorship :

1. Don't be an autocrat. Autocratic supervisor is self-defeating because the workers feel alienated and do not obey the supervisor willingly.

2. Listen carefully. The supervisor should be a good listener. He must listen carefully to everything told to him by his subordinates. He must accord full opportunity to the worker to present his case; only after it should the supervisor express his opinion.

3. Don't decide hurriedly. It is rash to form an opinion about some person hurriedly after a casual glance or brief hearing, as most of the complaints are not genuine. But some are certainly so and if these are not removed, the morale of the company would suffer.

4. Don't argue with subordinates. Under no circumstances supervisor should indulge in an argument with his subordinate, because if he fails to persuade or be convinced by his arguments, he is liable to issue orders to vindicate his point of view. This creates frustration and sense of insecurity among the workers. A good supervisor should not argue, but, listen carefully, and issue orders only after careful listening.

5. Don't criticize publicly. If a worker is rebuked publicly he feels insulted. The workers are usually rash and they tend to retaliate if they are wounded emotionally. Therefore a good leader avoids discussing the faults of workers in public. He points them out to him in private and in a direct manner.

SUPERVISION TECHNIQUES

The following are the important supervision techniques :

1. Autocratic technique.
2. Democratic technique.
3. Free-reign technique. Success of this technique depends on :
   - (i) Unrestricted supervision,
   - (ii) Free delegation of authority, and
   - (iii) Efficient and effective communication.

According to R. Lickert, "There is no one best way to supervise. Supervisory practices that are effective in some situations yield unsatisfactory results in the other." Indeed supervision is an individual trait and wisdom. Techniques are being developed by the supervisor himself in a given situation. His techniques differ from situation to situation, from work to work, from individual to individual, from group to group and from organisation to organisation. Under these circumstances, it is difficult to adjudge any one of the three as 'best'.

FACTORS AFFECTING SUPERVISION

1. Human relations skills. Supervision assimilates in itself the following functions :

- (i) Guiding the working force,
- (ii) Instructing them and
- (iii) Inspiring them for better performance.

The supervisor has to depend on the decisions of top and middle-order management for the following :

(i) Leadership

(ii) Counselling

(iii) Communication

(iv) Determinants of human relations

Without their guidelines, the supervisor remains handicapped. In modern set-up, he can take routine decisions within the framework provided for the purpose. But he cannot take a major decision without consulting his superiors in middle order and top management. He is the person who has to toe the lines as suggested by his superior though he is directly responsible to get the work done. But he is the person who is in direct touch with his men. He watches them to work. He knows their emotions, feelings and sentiments, notes them and shares them. He is on the spot. Therefore in these matters he is left with no alternative but to take quick decisions before any sparking situation arises. He is the best judge of human relations. He has to apply his skill, use his training, draw lessons from his experiences and handle the situation accordingly. So far as human relations are concerned it is a matter of skill.

2. Technical and managerial knowledge. The guidance and instructions are largely based on the technical knowledge and the managerial acumen. These helps the supervisor in serving his organisation well. His supervisory capabilities are increased by adequate training and sufficient technical and managerial skill.

3. Leadership position. The supervisor's ability of supervising his workmen depends on his position and status in the organisation. This position may either be delegated or may be acquired. The supervisor can improve his position provided a status worth of his responsibilities is given to him. This is fundamentally important and no organisation can afford to ignore it.

4. Improved upward relations. A supervisor is well heard and respected by his superiors at all levels of the management. His adverse reports as well as appreciations are equally respected to and action taken accordingly. He must have good relations with his superiors by way of encouragement. Thus helps him in establishing good relations with his workmen.

5. Relief from non-supervisory duties. A supervisor must be free from all duties except supervision and its related functions. Submission of reports, returns, etc. is not his job. If he is free from all these then he may devote more time with his workmen. Job training too is not his duty. Instead it should be given to instructional staff. The supervisor should be allowed to concentrate on directing functions for which he should be given sufficient authority under the basic norm of management — 'power with people'. This would ensure the maximum supervision from which results can be generally expected.

QUESTIONS FOR EXERCISE

1. What is supervision? Describe qualities of a supervisor.
2. Describe kinds of supervision. How can supervision be made effective?
3. What are the factors affecting supervision?

12
IMPACT OF INDIVIDUAL DIFFERENCES

Meaning of Individual Differences

According to Skinner, "Today we think of individual differences as including any measurable aspect of the total personality." From this definition of individual differences, it is evident that it comprehends every aspect of the human personality, albeit all aspects that are in some manner measurable. Aspects of this nature can be many such as variability, conformity, difference in the rate of learning and development, mutual relationship between the various characteristics of the personality, etc. In this manner, various individuals exhibit differences of physical and mental development, nature, rate of learning, ability, specific abilities, interest and personality, etc.

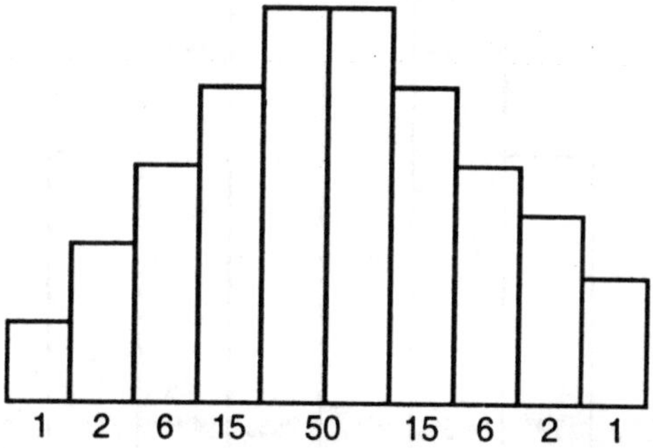

Fig. 12.1. Normal Probability Curve of Individual Differences

TYPES OF INDIVIDUAL DIFFERENCES

The following brief description may serve to make individual differences a simple concept that can easily be grasped :

1. Average intelligence. Individuals are seen differing in considerable measure in respect of their general intelligence. It is not possible to send children with a higher intelligence quotient to go to school. Children with intelligence quotients between 50

and 70 can learn only the simplest tasks. Even the small schools trouble children whose intelligence quotient varies between 70 and 80. Children between 75 and 90 I.Q. are considered morons and they have considerable difficulty in progressing, along with the other children, in their learning. Generally, 40 to 60 per cent of the children in school have I.Q.s varying between 95 and 105, being the children with average intelligence who form the basis for the formulation of the syllabus and curriculum as well as the method of teaching.

Children who are either above or below this level of intelligence require special educational methods and conditions. Children with intelligence quotient varying between 115 and 120 are considered brilliant or intelligent. The following facts have come to light concerning individual differences of intelligence in children :

(a) However good and beneficial the environmental and the method of education, the moron invariably reaches his highest level of learning much later than an average or the intelligent child.

(b) In favourable circumstances, the average child generally gives a good account of himself in his academic pursuits.

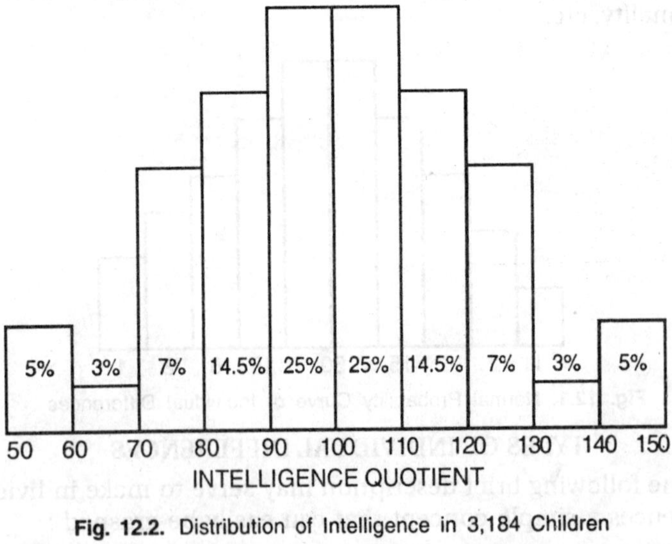

Fig. 12.2. Distribution of Intelligence in 3,184 Children

The height of the columns over each of the scores on the base-line indicates the number of children making a given score. (After J.P. Guilford, *General Psychology*, New York : D. Van Nostrand, 1939, p. 506; based on data from L.M. Terman and M.A. Merrill, *Measuring Human Intelligence*, Boston : Houghton Miffin, 1937.)

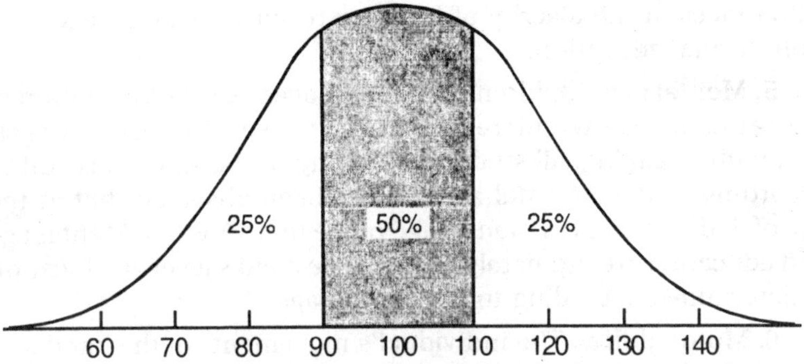

Fig. 12.3. Normal Distribution Curve

The height of the curve indicates the frequency with which the various scores shown on the base-line appear in population. Half of the people make scores which fall in a narrow band in the middle. The other two quarters make scores which are spread over a wider range, both above and below the middle band. If the middle half is divided into two quarters, the population is thereby divided into four groups of equal size.

(c) If the circumstances are favourable, the intelligent child shows great alacrity in the process of learning.

(d) Adverse circumstances have the worst effect on all children, and their learning activities are hindered.

2. Special abilities. During the junior and senior high school as well as at the college stage, the individual differences in respect of special abilities, in addition to the general intelligence, are also important, since special professions and specialized fields of vocation all need certain specific abilities. Abilities of this kind are concerned with mental, artistic or motor ability.

3. Differences of background. In school, the, differences that children exhibit are the outcome of their different families and their communities. Attitudes towards education and authority differ in each family, culture and class. Some of these attitudes are favourable while others are unfavourable to education. In either condition, the difference of attitudes results in differences among the children. Besides these attitudes, the child's emotional, social, aesthetic and moral development is influenced by his family and neighbourhood. Hence, differences of background are also manifested in individual differences.

4. Alacrity in learning. Difference in the quickness or alacrity in learning is visible, not only in children of different ages, but also among children in the same age group. This difference is dependent upon their maturity and educational background.

Differences in the alacrity of learning result in benefits accruing from formal education.

5. Mental age. Children of different ages as well as children of the same age show differences in their respective mental ages. Generally speaking, all students studying in the same class differ according to their mental ages. It has been observed that at the age of 6, differences in mental age range up to 5 years. Mental age and education are intimately related. The child's level of education is determined according to his mental age.

6. Motor ability. The individual's movements of the hand and feet and other physical abilities are seen to be very individual, as they do not resemble to another's to such a great extent. Till the individual attains adulthood, his manual dexterity, rate of muscular movement and resistance to fatigue develop continually. In this manner, the same individual in different ages and different individuals in the same age group manifest considerable differences in manual dexterity.

7. Sex differences. Makneimer and Terman discovered the following differences between men and women, on the basis of some studies :

(a) Women have greater skill in memory while men have greater motor ability.

(b) Female handwriting is superior while men excel in mathematical logic.

(c) Women show greater skill in making sensory distinctions of tastes, touch, smell, etc., while men show greater reaction and consciousness of size-weight illusion.

(d) Possessing greater linguistic ability, women are superior to men in languages, etc. On the other hand, men are superior in physics and chemistry.

(e) Women are better than men in mirror drawing. Faults of speech, etc., in men were found to be three times of such faults in women.

(f) Women are more susceptible to suggestion, while the colour-blind men are more than women.

(g) Young girls take interest in stories of love, fairy-tales, stories of the school and home and day dreaming, and show various levels in their play. On the other hand, boys take interest in stories of bravery, science, war and scouting, stories of games and sports, scouts stories and games of occupation and skill.

8. Racial differences. Many scientific studies have indicated the presence of various kinds of differences between individuals of different races, although differences of environment are a normal factor in causing these differences. Karl Brigham has composed a list on the basis of differences in levels of intelligence among people who have migrated to United States from other countries.

On the basis of these average differences between the races, the mental age of a particular individual of a definite race cannot be calculated since this difference is based on the environment.

9. Nationality. Many studies have led to the conclusion that individuals of different nations differ in respect of nature, physical and mental differences, interest and personality, etc. Such a difference is only natural since their culture and geographic environment are distinctive.

10. Economic situation. Economic differences are seen causing differences in the children's interests, tendencies and character, etc.

11. Differences relating to learning. In respect of learning, children manifest such differences as past experience and learning, ability in the use of various kinds of apparatus, rate of learning, interest in learning, etc.

12. Difference in respect of development. Difference in development is in evidence not only in individuals of different age groups but also between individuals of the same age.

13. Difference of interests. As has been pointed out, the difference in sex leads to a difference in interests. Similarly, factors such as family background, levels of development, differences of nationality and race, etc., cause differences of interests.

14. Personality. Differences in respects of personality have led psychologists to make in-depth study, and on the basis of this study, individuals have been classified into many groups. Jung, for example, has divided individuals into three groups : (a) Introvert, (b) Extrovert, and (c) Ambivert. This is the psychological classification of people. Stephenson has divided human beings into two categories — preservator and non-preservator. In this division, people of the first group are very sensitive and susceptible to experience while people of the second group are not influenced by it quite to that extent. Cattell has put people into the Surgent and the Surgeless or Non-surgent classes. The former is similar to Jung's extrovert while the surgeless resembles his introvert individual. Terman

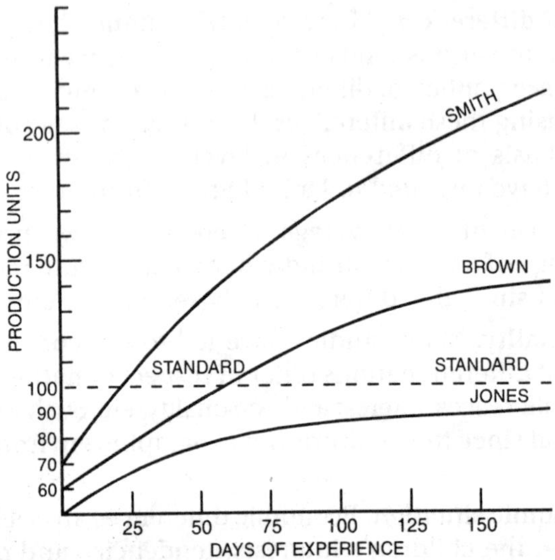

Fig. 12.4. Carves Showing Rates of Improvement with Experience

Although all people get profited by the job experience or training, some get profited more than others. The hypothetical curves of Jones, Brown and Smith differ in : (a) the points at which they begin, (b) the steepness of the progress, (c) the height at which the curve levels off to indicate the ceiling of their progress and (d) the length of time over which improvement will occur. Smith is superior on all counts, but Jones will never reach 100 units. Since 100 is the production standard, this means that Jones will never be satisfactory.

has put people into nine classes according to their level of intelligence : (a) Genius, (b) Near genius, (c) Very superior intelligence, (d) Superior, (e) Average, (f) Backward, (g) Feeble-minded, (h) Dull, (i) Idiot.

Thorndike has divided people into four categories on the basis of thinking : (a) Abstract thinkers, (b) Ideational thinkers, (c) Object thinkers, (d) Thinkers in whom sensory experience is predominant. These names indicate the peculiarities of thinking in these individuals.

Concerning these classifications of human personality, it should be remembered that although one specific person may exhibit the main broad characteristics of one class of personality, but the differences between various personalities are so subtle and minute that it is not scientifically feasible to divide them into classes.

CAUSES OF INDIVIDUAL DIFFERENCES

It is not even within the realm of possibility to describe all the causes of individual differences among the children, yet the main ones are the following :

1. Age. It is a matter of common knowledge that age creates differences of intelligence, abilities, physical capacity and maturity, etc., in different children.

2 Physical development. Differences in height, weight, physical structure, and the rate and quantity of development of the various parts of body lead to differences between the individuals.

3. Heredity. It has now been established that hereditary differences result in the quantity and rate of physical as well as mental development being different, in different individuals. Many physical as well as mental diseases are the result of heredity in persons. According to many scientists, a person inherits many mental peculiarities and abilities from his parents.

4. Environment or atmosphere. Modern psychologists do not believe heredity to be the only cause of individual differences. Personality is the outcome of mutual interaction between heredity and environment. Hence the influence of heredity and gradual changes in a child's environment can be seen reflected by the changes in his personality. An individual exhibits good and bad qualities as accruing from a good or bad environment. Generally speaking, environment comprehends family, school, neighbourhood, society and culture. The child is open to a very wide range of influences such as the social and economic level, standard of living, education, profession of parents, their mutual relationships, their relations with their children, and their personalities, nature of other people's character, personality and attitudes, etc.

5. Effect of race and nation. Although, modern psychologists believe that race does not lead to differences in the mental structure of individuals, yet it cannot be denied that individuals of different races exhibit very pronounced differences, even though, it may be induced by the environment. Similarly, individuals of different nations show differences in respect of their personality, character and mental abilities. These are the outcome of their geographical, social and cultural environment. Many scientific tests have established the existence of differences between Eastern and Western, Negro and American, Chinese and Japanese, English and Indian individuals.

6. Sex differences. Although modern psychologists are not prepared to accept sex differences as the basis of differentiation between boys and girls, yet sex does lead to differences between individuals, even though the family, social and cultural environment may play a major part in it. Development of boys and girls exhibits difference in sex.

7. Intelligence and mental Age. Many studies have indicated that many individuals differ because the differences of intelligence and mental age, and environment cannot be accepted to account for majority of such differences. Individuals who are well below the average of intelligence and mental age find much difficulty in learning and picking up easily.

8. Emotional stability. Due to many physical, mental and environmental factors, the emotional stability of individuals is differently affected, and this leads to differences in their respective natures.

9. Temperament. Medical men, and in particular Indians, believe that individuals have different temperaments. Some people are by temperament quick and short-tempered, while others are secretive, some active and others inactive.

10. Difference relating to learning. Individuals differ from each other because of their attitude to learning, their zeal, rate of progress and transfer of training, etc.

11. Other causes. In addition to the above causes, many other causes lead to differences among the individuals, *e.g.*, interest, attitudes, various sentiments of personality, communal circumstances, etc.

Value of Individual Differences in Industry

Individual differences have great importance in the field of industry. In an industry, different individuals with different qualities and abilities are required to perform various functions. If the work is to be of the best in quality and quantity, it is essential that each operation should be performed by the individuals best qualified to perform it. And the best person for a particular job can be located by testing individual differences through special tests. Any individual can be superior to others only when he is compared to them. How is such a comparison to be made? By studying the general distribution curve the superior can discover the kind of performance that can be expected from the average worker for a particular job. If, now, a particular individual gives a better performance than can be expected from the average worker for a particular job, he can be taken to be superior to average. On the other hand, an individual who shows result below the average can be classified as inferior. It is generally seen that the better qualified or able individuals do not put in all their time at work while the less able individuals continue to work for long hours without completing their assignments. And this can only be found by turning out the irresponsible worker and then finding out how many people are required to perform the same function that he was performing. Only then one can discover individual's level of efficiency. A job which can be performed only after many hours of labour by the inefficient worker, can be performed by the more able in a much shorter time, which is why he is seen roaming around and wasting his time. In fact, some people are so capable that the supervisor gets a headache in trying to keep them occupied. Such people become even more problematic when the work is measured in terms of time and not in quantity because then they are not inclined to produce more than the average, which takes them much less time than the average worker. Consequently, they loaf about, wasting their own time and that of the others.

Just as the exceptionally able proves to be a problem in industry, the less able worker is also a source of constant anxiety. When doing more work than they are capable of, they lower the quality of work. It is difficult to save them from accidents. Besides, they turn against the managers very often. Sometimes such inefficient individuals have an adverse influence upon the work of more efficient workers because then even the better worker reduces his own quality to suit theirs.

The importance of taking account of individual differences is evident from the above account. Many of the problems in industry have their origin in this difference between the individuals. The more efficient workers complete their task assignments within a short time and then roam around wasting the time of others. In offices, in particular, individuals of this kind can be seen sitting around at others' tables, taking tea or smoking cigarettes in the canteens, despite the fact that their daily assignments are invariably completed. Such behaviour hinders the working of the less efficient workers because the latter cannot achieve the same level of work despite complete application and dedication. Hence, the supervisor is forced to create work for efficient workers in order to keep them occupied but more often than not this work is also rapidly finished by them, after which they can again be seen roaming around. In such a situation, the able administrator must pay attention to the individual differences and divide the work according to the individual abilities. In the first place, he should conduct tests and find out the more appropriate function for each worker in the distribution cycle. This will help him to assign tasks according to the capacities of each worker and lead him to expect normal quality and quantity of production from each of them.

The importance of individual differences in the field of industry can be illustrated even better by the example given by Norman Meyer.

When a foreman in the telephone industry was asked about the production efficiency of the workers under him, he pointed out that six were above average and six below it. None of them was average. The above average individuals were installing four telephones a day while the below average workers were installing three. This report was obviously defective because half the workers cannot be above average. Besides, even among the six above average workers there might have been one or two who would be capable of installing more than four telephones a day. In the same way, one or two below average individuals must also have been installing less than three telephones a day. But this never occurred because whenever a worker failed to install three telephones he was either transferred or relieved of his job. But the most prominent fact was that, there was no individual who was installing between three and four telephones a day, implying the installation of 3-5 telephones per day. Hence, it became necessary to find out why all of them installed telephones only in round figures. Secondly, why were some of the individuals not taking interest in putting in more work? Thirdly, what was the foreman's behaviour towards those who failed to install three telephones? If the better workers were not giving optimum production merely in order to allow the less efficient workers to keep up with them, this fact was important and should have been noticed. It was also necessary to see the level of production below which a worker stood in danger of being thrown out of his job. This minimum level of acceptable production should never be of a kind so as to destroy the morale of other workers. To continue the above example, the installation of four telephones a day was essential because otherwise the workers were fired. Consequently, all the workers must necessarily have been worried about their security and many must have had to leave the job. In fact, industrial psychologists believe that it is improper, in any industry, to expect that all workers will provide the same level of production. Such a demand is in direct contradiction to facts. Since workers exhibit individual differences it is only natural to expect some to produce more than the average and others less than it. The sensible organiser is one who is not unnecessarily strict with the less efficient nor unnecessarily preoccupied with the more efficient. Actually, the average production does not suffer because the less efficient work of one is balanced by the more efficient work of another.

VALUE OF INDIVIDUAL DIFFERENCES IN VOCATIONAL GUIDANCE

Vocational guidance is the name given to the process of guiding an individual in his selection of a profession which will suit him. It is commonly accepted that every individual cannot perform every kind of task. Besides, different professions and different kinds of jobs require individuals with different aptitudes, qualities, personality, levels of intelligences, etc. Hence, the process of vocational guidance starts with the application of various tests for the measurement of the individual's intelligence, mental abilities, interests, aptitudes, physical development, qualities of personality, etc. Some jobs require mechanical ability while others require sociability or educational qualifications. Hence, to find the right man for the right job and right job for the right man, it is essential to test an individual to find out the qualities he possesses and the level of such qualities. For example, such professions as teaching, authorship, scientific research, legal practice, require a high degree of education, creative ability, power of reasoning and a high level of development. Only when a person possesses all these qualities that he can hope to find success in such professions. This happens because professions are categorised as mechanical, quantitative, scientific, creative, literary, social service oriented, etc., according to interests.

TESTS FOR MEASUREMENT

Now the most important question arises concerning the measurement of these individual differences. In recent times psychologists have constructed various kinds of psychological tests to measure these individual differences. Intelligence tests are used to discover differences in levels of intelligence. Differences in the subtle qualities of the personality are brought out into the open through personality tests. Specific tests have been devised to discover special abilities which may be latent. Mechanical tests are applied to test the mechanical aptitude of the individual. Interests are discovered through interest lists and scales. Various kinds of scales, such as rating scales, etc., are used to evaluate aptitudes.

In addition to the information being provided by the above-mentioned tests, individual differences are also exhibited through the diplomas and degrees that the individual acquires during the time he spends in colleges and universities. One of the best method of understanding individual differences is to interview the individual because in an interview it is possible to come to important conclusions about the individual's personality, interests, aptitudes, intelligence and many other personal factors. For this reason, almost all industrial organisations insist on an interview despite the written applications which provide a complete bio-data of the applicant. But, if the interview is to be successfully used to discover individual differences, the person conducting it must have psychological insight. It is only if he has this insight, that he can expect to find out the desired facts from the answers he has obtained. Only a person with psychological insight can correctly interpret the implication of the other person's behaviour at the time of interview.

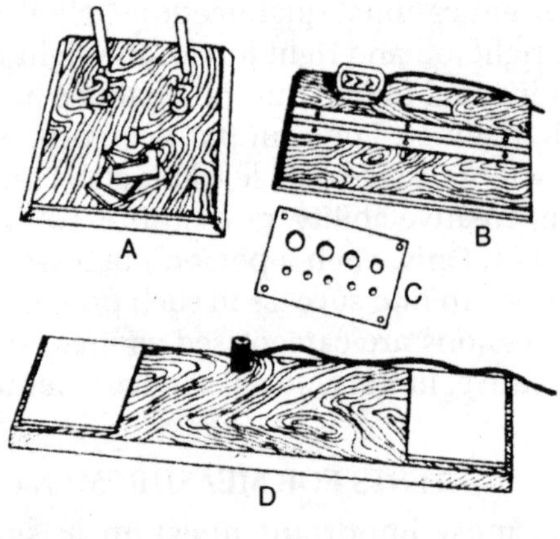

Fig. 12.5. Example of Aptitude Tests

A. Pyramid puzzle. The pyramid problem involves moving the blocks to a designated post without placing a larger block on a smaller one. Demonstrates problem-solving.

B. Steadiness tester. Groove type. Calibrated. Sides are electrified to activate buzzer of the electric counter.

C. Steadiness tester. Hole type. Conventional hole type with terminals for completing electric circuit to activate buzzer or counter.

D. Tapping board. Stainless steel metal plates at each end; completes circuit when stylus contacts each successive plate.

(From equipment made by Lafayette Instrument Co.)

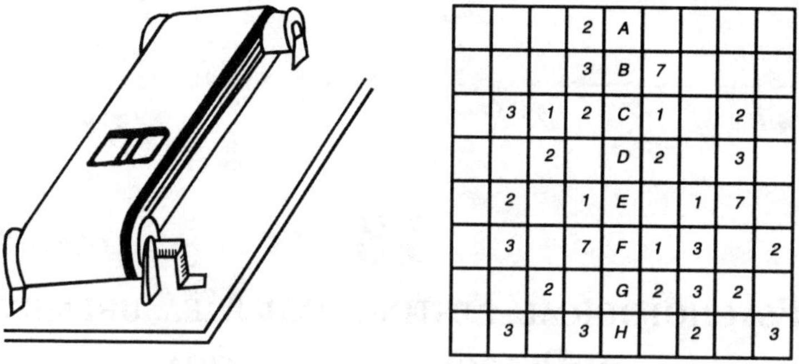

Fig. 12.6. Munsterbeg's Test of Motorman

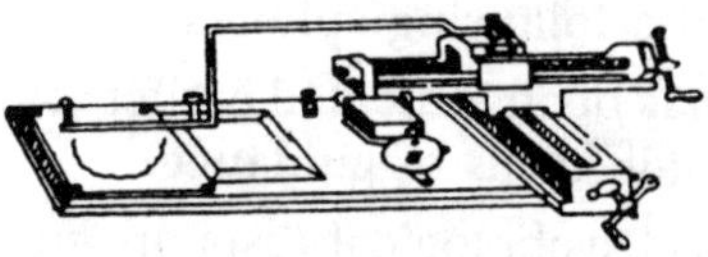

Fig. 12.7. Wiscounsin Test of Engine-lathe Aptitude

QUESTIONS FOR EXERCISE

1. What are individual differences? Describe their kinds.
2. Give two tests for measurement of individual differences.

13

Psychological Testing and Measurement in Personnel Selection

Psychological tests have proved to possess great utility in many spheres. Briefly, the utility and importance of mental tests can be observed in the following spheres :

1. Guidance. As has been indicated earlier, psychological tests are indispensable in all forms of guidance.

2. Appointments. Psychological tests are nowadays resorted to for the appointment of appropriate individuals to posts in offices, factories and government service. It has the doubly beneficial effect of securing proper and desirable jobs for individuals according to their interests, inclinations, intelligence and abilities, as well as ensuring that the highest level of efficiency is achieved by the right man being in the right job. In this way, both the employed as well as the employer are benefited.

3. Selection for training. An individual can be benefited from training for some particular job only if he is in possession of the requisite intelligence, abilities and qualities, besides the necessary interest in the work involved. It is evident that the individual should be tested in respect of these qualities before any training is imparted to him. Hence, in all advanced nations of the world, all kinds of training institutes make use of psychological tests for selecting the required candidates. In India, for example, the recruitment to the Police Training Colleges, the Government Teacher's Training Colleges, and other technical institutions is done only on the basis of psychological tests. In public schools, the students who receive scholarships are selected on the basis of psychological tests in order to ensure that the scholarships are not wasted, as they might be if they are provided to the wrong individuals. Psychological tests are further used for selection of candidates for the National Defence Academy in the country. Such use of psychological tests for the selection of persor nel in training schools is constantly on the increase.

4. Classification according to the level of intelligence. Nowadays, all educationists agree that the success of education depends upon the student being provided education of a kind that accords with his level of intelligence. Hence, individual students are classified and stratified according to their level of intelligence, and different curricular and extracurricular programmes devised for the three categories of students, the brilliant, the average and the retarded. The classification is based on intelligence tests. It is not only in the field of education but also in various vocations, armed forces and industries that intelligence tests are used to classify individuals so that they can be given the proper kind of work that is within their capacity to perform with reasonable success.

5. Prediction. The term indicates the forecasting of success in the case of an individual. While guiding the individual, a psychologist can normally make fairly accurate predictions as to the degree of success that one is likely to achieve. The prediction is based upon psychological tests; the greater the capacity of a psychological test to assist in prediction, the greater is validity and its reliability.

6. Diagnosis. Before giving any guidance, the directing psychologist makes a diagnosis of the problem present before him. He gives suggestions for alleviating a certain condition only after he has decided upon diagnosis, since it is only upon diagnosing some problem that he reaches the root causes. And psychological tests are essential for diagnosis; without them, a proper diagnosis cannot be achieved.

7. Research. Psychological tests are of use even in the field of psychological research. Intelligence tests, inventories, personality tests, tests of mental abilities and personal qualities, help in research in these specific directions.

WHAT ARE MENTAL TESTS?

Importance of psychological tests is fairly evident from the preceding exposition of the subject. Before proceeding to a study of the various kinds of tests, it is essential to know the kinds of psychological tests that are in use, and the principal elements active in them. Defining psychological tests, Mursell writes, "A psychological test, then, is a pattern of stimuli selected and organised to elicit responses which will reveal certain psychological characteristics of the person who takes them."[1] In this way psychological tests are an organisation of some stimuli. These stimuli are selected with some special objectives in view. The object is to discover some psychological characteristics of the person being tested. Stimuli present in psychological tests are called test items, and they can be of several kinds — pictures, figures, wooden blocks, word groups, sentences and figures, etc. And the way in which these stimuli cover psychological characteristics will be evident from a description of each of them.

Psychological Tests and Experimentation

What should here be kept well in mind is that psychological tests differ from psychological experimentation although in both cases some stimuli are given, and it is the reaction to them that is examined. As has been pointed out, the object of psychological tests is to ascertain the psychological characteristics of the subject, while in the case of psychological experimentation, the object is more purely academic as they aim at discovering a mental process concerned with the particular experiment. In this manner, it is evident that while psychological tests lead to the discovery of abilities or capabilities, the psychological experiments discover and confirm various mental processes. Nevertheless, the difference between the two is very subtle, since nowadays, psychological tests are also being used for discovering and identifying mental processes.

CHARACTERISTICS OF A GOOD TEST

Good tests of psychological nature bear the following features :

1. Reliability. The higher the degree of reliability that results of a test have, the greater is considered the reliability of the test itself. And the reliability of its conclusion means that if the same test is performed upon the same individual more than once, results obtained in each case should be the same or commensurate with the first one, if it is modified by changed circumstances.

2. Validity. The validity of a test lies in the fact that it succeeds in testing the particular quality which it is designed to test. For example, intelligence tests can be valid only if they, in fact, test correctly the intelligence level of the individual.

3. Objectivity. A test can achieve a high level of objectivity only if the answer to each of its various questions is distinct and

1. Mursel, J.L., *Psychological Testing*, New York, p. 1.

precise and if there no difference of opinion regarding it among the various examiners. Its efficacy lies in the fact that the conclusion or result is in no way influenced by the examiner's individual thoughts or opinions, so that the conclusions or results are obtained no matter what the number of examiners who examine the same subject.

4. Comprehensiveness. Another feature of good test is its comprehensive nature. This feature is inclusive of all features or qualities allied to the one in question. It will provide information of qualities concerned with the one quality actually being tested. In this manner, in a comprehensive test, questions cover the quality in question as well as allied qualities so that no aspect to be measured or tested ability escapes attention.

5. Discriminating Power. This applies to the ability which helps to distinguish between persons with greater or less ability so that they score more or less points or marks.

6. Utility. This feature concerns the extent to which a particular test can be used with facility. And for this, it is essential that the questions asked should be simple, the method easy, the time involved less and the expenses negligible.

Of the above, mentioned characteristics, the most important are validity and reliability. Hence, both these qualities will be described in detail here.

CLASSIFICATION OF PSYCHOLOGICAL TESTS

Mental tests are of various kinds. They have been classified from various different standpoints. Classifications are as follows:

1. Classification according to method of testing. Tests have been divided into two classes; in this case classification is based on the method involved.

(a) Individual tests. These tests are administered to one individual at one time, as indicated by the term denoting them. They include performance tests. In addition to these, they also include tests that require linguistic ability. Some examples of these are Stanford-Binet intelligence test, Wechsler-Bellevue intelligence tests, Kohez's block design test. These are particularly appropriate for testing of individuals, but they are not financially suitable as they are expensive, in addition to requiring more expert training than in many other cases. Secondly, they are less objective than group tests.

(b) Group tests. In this category, the tests included are performed upon a large number of people simultaneously. Some examples are the group intelligence tests of the Psychological Bureau of Uttar Pradesh, interest lists, vocational lists, etc. They are more objective and less expensive, requiring very little, if any, specialised training that may prove expensive. But in these tests, no real rapport between the subject and the examiner is established. Hence, they are less useful for solving problems of individuals, than are the individual tests. Nevertheless, they have proved really useful in the case of education and vocational guidance requirements.

2. Classification according to the medium of instruction. In these tests, classification is based upon the medium of leaching of the subjects. The psychological tests, from this viewpoint, are divided into following two classes :

(a) Verbal tests. This classification comprehends tests in which questions are orally asked, linguistic and concerned abilities being essentially required. One of the best examples of verbal tests is, Dr. Sohan Lal's intelligence test utilised at Uttar Pradesh Bureau of Psychology. These tests are not intended for and cannot be used in the case of illiterates, only slightly educated persons and small children, since such people lack linguistic ability.

(b) Non-verbal tests. This classification substitutes figures, which do not require the use of language, but substitutes figures, pictures, blocks and, other implements for it. Examples of it are Pidgon's non-verbal tests and Raven's progressive matrices. Their particular felicity lies in the fact that they can be applied to the testing of illiterates, very slightly educated individuals and very young children. This category includes all non-verbal tests.

(c) Interest tests. These tests help to discover the interest of the individual, some examples of which are Strong's Vocational Interest Blank, and Cudor's Vocational Inventory. Both of them are described in detail at a later stage. Besides these, the vocational interest list devised by the Bureau of Psychology, Uttar Pradesh, is also an effective test.

(d) Aptitude tests. These tests are devised by combining the different tests of mental abilities.

(e) Personality tests. These help to find out the individual's personality traits or characteristics. The main methods of personality testing are Rorschach's Ink Blot Test and T.A.T.

INTELLIGENCE TESTS

Historical Outline

As the new individual dissimilarities came to light, psychologists tried to measure the various individual differences, and to this end, different tests were evolved. Among these tests, those devised to measure intelligence achieved a lot of fame. Near the close of the 19th century, Galton developed some tests to measure the functions of the different organs. By these, Galton measured sensory discrimination, sensory perception and sensory acuity. Though, these measures are not directly related to intelligence, they may be accepted as the forerunners of intelligence tests.

In 1880, Ebbinghaus prepared several tests to measure the differences of intelligence in various individuals. In 1890, a famous American psychologist, Cattell, evolved some mental tests. On the basis of these, Cattell measured individual differences between some students of Columbia University, in respect of speed reactions, sensory acuity, memory and some other simple mental activities.

But, in fact, the first concrete step in the direction of intelligence tests was taken by a famous French psychologist Alfred Binet. Alfred Binet was conducting some research in the mental activities of school-going children. In the course of his research, he observed that, in order to give any useful education to the feeble-minded children, it is essential to put them in special classes. In order to investigate this subject, a committee headed by Binet was formed in 1904. The first difficulty concerning the study of feeble-minded children was need of a scale with which to measure the intelligence of children.

With Simon's assistance Binet developed and published a scale in 1905, what we know as the Binet-Simon Scale. In this scale, some 30 tasks, from the simplest to the most complex, were prescribed in a serial order. On the basis of experiments with the average and feeble-minded children carried out with the help of this scale, Binet and Simon determined norms by various age levels. According to the Binet-Simon intelligence tests, if a five-year old child is capable of performing tasks which an average child of three can perform, his mental age will be rated as three years and if that child fails to perform more than the first five among the thirty tasks he will be classed as idiot.

Binet and Simon made revisions in this scale from time to time. The first revised scale was published in 1980. From the success of this revision, psychologists of other countries developed intelligence tests suitable to the environment of their own countries. Among them, Hurt's London Revision and Terman's Standford Revision are well known. The modern revised edition was published in 1937 under the name of Terman-Merrill Scale.

In the Terman-Merrill Scale which was a revision of the Standford-Binet Scale, some more subjects, related to intelligence tests, were included. It now became useful for the age range of 2 to 18 years. In this scale, there were provisions for two types of two to four years. Many other subjects were included for the adult people. For every age group there were six to eight subjects. In this scale there are tests which enable the examiner to examine the intelligence of an individual in a very short span of time.

In Indian conditions, Binet's test was adopted for the first time by Dr. C. Herbert Rice. But its revised form is almost completely different from the Binet tests. These tests were compiled in Urdu and Punjabi. There are two types of scales in it, one having 10 tasks, the other 35 tasks, and it was the smaller scale of tests which proved dependable. In 1927, Dr. J. Munry of Christian College started verbal group tests in Urdu, English and Hindi. In 1933, Mr. Lajja Shankar developed group tests for children from 10 to 18, which adopted a revised and studied form of Terman's group tests. Besides these, the group tests started by Dr. Jalota of Lahore, in Hindi, Urdu and English proved to very valuable. In Bihar, under the direction of Dr. S.M. Mohsin, a test battery was constructed to measure mental abilities and intelligence of participants in many group tests. In the non-verbal group tests for college students, important contributions have come from Dr. Lalit Kumar Shah, C.T. Philip, H.C. Banerjee, D.H. Roy, T.P. Bhowimck and H.P. Maiti. The above description makes it quite clear that not much work has been done in the direction of non-verbal tests. There is a hope of development in this direction in future.

Types of Intelligence Tests

Intelligence tests are classified as follows according to the activities prescribed in them :

1. Verbal Tests.
2. Non-verbal Tests.

As the name itself suggests, verbal tests make use of language while the non-verbal include such activities which do not necessitate use of language. Both these types are suitable for individual as well as group tests. Consequently, verbal and non-verbal tests are further subdivided into two classes — individual and group. Thus, finally, there are four types of intelligence tests :

1. Verbal Individual Intelligence Tests
2. Non-verbal Individual Intelligence Tests
3. Verbal Group Intelligence Tests
4. Non-verbal Group Intelligence Tests

Verbal Individual Intelligence Tests

The very name of verbal individual intelligence tests suggests that these are intelligence tests given to individuals or in other words they are meant to test the intelligence of the individuals. Language finds adequate use in them. Binet-Simon tests and the various revisions are all included in this classification.

The State Bureau of Psychology of Uttar Pradesh has adopted a Hindi version of the Terman-Merrill Scale. This revision includes a variety of materials, from solid objects to difficult questions. The activity in the beginning is simple, like constructing a bridge or a tower of blocks or fitting an irregular wooden blocks in their proper places supplied to them. At the same time, at the end of the tests there are difficult questions which need considerable thinking. These tests are divided into several age groups. The higher groups use language and its use gradually declines with the age group. For example, the two years' group includes the following activities :

1. The form panel with three holes
2. Recognition of objects by name
3. Recognizing the organs of the body
4. Making a tower of blocks
5. Naming an object from its picture
6. Word-building

Non-verbal Individual Intelligence Tests

It is quite apparent from the above example that in verbal tests, the child's knowledge of language is more in demand, and therefore, the use of these tests is limited to students and literate persons. But these verbal tests cannot be used in the case of illiterate individuals as these tests involve an extensive use of language which fails as a medium to measure the individual differences between the illiterates. Consequently, illiterate individuals are tested with the help of non-verbal individual intelligence tests. The name itself indicates the nature of these tests. These tests involve the least possible use of the linguistic ability and are similarly almost unaffected by knowledge derived from books. An example of these non-verbal tests is the Performance Intelligence Tests.

Merrill-Palmer Block Building Test

One of the most important of performance tests for children is Merrill-Palmer Block Building Test. Besides Seguin Form Board, it includes block building test as well. In the figure given, a four-year old girl is making structure by means of blocks as demonstrated by the tester.

Fig. 13.1. Merrill-Palmer Block Building Test

Pintner-Paterson Performance Scale

An example of the performance intelligence tests is the Pintner-Paterson Performance Scale. It was evolved by Pintner and Paterson in 1917. In this scale there are 15 types of tests, of which 4 are form boards, 6 picture completion, memory span and the rest picture puzzles and imitations, etc.

Porteus Maze Test

Another example of the performance intelligence test is the Porteus Maze Test. In it, paper and pencil mazes are used. For his tests, Porteus created mazes for children from 3 to 14 years. It gets difficult, corresponding to the increase in age. The subject is allowed two chances and if he fails in the attempts then the conclusion is that his intelligence is not of that age level. Children of 12 to 14 years are given four opportunities. These tests designed by Porteus not only measure intelligence, but they also reflect the temperament of the individuals. It is distinguished from other tests as the Stanford-Binet test.

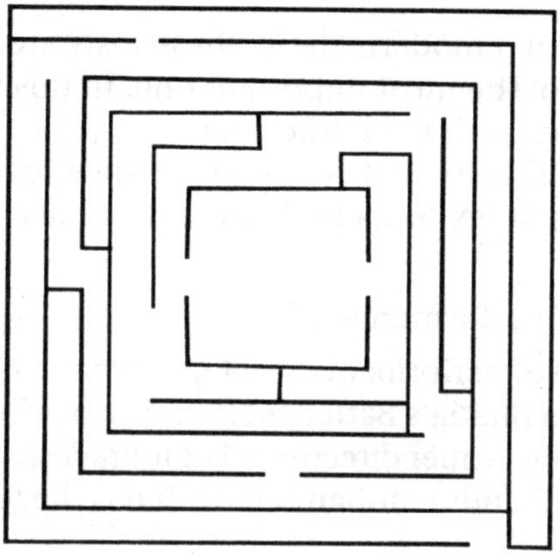

Fig. 13.2. Porteus Maze Test

Form Board Test

A comparatively simple of the performance intelligence tests is the form board tests; among them the test of Seguin and Goddard deserve special mention. In the form board test, there are numerous blocks and a board in which there are holes corresponding to this block. The subject as shown has to fit the blocks in these corresponding holes in the board, the time taken and mistakes committed being noted from which the score of the test is calculated.

Fig. 13.3. Seguin Form Board

Wechsler-Bellevue Test

Another example of the performance intelligence tests is the Wechsler-Bellevue test, evolved in 1939, meant for people from 10 to 60 years of age. In a modern clinic, these tests are included in Binet class, as one of the most important one. In this way it is the most apt test for measuring the intelligence of adults. In this test there are five verbal tests and five performance tests. This test affords not only an index to mental abilities but also a profile of abilities.

Bhatia's Battery of Performance Tests

The description of performance intelligence tests is incomplete without reference to Bhatia's Battery of Performance Tests. It is the battery created by the former director of Uttar Pradesh State Bureau of Psychology, Dr. Chandra Mohan Bhatia. It has the following five sub-tests :

1. Kohez block design test. Ten items of test out of the Kohez block design test have been included in the battery. There is one card on every subject upon which is depicted a colour design. The subject or the examinee sees this design and makes a similar one out of the blocks. These designs become correspondingly more and more complex, having been simple at the start.

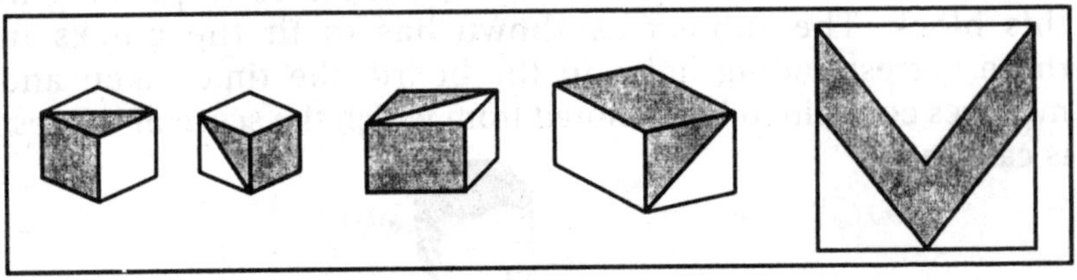

Fig. 13.4. Kohez Block Design Test

2. Alexander pass along test. The Bhatia's battery also includes Alexander pass along test, in which, too, there are some designs. The subject shifts coloured pieces in an open box and places them into a similar design.

3. Pattern drawing test. This test has been developed by Dr. Bhatia himself. In this there are eight cards on each of which there is a particular form. The subject draws a particular figure or pattern after seeing this form.

4. Immediate memory test. Some digits are recited, which are immediately repeated by the subject; this activity throws some light on the immediate memory of the subject.

5. Picture construction test. In this sub-test there are five subjects in which pictures relating to the rural life are fragmented into 2, 4, 6, 8 and 12 pieces respectively. At one time, piece of picture is placed before the subject, who puts them in order and constructs the picture.

Difficulties in the Individual Intelligence Tests

Some difficulties are faced in both the verbal and non-verbal types of individual intelligence tests. They are roughly as follows :

1. The difficulty of time. The individual intelligence test takes an hour usually and only one person can be tested at one time. Obviously, at this rate it would be essential to have a very big number of trained examiners and in spite of that it would be difficult to test all the people.

2. Need for experienced examiners. The second obstacle in the individual intelligence tests is the need of experienced examiners because the correct result cannot be arrived at if the examiners are inexperienced. At the same time, availability of such a large number of trained personnel is almost impossible.

Notwithstanding these difficulties, in some circumstances, the individual intelligence tests become unavoidable. This is because the level of accuracy reached by the individual intelligence tests, in the assessment of a person's intelligence, is beyond the reach of the group intelligence tests.

VERBAL GROUP INTELLIGENCE TESTS

The group intelligence tests owe their origin and development to the difficulties from which the individual tests suffer. As the name suggests, these tests are designed to test the intelligence of a group and not of an individual. All the people in the group are given the same directions and have to perform the same activities. Even the score of the result of group intelligence tests is calculated by machines thus dispensing with the necessity of skilled examiners, resulting in an economy of time.

Army Alpha and Beta Tests

An excellent example of group intelligence tests is afforded by the Army alpha and beta tests, which were evolved during the World War I in order to test the American soldiers. For example, it revealed separately the feeble-minded, men capable of becoming skilled specialists, men capable of becoming officers, men needing some training, etc.

Naval and Army General Classification Tests

Due to the success which attended these tests, some group tests for classification of naval or army soldiers were evolved during the World War II. Of these, two particular forms deserve mention. These two are : (1) Naval general classification tests and (2) Army general classification tests.

With the type of calculations made by Cruze, some one billion people were tested by the military general classification tests during the years 1941 to 1946. In these tests there are three subjects, *viz.*, those relating to vocabulary of counting blocks.

From the above example, it is quite clear that these verbal group intelligence tests examine the reasoning ability, ability of comparing and contrasting sense of directions, ability in numerals and language of the individuals who constitute the group. It is essential that the examiner should be fully acquainted with the test and he should also understand the corresponding directions. Thus, often the examiner examines himself to start with. At the same time, it is necessary for the examiner to have some knowledge of the mechanical aspects of the conditions of examination such as the proper seating arrangement of the examinees, the distribution of test blanks and the preparation of material related to the tests, like paper and pencil, etc.

Difficults in the Verbal Group Intelligence Tests

Even after taking in all the precautions, some difficulties are discernible in the verbal group intelligence tests which can be eliminated only by reverting to the individual intelligence tests. The difficulties of the verbal group tests are fundamentally as follows :

1. Difficulties related to co-operation in tests. In these tests it is difficult to judge whether the examinee is extending his full co-operation or not.

2. Difficulties related to the balance of the subject. In these tests it is difficult to determine whether the physical and emotional balance of the examinee is even or disturbed.

3. Difficulty related to the ease of the subject. In the verbal group intelligence tests, it is difficult to ascertain if the examinee is feeling at ease and free or restrained.

4. Possibility of cheating by the subject. Another difficulty is to ensure if the examinee has written the answer himself or copied it from his neighbour.

In spite of the difficulties which arise in the verbal group intelligence tests, they have their own advantages due to which they are used comprehensively. As has been said before, these advantages are the same as the difficulties, of the individual intelligence tests.

NON-VERBAL GROUP INTELLIGENCE TESTS

As has been mentioned earlier, the verbal intelligence tests are meant only for the literates because of the requirement of linguistic ability. It is for this reason that the non-verbal group intelligence tests have been developed, the examinee making a minimum use of language but performing, instead, many activities. One example of the non-verbal intelligence tests is Cattell's Culture Free test, Raven's Progressive Matrices and the N.I.I.P. test. In these non-verbal group intelligence tests, the examiners have to explain to the examinees even the simplest directions which are also demonstrated as far as possible. All this is done to make the least possible use of language. There are some performance tests in these group intelligence tests, in which the examinee draws some simple figures, or performs some simple activities. Some psychologists do not give credence to these non-verbal tests in their role of measuring intelligence of the subjects, while, on the other hand, some psychologists consider them to be better than verbal tests. For example, in Alexander's opinion, "A complete performance battery will be a better measure than a complete verbal battery."

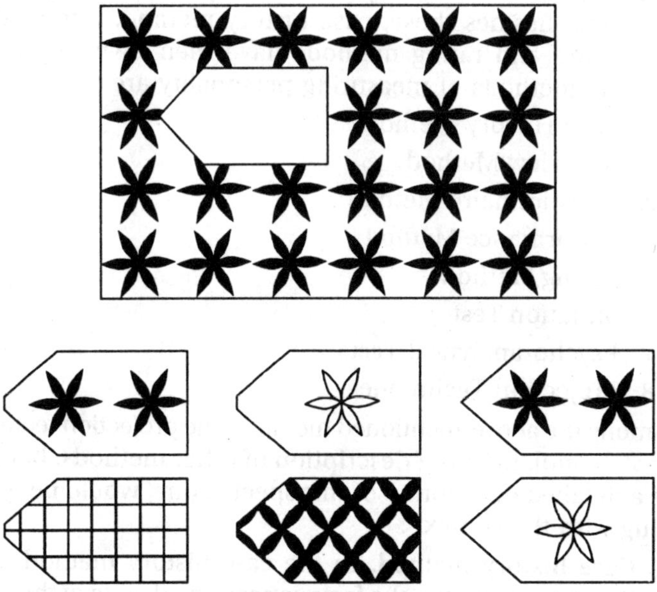

Fig. 13.5. Raven's Progressive Matrices

Characteristics of the Non-verbal Group Intelligence Tests

The truth is that even if non-verbal group intelligence tests are not more important than verbal tests, they are certainly not less important. Some of their characteristics are as follows :

1. Comparison of various human groups. The first obstacle in the comparison of human groups of various languages and cultures is the difference in their language. This obstacle can be overcome by the non-verbal group intelligence tests and a comparison between different human groups is rendered possible.

2. The testing of illiterate workers. The verbal group intelligence tests are manifestly inapplicable to illiterate workers for the testing of their intelligence. Consequently, the abilities of illiterate workers are assessed by employing the non-verbal group intelligence tests and the possibilities of learning are known.

3. Intelligence testing in children. The linguistic ability is very low in the case of children and consequently the verbal group intelligence tests cannot be given to them.

MEASUREMENT OF PERSONALITY

Psychologists employ a number of methods to measure personality, *e.g.*, situation test, psychoanalytic tests and projective method, etc. Besides these, case history method, interview and questionnaire and rating methods have their own importance. Briefly, the methods of measuring personality are :

1. Case History Method
2. Interview Method
3. Questionnaire Method
4. Performance Method
5. Rating Method
6. Situation Test
7. Psycho-analytical Tests
8. Projection Techniques

Among the above-mentioned methods, the projection techniques are most popular. A brief description of other methods, before we make a detailed description of this specific one, would be quite in keeping with the context :

1. Case history method. In the case history method, as the name obviously indicates, the facts concerning the life of the subject are collected. This case history supplies all the facts related to man's environment and heredity. This method can be employed to study both normal and abnormal personalities but it needs experienced testers.

2. Interview method. The interview method is the most common of all the methods for the study of personality. It is the method widely used in the selection of people for government, semi-government and private services. In this, the subject and the tester sit facing each other and the former answers questions asked by the latter. Besides the answer which the subject offers, his personality is indicated by his expression. The method, like the case history method, needs very experienced testers, who ask questions which may probe the correct thing, and enable the subject to express himself without any apprehension. Thus the interview method depends as much on the tester as it does on the subject.

3. Questionnaire method. Questionnaires have been used extensively in the investigation of personality. The name suggests that it is a list of selected questions, the answers to which throw light upon different traits of personality. 'Yes' and 'No' are written in front of these questions. The subject either strikes out the wrong answer or indicates the correct one. Questionnaires are used to gain knowledge of traits like self-confidence, sociability, introversion or extroversion, tendency to dominate or be dominated, etc.

There are some difficulties in the questionnaire method. It has the following limitations :

(a) Often the subjects conceal the fact and give wrong answers.

(b) Sometimes the framing of the questions is such that the tester takes them to mean one thing and the subject another.

(c) Usually the subjects write the answer without an adequate amount of thinking thus leaving possibility of mistakes.

Fig. 13.6. Minnesota Multiphasic Personality Inventory

In spite of these difficulties, the questionnaire method has proved to be of tremendous value. All port and Minnesota, etc., have formed questionnaires which help in the study of some subtle traits of personality. It affords a lot of assistance to comparative study because of various answers of the subjects to the same questions. The conclusions based on these questionnaires are comparative as well as numerical. They also facilitate wide study because a number of people can be studied simultaneously.

4. Performance method. The performance method was developed by May and Hartshorne. In this method the subject is given a variety of specific jobs to be performed and the particular trait of his personality is examined. For example, in order to test the honesty of children, some weights with little difference between them, were presented to them. The exact weight of each was written under it and the children were told to place them in the correct order. The honest children were told to place them in the correct order. The honest children experienced great difficulty while the dishonest read the weights under them and placed them in order promptly. A very simple method of judging the honesty of the students in the class could be something like this. Some piece should be dictated and the copies collected and examined. The mistakes of each should be secretly noted without any markings on the copy, following which the copies should be returned with the direction that the mistakes are to be noted and marks allocated. The dictation should be written on the blackboard. The honest will mark their mistakes while the dishonest will quietly correct them. The honesty of the students can be judged by comparing these with the mistakes previously noted.

5. Rating method. Another method of measuring personality is the rating method, in which the procedure is of two types: one, the subject is asked to answer questions related to traits of personality. The answers which the subject offers or selects exhibit his personality. Another way of applying the rating method is to place the subject in real situations and then study his behaviour and reactions. For example, in order to judge personality traits, a person is given a variety of jobs to perform.

The rating method is very simple. But it needs more skilful testers. Roughly speaking, it presents the following difficulties :

(a) Much skill and capability are essential in the tester.

(b) The possibility of prejudice is very great.

(c) It is very difficult to enumerate or evaluate the subtle traits. Mistakes are often made in this.

In spite of the above-mentioned difficulties, both social and industrial psychologists make much use of this method. As has been pointed out previously too, it can be made useful to a large extent if the tester is very skilful.

6. Situation test. As usual, the name suggests the nature of the method. In it, the subject is placed in some specific situations and the traits of his personality are ascertained. Actually, it resembles the performance method, the difference lying in the fact that in this case the person is placed in a situation while in the performance method he is given some work to do.

7. Psychoanalytic method. In the psychoanalytic method of measurement of personality, two types of tests are more popular — Free Association and Dream Analysis. Both these tests show the traits of the personality in its unconscious aspect. In dream analysis, the subject describes his dream and without using reasoning, associates freely the dream objects and activities. Because of the absence of reasoning, the truth of the unconscious mind is expressed by this association by which the psychoanalyst discovers many characteristics of personality. The psychoanalytic method is mostly used in discovering the personality traits and mental ailments of abnormal people. Its main condition lies in the need for a skilled and experienced psycho-analyst. Often, the psychoanalyst has to analyse his own mind in order to remove the possibility of any prejudice.

8. Projective techniques. The most popular of all the methods for the investigation of personality is the projective method. Its name suggests the fact that it is founded upon the element of projection. The Taj Mahal, to take an example, is a marble building many people go to see. Different people find in it different things, in keeping with the peculiarities of their personalities. An emotional person sees it in the form of a formal symbol of emotions while to the person who gives importance to political and economic questions, it may be a symbol of exploitation. This is an example of a material object but it does make clear the fact that a human being does not see an object as it is but also projects the traits of his own personality upon it. Many peculiarities of the personality are investigated by an analysis of this projection and a comparison of it with the projections effected by others.

Two tests in the projective techniques are more widely used :

1. Rorschach Ink-blot Test.

2. Murray's Thematic Apperception Test, known in brief as T.A.T. They are extensively used in the investigation of personality. These will, therefore, be described briefly here.

1. Rorschach Ink-blot test. This test was developed by the Swiss scientist Hermann Rorschach. He used ten original ink-blot cards which are still in use today. There is no picture made in these blots. Five of these are black, two black and red and the other three multicoloured. To investigate personality, they are exhibited before the subject one after the other and he is asked to describe everything he sees in the blot. These are shown for a definite interval of time. Then they are shown to the subject for a second time and he is asked to point out the location, of whatever he has seen, on the blot. In order to establish the meaning of the subject's reaction to the blots, the psychologist analyses the location, determining factors and the object. The analysis of the location serves to indicate whether the subject reacted to some particular spot on the blot or towards the blot as a whole. As a general rule, it is believed that the person who reacts more completely is more principled. The analysis of the determining factors is an attempt to find out whether the reaction of the subject is towards the shape of the blot or to the colour or motion in the blot. As to the object, the analysis shows whether the subject sees in it the figure of a man or an animal or anything else.

Besides the above analysis, facts like the time taken by the subject to react to the whole blot, the number of activities which he did and whether he did them normally or not, are also noted and observed. All these things tend to help in the analysis and investigation of the unconscious peculiarities of the subject.

The difficulty in the ink-blot test is that the description of the subject's reaction becomes quite subjective, which conceals to some extent the correct personality traits of the subject. But efforts are being made to make this test more objective.

Fig. 13.7. Rorschach's Ink-Blot

2. Murray's Thematic Apperception test. The founder of this test, Murray investigated the personality traits with the help of some pictures. These pictures are still considered to be standard. Observing these pictures, the subject, by projection, identifies himself with the characters in the picture. The pictures are presented one by one to the subject who has to compose a story on each of them within some fixed time period, say five minutes. He does not get time to think. Therefore the story expresses his natural desires, emotions, sentiments, etc. On the basis of these stories, the psychologist analyses the personality of the subject and uncovers his traits.

As in the Rorschach ink-blot test, there is some difficulty in Murray's thematic apperception test also, since the personality investigation done by it is not numerical but qualitative with possibility of mistakes. But there is no doubt that an experienced and skilful psychologist can use this method to uncover many hidden traits of the personality of the subject. This test helps in the discovery of many abnormalities of personality as well.

MEASUREMENT OF SPECIAL ABILITIES

Such problems as the profession an individual may adopt or the course of study a student may profitably pursue are ones that need guidance and for this guidance it is essential that in addition to measuring the individual's level of intelligence, his special abilities are investigated. Hence, efforts have been made to devise tests to discover special mental abilities and they are being extensively used.

Before going on to the testing of special mental abilities, it is necessary to know the age in which these tests can be suitably administered. This question arises for the simple reason that in childhood, these special abilities are not distinctly present and psychologists are not unanimous in their opinions regarding the age in which these abilities become distinct and separate. According to some, man's special mental abilities can be separately distinguished at the age of 11, while in the opinion of Cyril Burt, it is at 13 that these abilities become distinct. Generally, it is the former opinion that is accepted. Accordingly, all educational guidance is rendered at the age of 11 or thereabouts.

Number of Special Mental Abilities

Having determined the age at which the special mental abilities become distinct, it is now essential that their number also be determined. In fact, it is very difficult to determine the exact number of special abilities, and there is no unanimity of opinion on this question. In 1938 Thurston and his associates fixed the number of special fundamental abilities at seven, calling them Primary Mental Abilities — verbal abilities or V, numerical ability or N, reasoning or R, memory or M, word fluency or W, and spatial ability or S, and perceptual speed based on these mental abilities. Another test battery formed on the same principle is used in the American Psychological Corporation. It contains the following seven tests :

1. Verbal reasoning,
2. Numerical ability,
3. Abstract reasoning,
4. Space relation,
5. Mechanical reasoning,
6. Clerical speed and accuracy,
7. Language uses.

Now, we can go on to a slightly detailed account of some special abilities tests.

Thurston's S.R.A. Tests of Primary Mental Abilities

To repeat, Thurston has discovered the presence of seven fundamental mental abilities through his study. This conception of primary mental abilities wrought a great change in the field of guidance and counselling. Following this discovery, in the field of guidance even more importance began to be attached to these abilities, than to intelligence, since mental abilities of different individuals with similar levels of intelligence were found to differ at the extreme. On the other hand, people with the same mental abilities were found to have different levels of intelligence. In fact, the choice of a course of study to be taken up by a student or the choice of a profession by a person requires a test since success in these fields depends more upon innate as well as acquired ability than upon intelligence. Hence in England and America, many tests of mental abilities were evolved, and they were combined to from test batteries. Then, these test batteries were used extensively in the field of education and professions.

Thurston constructed three batteries of tests for special abilities for various children in the following three age divisions and used different test items in each of them :

(a) For children between 5 and 7. In the test battery for this division, he included tests of verbal reasoning, spatial ability, speed of perceptual knowledge and tests of motor ability.

(b) For children between 7 and 11. Test battery for this classification includes tests of verbal ability, numerical ability, speed of logic and perceptual knowledge.

(c) For children between 11 and 17. Test battery for this division includes tests of verbal ability, numerical ability, word fluency, spatial ability and power of abstract reasoning.

TESTS FOR INDIVIDUAL ABILITIES

Test batteries devised by Thurston reveal the main mental abilities of children of different ages, but in addition to this, there are individual tests for separate mental abilities. It would be in keeping with the context to describe them also.

1. Spatial ability tests. This reveals the person's spatial or form ability. One example of this is the N.I.I.P. form relation test devised by the National Institute of Industrial Psychology, London. It has been described earlier. The Psychological Bureau of Uttar Pradesh has been making use of it for quite some time; besides the Bureau has also formulated its own test for measuring spatial ability. Another example of such a test is the Minnesota Paper Form Board which includes 64 test items in which one has to combine various incomplete geometrical forms to complete the figures. In the Minnesota Spatial Relation Test, there are four tests of the form board. Both these tests have proved to be of immense value.

2. Mechanical ability tests. Through these tests, the person's ability of handling mechanical devices is measured. For this, some laboratories use paper and pencil while others use mechanical tools and objects. One example of this is the Minnesota Mechanical Assembly test. In this there are three boxes that contain the various parts of some common mechanical device. In the test, these parts have to be put together to form the complete object. Other tests of mechanical ability that are famous are the Bennett Test of Mechanical Comprehension, and MacQuarrie Test for mechanical ability.

3. Motor dexterity tests. In these tests, the motor ability of the hands and figures is measured. Examples of such tests are Bennett Hand Tool Dexterity Test, Purdue Peg Board, Steadiness Tester

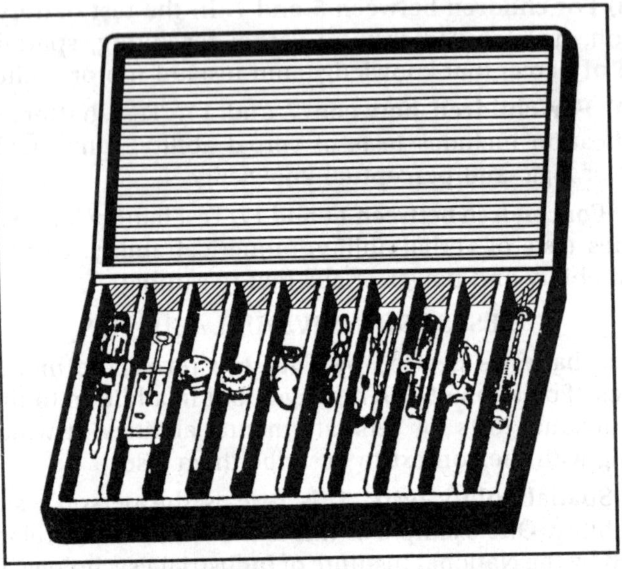

Fig. 13.8. Minnesota Mechanical Assembly Box

and O'Conor Tweezer Dexterity Test. Only the first two will be described here :

(a) ***Steadiness tester*** : This device examines the steadiness of the hand and the fingers. In this, there is a box on one side of which there are numerous holes arranged systematically so that they proceed from the widest to the smallest. The subject takes an instrument called the stylus into his hand and inserts it completely and draws it out, of these holes successively. If in doing so the stylus touches any of the walls of the hole, a bell rings. The test consists in the ability to prevent the stylus touching the wall while inserting it into the hole and drawing it out. The hole in which the bell rings is tried thrice by the subject. This test helps to discover the individual's dexterity with his hands and fingers and the extent to which he can handle minute instruments.

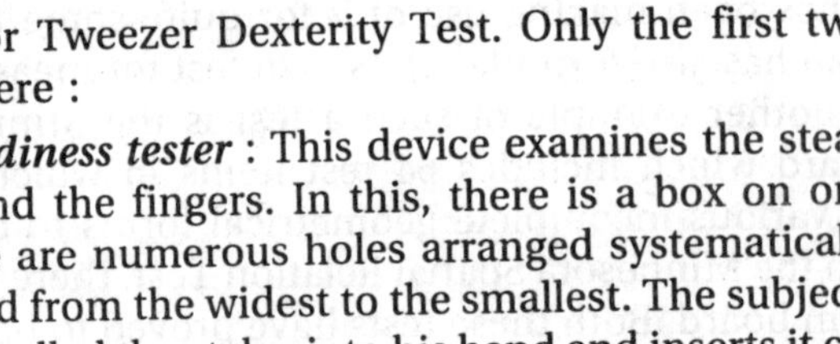

Fig. 13.9. Steadiness Tester

(b) ***O'Conor's Tweezer Dexterity test*** : In this test, there are 100 small holes on a board, in rows of ten each. There are 100 pins placed by the side. The subject has to use a tweezer to place each of these pins in this board, one in each hole. He scores according to the time he takes to complete this task.

4. Clerical tests. These tests measure the individual's ability concerning writing and composition. It is composed of tests in arithmetic, word groups, distinct reading and good writing, tests in direct knowledge, etc. One example of the clerical test is the Minnesota Clerical test which has two parts. In one part there are pairs of numbers, the correct pair having to be marked in which both numbers are given. In the other part, one has to point out pairs of names that are similar.

5. Artistic or aesthetic ability test. In these, the individual's ability concerning art is tested. One example of this is the McAdory Art Test. Sea Shore Measure of Musical Talent measures the individual's ability in respect of music. Meier Art Judgement Test is another test of artistic and aesthetic ability. In this test there are 100 pairs of pictures. In every pair there is one original and the other copy, and the student has to select the original and its copy in respect of every pair. Success in this depends upon his aesthetic ability and acuity since the original has more beauty than the copy.

MEASUREMENT OF ATTITUDES

Difficulties in Measuring Attitudes

Attitudes contain many elements which are very difficult to measure. To take but one, the emotions and feelings involved in attitudes cannot be measured and hence attitudes can be measured only by internal systems. In this form, they do not admit of any measurement, but the individual's external behaviour is generated by inner tendencies. Hence, attitudes can be measured from the external behaviour. For the measurement of attitudes, it is necessary that the immediate circumstances be controlled. The greater the amount or extent of control upon these immediate circumstances, the greater will be their success and their reliability. Hence, the conditions which defy any attempts at controlling them must be eliminated. For example, it would be difficult to generate communal attitudes in the laboratory, or artificially anywhere else. In a situation of this kind, the experimenter should keep in mind all these details of the actual circumstances in conducting the experiment upon the attitude. It is therefore evident that the degree of reality which can be obtained in the measurement of external behaviour cannot be expected in the measurement of attitudes, which in addition, do not offer the same degree of reliability. Yet it is too precipitate to conclude from this that no reliability at all can be expected in the measurement of attitudes. The accuracy of the measurement of attitudes can be tested by the capacity of prediction. The extent to which any measurement can forecast and predict the future conduct of any individual is accurate.

Limit to measurement of attitudes. The following conclusions are to be drawn from the preceding discussion on the measurement of attitudes :

1. Attitudes can be measured only indirectly.
2. The greatest possible degree and extent of control should be levied upon the immediate circumstances in the measurement of attitudes.
3. In studying attitudes, the uncontrolled circumstances should be carefully studied.
4. The measurement of attitudes cannot be as reliable or accurate as the measurement of external behaviour.
5. The accuracy of the measurement of attitude can be judged from the accuracy of prediction of the individual's subsequent behaviour.

METHODS OF MEASURING ATTITUDES

Hence, the social psychologist has evolved various methods for the measurement of attitudes. The major ones are :

(a) Opinion Scales
(b) Rating Scales
(c) Indirect Scales.

(a) Option Scales

Opinion scales are methods of measuring attitude through the medium of opinions. That accounts for the name. Our attitudes towards some specific person or subject can be known by analysing our opinions concerning them. Hence psychologists evolve scales for discovering the opinions of individuals concerning different objects, problems and persons. These standards differ in respect of the method of their construction and kind. But the aim of every standard is to locate and determine the position of an individual upon a measure extending from one limit of acceptance to the other limit of refusal. We have had an occasion to point out before that it is not possible to measure attitude directly by means of any available standard. The opinion scales reveal the reactions of the individual towards some particular things, and from the reactions his attitude can be deduced. Obviously, the scale should be so devised as to throw the maximum possible light upon the attitudes of the individual. For this there should be, in the scales, a selection of statements which can efficiently give expression to the concurrence or otherwise of the attitude of the person.

Characteristics of an Adequate Scale

A scale which has any claims to adequacy in serving the purpose for which it is intended must possess the following characteristics :

1. Reliability. The most prominent characteristic of the scale is its reliability. Reliability means that the scores obtained under two distinct but similar circumstances should not be too different. The more this quality is present in a scale, the greater will be its reliability.

2. Exactness. Besides being reliable, the scale should also be accurate and exact. For this the scale should possess elements which can indicate the actual mental tendency of the person.

3. Objectivity. The construction of the scale should be objective and relative to the subject matter. The choice of its various questions should not reflect and should not be influenced by the mental tendencies of the subjects or testers.

4. Psychological quality. The scale can be a success only when the questions contained in it and the answers which are forthcoming to them have a psychological relation with the attitudes of the individual. The choice and selection of questions of this nature depend upon the capability of the person constructing the scale.

5. Distinction in different items. In order to be exact, the questions, items, statements, etc., should be mutually distinct. If this is not so, the answers will also not be clear. This can lead to mistakes in the result.

Various scales. Many forms of opinion scales are prevalent in social psychology, but the main among them are the following :

1. Thurston Scale Construction Method
2. Likert Scale Construction Method
3. Guttman Scale Construction Method

In addition to these methods, the Borgardus Scale, Rank Order Scale and Paired Comparison Scale are also important, but they are not described here due to lack of space.

1. Thurston Scale

Thurston and his colleagues constructed scales for the measurement of opinions and beliefs of human groups concerning such varied questions as war, the church, Negroes, capital punishment, birth control, etc., in 1929 and 1931.

Construction method. The Thurston Scale Construction Method was constituted of the following items :

1. Collection of numerous simple opinions related to the question or object presented.

2. To determine the value of the scale for these opinions by some definite determinant. This evaluation leads to the elimination of controversial statements, leaving only statements concerning which all specialists are unanimous. Opinions extend between a negative and a positive limit.

3. To determine the median point for every statement according to the opinions of the specialist judges.

4. Finally, it is necessary to see whether the questions contained in the scale are in a definite order or not. The order of statements should be such that they proceed from maximum to minimum acceptance. For this, in the beginning of the scale, those questions are arranged concerning which all specialists are agreed while at the end questions concerning which all specialists are disagreed are arranged.

Precautions. The following precautions are observed in the construction of the Thurston Scale Construction Method :

1. Every statement of the scale should be clearly worded.

2. The number of determining specialists should be large enough to indicate clearly the position which should be given to the opinion professed by the subject. For this, the number of judges is usually above hundred.

3. The scale should comprised only those statements concerning which the judges are unanimous. For this, every specialist places all statements of maximum and minimum acceptability in eleven classes. If a particular statement is placed in the same class by each of the specialists, it should be definitely chosen. But if the statement is placed in a different class by each of the specialists, it should be rejected because it is controversial.

Examples. One example of the Thurston Scale Construction Method is the scale constructed by Droba. It has 22 statements, and was constructed in 1930. This printed scale is given to an individual in order to find his attitude score. The statements which the individual finds correct, he marks them right. The median of the scale score of these statements shows the attitude of the person.

Some of the statements of Droba's scale are the following :

1. No country can gain prestige without national respect, and war is the only means by which national respect can be defended.
2. If war is declared we also should enlist.
3. It is right to start a war only if the weaker nation is protected.
4. War and peace are necessary for progress.
5. The most that we can expect is that war be partially destroyed.
6. Lack of respect for life on the part of people engaged in war results in a wave of crime.
7. Every nation should immediately disarm itself.

2. Likert Scale

In 1932, Likert constructed a scale which differed from the one given by Thurston. This scale aimed at discovering the attitudes of various human groups concerning imperialism, internationalism and Negroes.

Construction method. The following are the items in the Likert Scale Construction Method :

1. To construct many statements related to the object or a problem, the attitudes towards which are to be studied.

2. To show these statements to the subject and to get them classified into the following groups :

(Strongly approve)	(Undecided)	(Disapprove)	(Strongly disapprove)	(Approve)
5	4	3	2	1

3. To award points to the above classifications in the following manner :

(a) To find the correlation between the total score of the subject and the score of the statements individually.

(b) To exclude those statements which bear a negligible correlation to the total score.

3. Guttman Scale

In 1941, Guttman constructed a scale to measure and study the level of morale in American soldiers. Guttman's scale possesses the following main elements :

1. To determine whether any statement can be shown upon by the scale or not.
2. To prepare scalogram to test the consistency of any statements.
3. To vary the questions concerning the same problem in such a manner as to determine that the opinion of the subject is consistent.

Fastigner bitterly criticised Guttman's scale in 1947.

(b) Rating Scales

As was stated at the outset, the second method of measuring attitude, after the opinion scales, is that of rating scales. The special feature of the rating scale is that the attitudes are evaluated not on the basis of the opinions of the subjects but on the basis of the opinion and judgements of the experimenter himself.

Means of collecting data. In the rating scale, the experimenter collects the data by following means :

1. Non-verbal behaviour, such as accepting or rejecting customs.
2. Verbal behaviour, such as expressing concurrence or objection.
3. Secondary expressive cues such as facial expression, etc.
4. Conical type interview.
5. Personal documents, such as autobiography, letters, diary, etc.
6. Projective techniques — such as ink-blot test.
7. Immediate experience, such as the emotions, thought, perception, imagination of the individual, etc.

From the above source, the experimenter gets enough data concerning the attitude. The speechless behaviour of the individual also provides a lot of information though of course precautions must be taken while interpreting it. Compared to speechless behaviour, the easier method of understanding attitude is that of conversation. In addition to conversation, various facial expressions and the fluctuations in the volume of sound are also good indicators of attitude. "It is a commonplace belief that what a man says may be less revealing than how he says it," say Krech and Crutchfield, with a happier choice of phrase. In this way, the manner of expressing an opinion may be more informative than the verbal expression itself. In a clinical interview, the subject can be made to respond to questions from which he would normally hesitate, but does so now under the belief that the answers are necessary for his treatment. Diary, essays, letters, poetry, story and other kinds of individual writings manifest the attitude of the individual. Among them, diary is of the greatest importance since it is the most personal. An autobiography also reveals the attitudes of the author. Projective techniques have also proved very useful in revealing attitudes. Two among them are : (a) Rorschach's Ink-blot Test, and (b) Murray's Thematic Apperception Test or T.A.T. In Rorschach's Ink-blot, the subject is given ten original cards with ink-blots on them and he is asked to describe what he sees on them. In Murrary's Thematic Apperception Test, the individual is presented ten original picture cards one after the another and is asked to write a story on each of them in short but indefinite period of time. In the projective techniques, the subjects, thoughts, perceptions, etc., of the individual also help in revealing his attitude to the experimenter.

Types of Rating Scales

Roughly, rating scales are of two kinds — relative and absolute. One example of the relative method is the Rank Order Scale, while one example of the absolute type is the Percentage of Population. It would be opportune to describe both of these scales briefly :

Rank order scale. In this scale the experimenter gives to the individual's attitude, a position in the scale extending from the highest quality to the lowest quality. In examining the individual in the circumstances of the human group, his position, relatively to the position of others, is kept in view. In this way, in the Rank Order method, the individual is given a relative position in the population. In this method, a definite population is put to the test and then the opinions of one individual are examined. Now the examiner places the opinions of the individual on the scale, which shows the percentage of the population concurring with his opinions as well as the percentage differing from him. This also reveals the percentage of his opinions in which he leads the population and the percentage in which he is behind the population.

(c) Indirect Scales

The third method for the measurement of attitudes is that of the indirect scales. All the methods so far mentioned for the measurement of attitude suffer from the defect that the subject generally realizes that he is being examined and he therefore tries to conceal his real attitudes. Hence, psychologists have favoured the indirect scales for the measurement of attitudes, in which it cannot be guessed that tendencies are being examined. In 1938 Asch, Hertzman, and other scientists attempted to study attitudes by means of the indirect scales. With the help of signs they studied changes in opinions in industrial groups. Nowadays, many social psychologists are making efforts to study attitudes by indirect methods.

Importance of Measuring Interests

Knowledge of interests is important for the task of guidance. The task that an individual can perform with success and efficiency depends upon his interests, besides his intelligence and general abilities. In suggesting any particular course of study or subject, that an individual student should pursue, one must keep in mind his intelligence, his ability and also his interests. In this respect, whether the guidance be educational or vocational, it is essential for the guide to be aware of the interests of the individual whom he has undertaken to advise. Normally, most novices to the intricacies of psychology think that the only way of knowing a person's interests is to enquire them from him. People are normally seen asking each other as to their respective interests and inclinations or the task that suits them best. But science cannot rest satisfied with such inane and cursory enquiry. It requires that every element, with which it is required to deal, should be as objectively determined as possible. Hence, psychology has invented many tests whereby it discovers and measures interests.

Lists of Interests

The simplest and most prevalent test of interests is asking the individual himself. The subject is equipped with a long list of interests and he is required to pick out the vocations that interest him, the psychologist thereby coming to know what interests the subject, or at least, what the subject thinks is of interest to him. Of the many such lists that are in use, Margaret E. Hoppock's check-list of occupations is of particular importance and deserves mention.

Limitations of Interest Inventories

The above described inventories of interests do, to a certain extent, help in guiding an individual regarding his occupation, but these lists have some limitations that are natural to them, and which must be kept in mind in making use of them. Roughly speaking, they are subject to the following limitations :

1. Difficulty in collecting description of vocation. As has been pointed out, vocational inventories or lists provide description of vocations. But it is manifestly difficult to collect a complete description of any vocation, that is a description of all activities undertaken in it, the natural abilities required for those functions and the interests required, and other equally nebulous details. Let alone any psychologist, probably even the people engaged in these professions themselves could not provide a detailed account of them.

2. Suspect responses. The subject to be guided is not examined as to the various occupations, interests area and functions, but his reactions are enquired from him. Evidently, such material as yielded by him is not sufficiently scientific since the individual's responses are questionable, being always 'open to doubt. In addition to this problem, there is no way of ascertaining the accuracy and validity of the answers provided.

3. Variability of interests. Interest inventories provide information concerning interests, but interest is no permanent part or trait of the individual's nature. Interests keep on varying. To maintain the individual's interests creates a problem since it is not reasonable to determine from his interests of the check-list the profession into which he should put himself. It is quite possible that his abilities may fit him for a particular profession in which he shows no interest at present but he may develop affection for it when he actually gets into it. It may grow on him, as they say. Of vocations, it is usually observed that one which did not interest the individual in the beginning later on interested him if he had persevered with it for some time. On the contrary, there are other vacillating individuals who profess the deepest interest in some profession so long as they have nothing to do with it, but once they have been in it, they change their minds and decide not to like it. Hence, these vocational lists or inventories are no foolproof or even provisionally reliable methods of determining a person's interest in a particular profession.

4. No relation of invariable concomitance between Interest and Success. To forecast success on the basis of interest shown in the vocational preference lists is not scientific. That an individual is definitely interested in a particular profession is no guarantee that he will also succeed in it.

5. Classification of occupations is not scientific. Another major fault in these inventories of occupations is that the classification by which the professions have been divided is not scientific. Truly speaking, no two occupations included in them are the same. Every profession has its own specific functions, its responsibilities and its specific qualities that lead to success, and such independent occupations number in hundreds if not thousands. To prepare a list of all these occupations, and then to include a detailed description of each, is a difficult task.

It is improper to conclude from the above description of the shortcomings of vocational preference list that they are completely worthless. In fact, interest itself is a subject in which the decisions reached cannot be expected to contain a high degree of objectivity. As a makeshift method, these interest inventories are important, but when putting them to use, it is essential that the above shortcomings be kept well in mind.

QUESTIONS FOR EXERCISE

1. Describe in brief the role of psychological testing in personnel selection.
2. Evaluate the significance of psychological testing in measuring fitness for work.
3. "The need for evaluating the potentialities of men is as great in business and industry as in any field of human activities." Discuss and evaluate the part played by psychological tests in solving the problem in industry.
4. What kinds of tests are needed for measuring individual differences in the field of industry?
5. Discuss and evaluate the part played by psychological tests in solving the problem of selection of personnel in industry.
6. What kinds of tests are needed for measuring individual differences in the field of industry?

14

PERSONNEL SELECTION TESTS AND INTERVIEWS

Testing is the most vital technique of selection gaining significance in recent years. As it is difficult for the organisations to evaluate the candidate's performance only on the basis of application blank and/or interviews, selection tests help the management in evaluating the candidate's suitability to the job. According to Dale S. Beach these tests are also called psychological tests because psychologists have contributed a lot in developing these tests. Edwin B. Flippo defines selection test as an instrument designed to measure the nature and degree of one's psychological potentialities, based on psychological factors, essential to perform a given job efficiently. Their purpose is to help in judging the ability of a candidate in a given job-situation. According to Daniel Golman, the tests are useful in selection, placement, promotions, performance appraisal and potential appraisal, help in ranking candidates and are valuable in determining subsequent success on the job. Monappa and Saiyadain write, "Psychological tests are an objective and standardised measure of a sample of behaviour".

GUIDELINES TO TESTING

Dale S. Beach has suggested the following guidelines for the employment tests :

1. Tests should be in addition to other selection techniques as entire tests can only provide information about a part of total behaviour of candidate.

2. Test information should be taken into consideration to find out candidate's weaknesses rather than strength (as tests are more accurate at predicting failures than success).

3. Tests are helpful in picking a most likely successful group from a larger group rather than successful individuals.

4. A test should be conducted in one's own organisation as "a valid test is one that measures what it is supposed to measure".

5. Tests can be held only in case of failure of other selection devices in providing satisfactory information.

6. Test administrators should not heavily depend upon test score in making-decisions regarding selection of a candidate.

7. As relationship between test score and job success is not always linear, decision-makers should use the test score judiciously.

STEPS IN TESTING

1. Job analysis. It provides basic information about the type of the candidate needed by the organisation. Job analysis includes job specialisation and employee specification. Job specification and job requirements provide information about the demands made by a job on the incumbent. Employees specification provides the information about the characteristics, qualities, behaviour of the employee needed to perform a job successfully. It is the basis to decide upon a particular test or tests. It provides minimum acceptable score required to test whether the candidate possesses the required amount and degree of behaviour and qualities like intelligence, aptitude to perform the job successfully.

2. Reliability. After identifying the test(s), the administrator should ensure the reliability of test/instrument. It refers to the level of consistency of score or results obtained throughout a series of measurements. The test is reliable if a person obtains same or similar score in the tests conducted in first, second and third time, under the same conditions. The reliability of any selection technique/test means its freedom from systematic errors of measurement or its consistency under different conditions. If the score differs considerably in first, second and third measurements, a test is unreliable. The causes of low reliability are : conducting the test under non-standardised conditions, administering the test by different persons and under different psychological states of candidate, existence of factor of luck and ill-luck, etc.

As suggested by Beach, the reliability coefficient should be between +0.85 and +1.00. Higher reliability can be obtained from written tests.

3. Validity. A selection device aims at finding out whether a candidate possesses the skills or talents required by a particular job. Each selection test aims at finding out whether a candidate possesses that particular skill/talent. For example, intelligence test aims at testing whether a particular candidate possesses the nature and level of intelligence essential to perform a job. An intelligence test effective in measuring the level of intelligence is a valid one. According to Dale S. Beach, "The validity of a test is the degree to which it measures what it is intended to measure". A valid test accurately predicts the level of success or failure of a candidate on the job. According to Dale S. Beach, there are five kinds of validity *viz.*, concurrent validity, predictive validity, content validity, construct validity and face validity.

4. Personnel Programme. Now the personnel manager has to develop a testing programme with the following steps :

(i) Formulation of the objectives of testing programme.

(ii) Analysis of jobs to identify those characteristics that appear necessary for job success.

(iii) Making of a tentative choice of tests for a try-out.

(iv) Administering of those tests to an experimental group of people.

(v) Establishing of criteria for job success.

(vi) Analysis of results and making of decisions regarding test application.

TYPES OF SELECTION TESTS

1. Aptitude Tests

(a) Intelligence test

(b) Mechanical aptitude

(c) Clerical aptitude tests

2. Achievement Tests

(a) Job knowledge test

(b) Work sample test

3. Situational Tests

(a) Group discussion

(b) In-basket

4. Interest Test

5. Personality Tests

(a) Objective tests

(b) Projective tests

1. Aptitude test. Aptitude tests measure whether an individual has the capacity or latent ability to learn a given job. Aptitudes can be divided into general and mental ability or intelligence and specific aptitudes, such as mechanical, clerical, manipulative capacity, etc.

(i) ***Intelligence test*** : Intelligence tests measure intelligence quotient (IQ) of a candidate. IQ is the capacity for comprehension, reasoning, word fluency, verbal comprehension, numbers, memory and space, etc. Other factors such as both forward and backward digit spans, information known, comprehension, vocabulary, picture-arrangement and object assembly are also included in intelligence.

Intelligence tests are verbal and non-verbal meant for literate and illiterate employees respectively.

(ii) ***Mechanical aptitude test*** : Measuring the capacities of spatial visualisation, perceptual speed and knowledge of mechanical matter, these tests are useful for selecting apprentices, skilled, mechanical employees, technicians, etc.

(iii) ***Psychomotor test*** : Measuring abilities like manual dexterity, motor ability and eye-hand coordination of candidates, these tests are useful to select semi-skilled workers and workers for repetitive operations like packing, watch assembly, etc.

(iv) ***Clerical aptitude test*** : Measuring specific capacities involved in office work, items of these tests include spelling, computation, comprehension, copying, word measuring, etc.

2. Achievement test. Conducted when applicants claim to know something, these tests are more useful to measure the value of specific achievement, when an organisation wishes to employ experienced candidates. These tests are classified into :

(i) ***Job knowledge test*** : It tests a candidate in the knowledge of a particular job. For example, if a junior foreman applies for the job of a senior foreman, he may be tested in job knowledge, where he is asked questions about the job for which he has applied.

(ii) ***Work sample test*** : In this test, a portion of the actual work is given to the candidate, and the candidate is asked to do it. If candidate applies for a post of mechanic, he may be asked to operate specific machine as a work sample test. Thus the candidate's achievement is tested regarding his knowledge about the job and actual work experience.

3. Situational test. It evaluates a candidate in a similar real life situation. The candidate is asked either to cope with the situation or solve critical situations of the job. Situation tests are of two types :

(i) *Group discussion*: It is administered through group discussion. This test needs to solve a problem under which candidates are observed in the areas of initiating, leading, proposing valuable ideas, conciliating skills, oral communicating skills, coordinating and concluding skills.

(ii) *In-basket* : In situational test administered through in-basket, the candidate is supplied with actual letters, telephone and telegraphic message, reports and requirements by various officers of the organisation along with adequate information about the job and organisation. The candidate is asked to take decisions on various items based on the in-basket information regarding requirements in the memoranda.

4. Interest test. Consisting of inventories of the likes and dislikes of candidates in relation to work, job, occupations, hobbies and recreational activities, this test seeks to find out whether a candidate is interested or disinterested in the job for which he/she is a candidate and in which area of the job range/occupation is he/she interested. The assumption of this test is that there is a high correlation between the interest of a candidate in a job and job success. Interest inventories may not fluctuate after the age of 30.

5. Personality test. To discover clues to an individual's value system, his emotional reactions and maturity and characteristic mood, these tests probe deeply traits like self-confidence, tact, emotional control, optimism, decisiveness, sociability, conformity, objectivity, patience, fear, distrust, initiative, judgement, dominance or submission, impulsiveness, sympathy, integrity and stability.

(i) *Objective test* : Most personality tests are objective tests suitable for group testing and can be scored objectively.

(ii) *Projective test* : Under these tests candidates are asked to project their own interpretation of certain standard stimulus situations, basing on ambiguous pictures, figures, etc.

Personality tests can be faked by sophisticated candidates. Most candidates give socially acceptable answers.

DEVELOPING A TESTING PROGRAMME

As the most valid test for a particular job may be quite unreliable for another job, the suitability of a candidate for a job cannot be judged on the basis of a single test. A group or battery of tests alone can give useful results to judge the suitability of a candidate. Rather than an individual specialist, a team of specialists like technical specialist, industrial psychologist, personnel psychologist, etc. can develop and administer a test more successfully.

PRECAUTIONS IN USING TESTS

Certain precautions should be taken in using tests in different areas. These areas are : human relations aspects, operational suggestions and uses of test scores.

1. Preserving privacy. Some people, particularly deprived people, do not want to reveal all about themselves. This is more so because of their caste, community, economic background etc. This category of people may feel that tests discriminate them against forward classes. Such people fear and suspect the test secrecy and validity. It affects privacy. The test administrator should take steps to reduce the fear and to maintain fair human relations so as to infuse confidence into the applicants.

2. Operational precaution. Without pre-testing, same tests should not be used even for the same job in the same organisation again and again. Tests should be pre-tested on experimental basis. Sufficient time and resources should be provided for designing, developing, testing for validity and reliability, and administering a test or a battery of tests.

3. Care in use. Much care should be taken in deciding upon cut-off score which would be the lowest score beyond which a candidate is totally misfit. Correlation figures should be properly interpreted and used with much care. A team of specialists should design, develop and administer the tests. Tests should be used to find solutions to the problems of selection, placement, performance and potential appraisals, training, development, accidents, operational problems, etc.

WHAT IS SELECTION INTERVIEW?

According to William L. Donoghy, studies indicates that over 90 per cent of selection decisions involve interviews. Though they may not resort to any one or all other selection techniques, almost all the organisations, big or small, in organised and unorganised sectors, managed on traditional or modern lines, adopt interview technique. Interview measures all relevant traits and factors. It integrates all necessary information about the candidates, collected through various means. Its scope is wider than any other selection technique. Dale S. Beach has defined interview as "a conversation or verbal interaction, normally between two people, for a particular purpose". It is an open exchange between persons of unequal status for a mutually agreed upon position. It may also take place between a person and group of people and between two groups of people.

Objectives of Selection Interview

1. To collect accurate and essential information about the candidates;

2. To provide the candidates with the facts of the job and the organisation;

3. To establish a rapport with the prospective employees;

4. To sell the company at a premium to the candidates;

5. To judge and evaluate the suitability of the candidate to the job, based on job and organisational requirements;

6. To see the inner view and feeling of the candidates.

Types of Interviews

1. **Selection interviews.** These are for selecting the most suitable candidate for a job;

2. **Appraisal interviews.** These are for appraising the performance of a subordinate by superior;

3. **Sales interviews.** These are for convincing a customer by a salesman.

4. **Counselling interviews.** These are for counselling the employees regarding their family, personal and career problems by the Personnel Manager.

5. **Grievance interview/disciplinary interviews.** These are interviews discussing and enquiring about the grievance or a disciplinary case.

6. **Data collection interviews.** These interviews seek collection of data and information for a research study.

Types of Selection Interview

Various types of selection interviews are adopted to solicit different kinds of information and to measure the candidates, skills, knowledge, etc., at different planes. Selection interviews can be divided into preliminary interview, core interview and decision-making interview :

1. **Preliminary interview.** An exchange of basic information between the candidate and the Personnel Manager about the job and organisation. Like job nature, salary, working conditions, benefits, etc., it is helpful to the organisation to weed out unwanted hands

and to the candidate to select or reject the job. When the exchange of information between the candidate and the organisation is not true, it may prove to be unsatisfactory. This interview may generally be informal and unstructured :

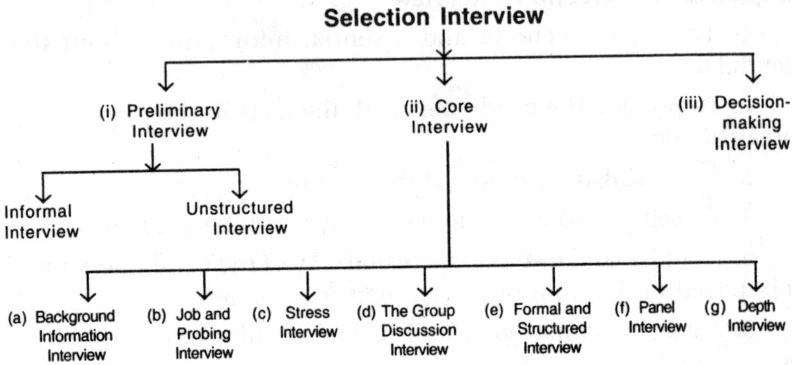

Chart 14.1. Types of Selection Interview

(i) ***Informal interview*** : Informal interview can be conducted at any place by any person to secure the basic and non-job related information. It is the interaction between the candidate and the Personnel Manager when the former meets the latter to enquire about the vacancies or additional particulars in connection with the employment advertisement.

(ii) ***Unstructured interview*** : In unstructured interview the candidate is given the freedom to tell about himself by revealing his knowledge on various items/areas, his background, expectations, interests, etc. On the other hand, the interviewer provides information on various items required by the candidate.

2. Core interview. An interaction between the candidate and the line executive or experts on various areas of job knowledge, skill, talent, etc. This interview may take the following forms :

(i) ***Background information interview*** : This interview is intended to collect the information which is not available in the application blank and to check information provided in the application blank, it is regarding education, place of domicile, family, health, interests, hobbies, likes, dislikes, extracurricular activities of the applicant.

(ii) ***Job and probing interview*** : It aims at testing the candidate's job knowledge about duties, activities, methods of doing the job, critical/ problematic areas, methods of handling those areas, etc.

(iii) ***Stress interview*** : It seeks to test the candidate's job behaviour and level of withstanding during the period of stress and strain.

It puts the candidate under stress and strain by interrupting him from answering, criticising his opinions, asking questions pertaining to unrelated areas, keeping silent for unduly long period after he has finished speaking, etc. Stress during the middle portion of the interview gives effective results. Stress interview should be handled with utmost care and skill. It is often invalid, as the interviewee's need for a job, his previous experience in such type of interviews may inhibit his actual behaviour under such situations.

(iv) ***Group discussion interview*** : Group interview method and discussion interview method are two methods of conducting group discussion interviews.

(a) *Group interview :* Under group interview, all the candidates are brought into interview room and are interviewed one by one. It helps busy executives to save valuable time. It gives a fair account of the objectivity of the interview to the candidates.

(b) *Discussion interview :* Under the discussion interview, a simple topic is given for discussion to the candidates who assemble in a room and are asked to discuss the topic in detail. Discussion interview helps the interviewer in appraising, certain skills of the candidates like initiative, interpersonal skills, dynamism, presentation, leading, comprehension, collaboration, etc.

Because of its informality and flexibility interviewees are at ease in this category of interview However, it may fail to cover some significant portions of the candidates' background and skills.

(v) ***Formal and structured interview*** : In formal interview, all the formalities and procedures like fixing the value, time, panel of interviewers, opening and closing, intimating the candidates officially, etc., are strictly followed. Depending on job requirements, the course of the interview is preplanned and structured in advance. The questions/items for discussion are structured. Experts are allotted different areas and questions to be asked. There is very little room for the interviewers to deviate from the questions prepared in advanced.

(vi) ***Panel interview*** : Owing to lack of knowledge and competence in multiple disciplines and areas, one person may not be effective in judging the candidates in different areas/skills. Therefore, most organisations invite a panel of experts, specialised in different areas, fields and disciplines, to interview candidates. The panel interviews each candidate, judges his performance individually and prepares a consolidated judgement based on each expert's judgement and weightage of each factor. Known as panel interview, this type of interview is more effective as each candidate is appraised by an expert in relevant areas. Experts should not try to achieve over accuracy, excessive weightage to a particular factor and domination of other experts, etc.

(vii) *Depth interview* : In depth interview, the candidates are examined by experts in that particular field in core areas of knowledge and skills of the job by posing relevant questions in order to extract critical answers initiating discussions regarding critical areas of the job and asking the candidates to explain even minute operations of the job performance.

3. Decision-making interview. Now the head of the department/ section concerned interviews the candidates once again, mostly through informal discussion. He examines the interest of the candidate in the job and organisation, his reaction and adaptability to the working conditions and his career planning, promotional opportunities, work adjustment and allotment, etc. The Personnel Manager interviews the candidates to find out his expectations/ acceptance of salary, allowances, benefits, promotions, opportunities, etc. After exchanging their views, the head of the department and the Personnel Manager jointly inform their decision to the chairman of the interview board, who finally takes the decision about the candidates performance and their ranks in the

INTERVIEW PROCESS

Interview is a process consisting of several steps. The major steps are grouped into four categories shown in Chart 14.2.

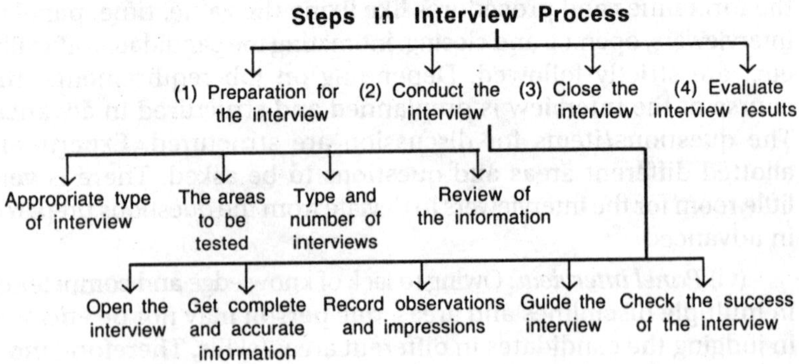

Chart 14.2. Steps in Interview

1. Preparation for the interview. Advance preparation for interview focuses its coverage on the vital aspects and helps the interviewer to remember and absorb many impressions and facts.

Before starting an interview the following preparations have to be made by the organisation :

(i) ***Appropriate type*** : Choose the appropriate types of interviews based on job requirements and the nature of the interviews discussed earlier.

(ii) ***Areas to be tested*** : Identify the knowledge, skill areas to be examined through interviews based on job requirements.

(iii) ***Types and number of interviewers*** : Interviewers should be selected on the basis of personal characteristics, technical competence, initiative, common sense, general smartness, ability to inspire confidence, capacity to work in a team and potential for growth.

Interviewers may be drawn from personnel specialists, line managers, experts in the discipline concerned, academicians, practitioners and psychologists.

Research studies and observations by Milton M. Mandell regarding the effectiveness of psychologist conclude that :

(a) As in case of other specialists, there is a wide variation in the abilities of psychologists;

(b) If he has got knowledge of job requirements and organisational interests, the psychologist would be a competent interviewer;

(c) If he is qualified, experienced and trained, psychologist's ability as an interviewer is higher than non-psychologists;

(d) Rather than a deciding factor, psychologists would act as an additional source of information.

Therefore, psychologists may also be included among interviewers.

Interviewers may interview the candidates either jointly or separately, but a panel interview is preferable to individual interview. The number of interviewers should be decided on the basis of number and nature of areas to be covered by the interview, number of candidates to be interviewed and the time available for interviewing.

(iv) ***Review of the information*** : Collected in advance through other selection methods, finding out the validity of those methods, the scores obtained etc., the information available in the application blank is thoroughly checked. It is as follows :

(a) Accuracy and validity.

(b) Acquainting about the applicant.

(c) Finding out stability, reviewing the number of positions and length of time held in each of the past jobs.

(d) Comparing the nature of positions in the previous employment with that of proposed employment.

(e) Checking the employee growth with the organisational progression in the past employment.

(f) Finding out discharges, etc., through unexplained breaks.

This helps in avoiding further evaluation of those areas appraised effectively by other means through interviews.

(v) ***Decision*** : Decide upon the administrative arrangements,

(vi) ***Finalisation*** : Finalise the physical setting including time convenient to interviewees and interviewers.

(vii) ***Determining the coverage of the interview*** : Generally the interview should cover the areas like relevance of qualifications and experience to job requirements, gaps in employment history and causes, reasons for choosing course, school, occupation, etc., likes and dislikes, sense of humour, quickness of reaction, ability to recognise thoughts, manner and poise, cultural level, etc.

(viii) Finding out the conditions under which the interview technique is effective. This includes :

(a) Consistency in the results of various selection techniques.

(b) Using the interview technique to test the candidate in those areas where other techniques are ineffective.

(c) The purpose of the interview is to find out the most suitable position to the applicant.

2. Conduct the interview. The next major step in the interview process is conducting the interview. As it is difficult, most of the line managers avoid this task. In the process of conducting interview, the interviewers should take much care because there is much scope for committing mistake at various levels. Adequate information can be obtained from the candidate by listening to and observing rather than talking too much. Interviewers very often commit the following mistakes :

(a) Indulging in discourtesy and rudeness.

(b) Arriving at conclusions before the interview is over.

(c) Asking questions mechanically.

(d) Feeling shyness in asking questions.

(e) Failing to observe the behaviour and tap the unexplored areas.

Mistakes by interviewer can be avoided by selecting competent interviewers, training and developing them.

SUBDIVISION OF INTERVIEW

(i) ***Open the interview*** : During the first few minutes of the interview, the interviewer has to open the interview with a conscious effort and with Conducive voice, speech and appearance. This helps the interviewer to establish a rapport with and gain the confidence of the interviewee.

(ii) ***Get complete and accurate information*** : The interviewer should get full information by structured interview relating to skill, knowledge, aptitude, attitude and traits of the candidate. In order to get complete and accurate information, the interviewer must do the following :

(a) Be alert for pauses, omissions and diversion of discussion.

(b) Use the language which is clear to the interviewee.

(c) Ask direct and straight questions in order to avoid ambiguous answers.

(d) Make unjustifiably favourable remarks or unfavourable comments about the applicant's motives or actions with a view to obtain truthful information.

(e) Frame the questions in such a way that the candidate's answers should be elaborate.

(iii) ***Record observations and impressions*** : In order to manage the information system for evaluating the candidate's suitability at the later stage, the interviewer should record his observations and impressions in the course of interview.

(iv) ***Guide the interview*** : Guiding the interview is essential to have just sufficient (neither too much nor too less) discussion on a topic. It should lead the applicant tactfully and surely towards the interview goals while some applicants are talkative and others are intelligent in giving information which they know and in avoiding other areas. The applicant is sometimes reticent.

While aiming at getting complete and reliable information, the interviewer has to guide the interview tactfully without causing much psychological inconvenience to the interviewee.

(v) ***Check the success of the interviewer*** : The next major step of the interview is to check the success of the interviewer in conducting the interview. The success of the interviewer in conducting the interview can be checked through the following items :

(a) Making favourable impression on the candidate at the beginning of the interview;

(b) Refraining from making judgement at the beginning;

(c) Putting the candidate at ease;

(d) Giving chance for further discussion;

(e) Asking questions at right time, clearly and in appropriate language;

(f) Avoiding unnecessary interference;

(g) Avoiding expression of approval or disapproval of any attitude;

(h) Talking to a minimum;

(i) Guiding the interview;

(j) Obtaining relevant and adequate information;

(k) Following up leads;

(1) Taking notes;

(m) Giving opportunity to the candidates to ask questions;

(n) Creating and keeping good impression throughout the interview;

(o) Giving the candidate a feeling of fair and just in conducting the interview.

3. Close the interview. Closing of interview should end pleasantly. It is as important as its commencement. The interviewer may show some signs of the close of the interview at an appropriate time. After closing the interview, interview results should be evaluated.

4. Evaluate interview results. The interviewer or the board of interviewers evaluate the candidates, strengths and weaknesses against the job and organisational requirements. Their evaluation is based on the observations, impressions and information collected during the course of interview. The final decision about the suitability of candidate is made on the basis of the results of all selection techniques. Much more than any other technique, the interview results influence the selection decision. The evaluation may be in descriptive grading or rating form. The interviewer has to strike a fine balance between the job requirements and employees, values, skills, knowledge, etc. He should give explanation of rating on each factor. This clarifies his thinking and enables discussion among the interviewers. To minimise errors in evaluation and to evaluate the candidate effectively, in general, the interviewer should also take into consideration the equational record, physical attributes, attitudes, sociability and social intelligence, flexibility in behaviour, tact, manners, temperament, dependability, self-confidence of the candidate.

LIMITATIONS OF THE INTERVIEW METHOD

1. Validity and reliability. Research has indicated the questionable nature of the validity and reliability of interviews.

2. Impression. Often the interviewer gets impressed favourably or unfavourably with the job applicant for wrong reasons. For example, a qualified male applicant should not be rejected merely because the interviewer dislikes his long hair.

3. Bias. Like all people, interviewers have personal biases. They react, positively or negatively, to fluency of speech, correctness of grammar and punctuation, poise and other characteristics.

4. Inbred notion. There are probably several inbred notions the interviewer holds that will colour the company's selection of a candidate.

5. Non-verbal behaviour. According to Dale and H.G. Heneman, interviewers often use non-verbal behaviour patterns as a basis of reaching a decision. These are, how the person looks, sits in the chair, and maintains eye contact.

6. Halo effect. The problem of the halo effect occurs when the interviewer allows a single prominent characteristic to dominate judgement of all other traits. For example, it is easy to discount other characteristics when a person has a pleasing personality, though having a pleasant personality does not necessarily ensure that the person would fit in the organisation. Sometimes the halo error can work in the opposite direction. According to Richard Arvey and James Champion, an interviewer may assume that a poorly groomed individual is stupid and dishonest.

7. Contrast errors. According to Jack Hallovan, these errors take place when an interviewer is overly influenced, in favour or against, by the interviews of previous applicants. For instance, if a qualified applicant follows a brilliant applicant, his qualifications tend to pale in comparison. This is unfortunate, since the qualified candidate may be rejected because of the contrast error.

The above limitations can be minimised by appointing trained and qualified interviewers. A trained interviewer is likely to make fewer errors because he understands potential errors, has learned how to ask questions effectively, is able to establish a positive relationship with applicants, and has systematically organised the interview.

QUALITIES OF A SUCCESSFUL INTERVIEWER

To be successful, the interviewer should possess the following qualities :

1. Elderly outlook, social detachment, intelligent, emotionally matured, interest in understanding human behaviour, sociability, active interaction, judgement, expressing of genuine feelings, etc.

2. He should be well-educated and trained. He should show interest in reading latest literature, equipping himself with latest knowledge and should have thirst for knowledge.

3. He should have thorough understanding of jobs, organisation, human behaviour, human qualities, etc.

MEANS TO MAKE THE INTERVIEW EFFECTIVE

According to Michael Jucius, the interview technique can be effectively used through the following means :

1. Selecting the interviewers with higher status, calibre, skill and knowledge.
2. Resorting to right type of interview depending upon the situation.
3. Studying the background information data, facts about the candidates before the interview.
4. Assessing and evaluating the characteristics and traits of the candidates accurately.
5. Basing interview coverage on job and organisational requirements.
6. Following time management techniques, to collect as much important information as possible within the available time.
7. Checking before hand the reliability and validity of the interview and method.
8. Respecting interviewee's interest and individuality.
9. Clearly informing the interviewee the purpose of the interview.
10. Making interviewee feel ease throughout the interview.
11. Encouraging interviewee to speak freely.

12. Interviewer should try to understand the words used by the interviewees.
13. Interviewer should not have personal views and opinions.

QUESTIONS FOR EXERCISE

1. Define Selection Test and give guidelines to testing. Outline various steps in testing.
2. Describe important types of Selection Tests. How are they developed? What precautions should be taken in using them?
3. What is Selection Interview? Explain its objectives and types.
4. Explain various types of selection interviews.
5. Describe the steps in interview process for selection of jobs.
6. What are the limitations of the Interview Method? Describe qualities of a successful interviewer and point out means to make interview effective.

15

VOCATIONAL GUIDANCE

WHAT IS GUIDANCE?

Guidance may be defined as the process of helping the individual in selecting, preparing, entering and progressing in the behaviour patterns which comprise human activities in the educational, vocational, recreational fields as well as in connection with community service group. This help takes the form of personal help on the psychologist's part. It is, again, in the form of advice. This does not solve problems but only helps the individual in solving his problems. In this way, guidance prepares the individual for his adjustment. It informs the individual of the kind of education that he requires, the subjects that he would be advised to choose in his study, the vocation to which he should employ when faced with problems that he must solve. In society every individual has a specific status and certain roles that are concomitnant with it. For example, a male member is the head of his family, and from this position is derived his responsibility of providing for the needs of the family and keeping in mind the proper development of every member. But an individual does not maintain the same status throughout his life. At one and the same or at different times, he passes through stages where he occupies the status of son, father, husband, teacher or advocate, a citizen of the nation, etc. In each of these different statuses, he has distinct and definite roles to play. The person who has ability or sense enough to work as benefits his status in society is the one who wins the acclaim of society and its approval as well. It is in the performance of these various roles and duties, which conform to his differing statuses, that he needs guidance. In this way, the psychologist's guidance helps the individual fit into his role and status in society. Every individual is not fit to take up any and every position in society. Teaching, doctoring, advocacy and a variety of other professions are not jobs that require the same individual qualities from the person occupied in doing them. Introducing fitness in an individual to occupy some position is a matter that has two aspects. The first is that his ability should be commensurate with the requirement of the job and the second that he should try to become qualified to occupy that position. The second of these aspects has some limitations. Whatever the effort expended, every person cannot become an artist or author, because every individual does not have the ability or quality to adopt any and every profession. Even every individual cannot become a successful trader as that requires a definite shrewd and calculating mentality that is not possessed by everyone. Hence, in order to prove able for some particular position, a person should choice the position that concurs with his capabilities and qualities. Educational psychology helps the individual in his choice. In this way, guidance helps the individual to settle down into the positions that are, or are not, of his own choose. As has been said in the preceding definition, guidance helps to prepare the individual for his future life. Preparation for the future life implies creating abilities in the individual to bear responsibilities and this can take a variety of forms. Normally, for example, every boy and girl gets married when he and she grow up, creates a family and indulges in prolific procreation. In this manner, every individual is to face in the future responsibilities concerning his children, responsibilities concerning the partner he has chosen for life as well as future responsibilities of the family in general. And in the normal circumstances, again, most young men and some young women have also to adopt some or the other profession, whether to their liking or not. A child grows up to be not only a man but also a citizen of his country and in this position certain rights develop upon him that bring with them some additional responsibilities. Consequently, when we talk of preparing an individual for the future, we mean to prepare him for bearing his responsibilities ably and sufficiently whether he be called upon to do so in the field of family relations, the economic sphere, the political field or any other situation of life. For this every individual boy or a girl should turn to a profession that conforms to the education they have had so that they may be in positions for which they have been prepared and act with skill and confidence. They should decide upon the profession that they would like to adopt. They should have the capacity to face and solve their own problems as well as the problems that are likely to arise in their relations with the others. Guidance helps the individual in all these kinds of efforts.

It should be quite apparent from the above detailed discussion on the meaning of the term that guidance helps in determining the objective of life, in establishing a synthesis in life and in solving various kinds of problems. In the words of Jones, "Guidance is the personal help that is given by one person to another in developing life goals, in making adjustment and in solving problems that confront him in the attainment of goals."[1] In this manner guidance is the personal assistance. Although guidance is sometimes offered at the group level, yet even in these matters, every member of the group is also individually given advice. Applied psychology is based on the conception of individual differences. General experience and scientific research have both established that every single individual has certain abilities, problems and difficulties that are distinctly his own, as distinct from those of others. Evidently, if any advice or guidance is to be rendered, it must be rendered individually and personally. This personal help is forthcoming from one individual to another. One of these two individuals is a psychologist, or one who knows psychology and the other a person who is in need of psychological guidance. Guidance, then, is the help rendered to an individual by the psychologist. In its more extensive sense, the term may be taken to comprehend the advice rendered by any individual who is in the know concerning psychology to another who is in need of it. For example, if a father guides his son in solving a problem, this, too, amounts to guidance, irrespective of the fact that it may or may not be based on the most correct notion of psychological principles. But this extensive meaning of the term has its general meaning and implication. In a scientific analysis it is not taken in its general meaning but reduced to more definite and precise terms whereby its meaning becomes limited. That is why it is first defined. Guidance, in psychology, means a particular thing. It is the personal advice or service rendered by a psychologist, and not by any Tom, Dick or Harry, to another person. This guidance takes the form of advice which helps the guided individual to adjust to various conditions and circumstances. If one would only look at it that way, it would become evident that adjustment is the basic problem of human life. The person who fails to adjust to his circumstances becomes a failure, suffers pain himself and inflicts it upon others, and is branded as an abnormal being. In this way, educational psychology, through its helping the

1. Jones, A.J., *Principles of Guidance*, McGrew Hill Book Co., New York, p. 85.

individual in adjusting himself, helps to spread happiness, peace and organisation in the society. Problems in human life do not come to an end, because new ones keep on arising. There is no end to trouble. A child, for example, is faced by very few problems, much of his anxiety being centred around the work forced upon him by the teacher, or the means of dealing with more recalcitrant of his friends and such minor things. He has not to worry about keeping the home fires burning. But these are problems that gradually engulf every individual as he grows older. As a general rule most people marry and have children who go to school and with equal inevitability fall ill and be treated for it, only to grow up and get married themselves and keep the almost eternal circle moving forward. Thus, one trouble grows out of the other, and never lets the individual being sit back contented and unharried. Human psychology is much like this. One's desire arises and destroys the being's peace till it is satisfied. Hence he immediately busies himself in searching for the means to satisfy this desire and achieves this after more or less trouble. But the story does not end here; it is followed by the arising of another desire, and the inevitable circle of objective, search for objective, obstacles in search for means of solving the desire, overcoming of the desire, and the arising of another desire. It is evident that every individual is continually faced with new objectives, achievement of which entails the facing of many other difficulties. As Jones has stated in his definition, guidance helps in overcoming these difficulties that beset the achievement of an objective.

KINDS OF GUIDANCE

As has been pointed out, an individual has to turn to the psychologist, in the latter's role as a specialist, for personal advice when he fails to solve the problems that confront him. This personal advice is guidance. How this guidance can take effect depends on the fact that it is given in the context of some problem the solution of which is being sought. As a matter of fact, it is no easy matter to recount all the possible problems that arise in various spheres of human life, but some psychologists have attempted a classification of them. For example, Jones has divided the problems of life into eight spheres on the basis of their nature : (1) Related to health and psychological development, (2) Related to house and family, (3) Related to time for recreation, (4) Concerned with personality, (5) Religious, (6) Education, (7) Social and (8) Vocational or occupational. Having achieved the classification of problems, it becomes possible to classify the kinds or forms of guidance that is to be given correspondingly. For example, vocational guidance is required in connection with profession and educational guidance in the field of education. Psychologists have professed many and various kinds of guidance. For example, Myers has mentioned the following eight kinds of guidance :

1. Vocational Guidance,
2. Educational Guidance,
3. Recreational Guidance,
4. Civic Guidance,
5. Community Service Guidance,
6. Social and Moral Guidance,
7. Health Guidance,
8. Leadership Guidance.

The present discussion makes a study of three kinds of guidance. The Bureau of Psychology, Uttar Pradesh, has also put guidance in these three categories, and much the same classification of guidance kinds has been followed in the other Indian states as well. These three kinds are : (1) Educational guidance, (2) Vocational guidance and (3) Personal guidance.

If the matter is looked at closely it will be seen that the above three classes in fact include all kinds of classification. If child guidance is considered, for example, and this guidance requires the opening of clinics in various places, it will be found that problems concerning the children are either concerned with education or are of the personal nature. Hence, child guidance is jointly comprehended under education and personal guidance. Similarly, the various forms of guidance, such as health guidance, recreational guidance, civic guidance, social and moral guidance, community service guidance and leadership guidance are all comprehended in personal guidance.

Dividing of the various spheres of guidance does not imply that these spheres are completely separated and unconnected. In fact, guidance is a dynamic and progressive concept in which advice given on every aspect of human life is comprehended, but, nevertheless, with a view to convenience in discussion, its aspects and spheres have been differentiated. Educational guidance and vocational guidance are closely related, and both of them are very intimately concerned with personal guidance. The basis of this correlation between the various spheres is that all problems of human beings are connected with each other. For example, when a person experiences difficulty in selecting a particular curriculum or a definite profession, his indecision may stem from certain personal difficulties. It happens quite often that young men become so engrossed in their careers and future. Death of a close and loved relative may be another reason why he may be at a loss and groping in dark. The fundamental problem here is of a personal nature, with the result that all education or vocational guidance to such an individual will be modified by the personal guidance given to him. On the other hand, many personal problems may be the consequence of certain deficiencies of education and the lack of educational guidance. If a child runs away from school and becomes vagrant, finds no interest in study but chooses to pursue a life of crime or one of anti-social conduct, then it is evident that there is something wrong somewhere and as likely as not it may be that his choice of curriculum may have been undesirable. In much the same manner, certain individual and personal problems may be the outcome of an absence of vocational guidance. A young man, for example, in his school days may have been a very fine sportman, and by its virtue he would naturally not appreciate a job that ties him down, offers no opportunity of leadership, and does not allow the development of any of his sportman-like qualities like motivation, patience, adventure and courage. If he is forced to take on such a job for a variety of reasons, it would be natural for him to become irritable and lose his mental balance and calm to some extent. This may lead to further complications in the form of personal problems. Here the personal problems have been caused by lack of proper vocational guidance. Similarly, educational, vocational and personal guidance is mutually related.

CLASSIFICATION ACCORDING TO THE MODE OF GUIDANCE

The above classification that we have been viewing is made on the basis of problems for which guidance is required. If the mode of guidance is taken into consideration, guidance can be classified in the following manner :

1. Individual Guidance,
2. Group Guidance.

Before going on to a detailed description of educational, vocational and personal guidance, it would be advisable to comprehend this classification of guidance made on the basis of its modes :

1. Individual guidance method. In the individual guidance method, the person to be guided and his guide, the psychologist are in direct and personal contact with each other. He invades the ill person's house and makes a study of his family conditions, and for this purpose he interviews the various members of the individual's family. His social, financial and cultural background is also investigated so that no possible source of information is left untapped. And for this it becomes essential to study his neighbourhood and to collect as many facts of his life as are possible so as to build up a fairly complete case history. The schools and colleges that he has attended are contacted in scholastic attainments there. His teachers, too, are consulted on the matter.

Study of this type and the collection of all possible information concerning the individual is followed by testing of the individual himself. He is made to take tests of intelligence, specific mental abilities, interests, attitudes, and personality. Interview is another weapon that is used to uncover much information and, incidentally, to learn the person opinion about himself. Accordingly, then, in an individual guidance, the following information concerning the individual is gathered :

1. Information concerning his intelligence, mental abilities, interests, attitudes and personality.

2. Information concerning family conditions.

3. Information concerning the social, financial and cultural background.

4. Other relevant information.

Having gathered all this information, it is subjected to close and intelligent scrutiny, and then curative measures are introduced to remove the problems which have made this guidance necessary. Among these efforts are logical arguments, suggestions, psychoanalysis, etc.

The individual guidance method has the following qualities :

1. It renders almost complete information concerning the individual. Hence a proper cure can be effected.

2. Cures in this method are simpler and more effective.

Despite these advantages, the method suffers from the following drawbacks :

1. It consumes much time, with the result that a very large number of psychologists are required if there is a big number of patients.

2. Accordingly, this method is extremely expensive also.

3. It needs highly trained and specialist psychologists.

2. Group guidance method. These shortcomings of the individual guidance method are not found in group method because in this, a number of people are guided simultaneously. Group guidance should not be interpreted to imply that it involves guiding the group. Actually, the guidance is aimed at the individual because it consists of the personal assistance rendered by a psychologist. In the group guidance technique, a complete group is guided. But this guidance is intended to help the individual member of the group to solve his own problems, the sole difference being that the group comprises individuals facing more or less the same problems. Evidently, then, there is no need to waste money and time in giving individual guidance to individuals who are facing similar problems and the advice given is likely to be similar. Hence, there can be no questioning of the importance of the group guidance technique. It economises upon time and money.

Nevertheless, group guidance technique lacks all the advantages that accrue from an application of the individual guidance method. Due to the smaller degree of personal contact between the psychologist and his subjects, the cures are not quite so effective as in the case of individual guidance. When group guidance is administered it is also not possible to gather the same amount of authentic information concerning the subject as is feasible in the individual guidance method. Hence, it may be tentatively concluded that group guidance method can be of value only in circumstances in which the problems faced are similar to a degree without wide individual differences and are also not particularly complex.

VOCATIONAL GUIDANCE : ITS HISTORY

Vocational guidance was defined by the 1954 Committee of the International Labour Organisation in its suggestions concerning vocational guidance, as assistance rendered by an individual to another in the latter's solving of problems related to his progress and vocational selection, keeping in mind the individual's peculiarities or special abilities and their relations with their occupational opportunities. In this manner, the objective of vocational guidance is the proper and complete utilization of a nation's manpower through helping the individual to achieve his development and satisfaction in his profession. An individual should choose a profession that suits his abilities in order that both he and the nation may profit. It is not possible for any one individual to be capable of doing every job. Special kinds of job require particular kinds of skills and special know-how. It is possible that it may be asked why guidance thereby becomes necessary since every individual can tell the kind of skill he has and choose a profession accordingly. But if the situation is objectively viewed, it will be found that it is not precisely of this nature, as only few people are able to gauge their own abilities and capabilities. A large majority of persons are wrong in their estimate, of their own capabilities, many of them overestimating while a fair number denigrating themselves. It is not possible for the proverbial human eye to see the very grit, that is, that the human eye rarely lights upon the individual's own defects. If one were to go to any student doing post-graduate work in the university and ask him as to what he proposes to do after obtaining the degree, the most likely reply would be that he would take one of the competitive examinations, preferably the administrative service, and if not fortunate enough to be selected, carry on to do research and finally become a teacher. The audacity and overweening self-confidence of the students is stupendous. If you were to ask him as to what he will do if neither of these contingencies comes about, then it will only be a regard for your social standing that will prevent him from denouncing you on the spot. The implication is that very few of the students who fail in these and other competitive examinations realise that they do not possess the requisite qualities. When they fail, they turn their wrath upon the examiner while the more charitable abuse only their bad luck. There will hardly be one student who will acquiesce in the knowledge that it was he himself who was lacking in the qualities required for the job. Again, to prevent unnecessary meanings being read into these statements it must be pointed out that the competitive examinations held in the present era can hardly be considered sufficient to gauge an individual's inherent merit. The sole intention of introducing this example is to point out the fact that young men and women do not think rationally and scientifically when faced with the choice of a profession. Vocational guidance helps in the solution of this problem. Scientific testing reveals all that there is to know of the individual and then advise the former as to the profession most suitable for him. Experiments have succeeded in pointing out roughly the qualities that a particular kind of profession requires in the individual. For example, efforts were made to establish the intelligence level required for various kinds of jobs.

The following table states the intelligence quotient that a person should possess in order to go in for one or the other profession :

S.No.	*Professional Class*	*I.Q.*
1.	Administrative work and high level professional work	150 or more
2.	Low level professional and technical work	130 to 150
3.	Clerical or high level skilled labour	115 to 130
4.	Skilled work	100 to 115
5.	Semi-skilled work	85 to 100
6.	Work not requiring intelligence	70 to 85
7.	Labour work	50 to 70

Similarly, other tests and experiments have been conducted to establish some relationship between vocational and other mental abilities. For example, engineering and other industrial work requires mechanical skill in the individual, with the result that persons who possess it in a slight degree cannot in the normal course be expected to become successful engineers or skilled technicians. Some kinds of work, for example, the repair of chronometers and surgery, require the ability to do minute work skilfully. Lacking this quality, no individual can become a good surgeon, watch-repairer or experimenter or research worker. In much the same manner, other industries and professions require different kinds of expertise and skill.

The above description makes evident the importance inherent in vocational guidance. But this hardly means that the guide pays no attention to the person's aptitude. Aptitude is one of the basis of guidance, but one thing that is beyond question is that no individual can attain much success on the sole basis of aptitude. Accordingly, the guide has to collect elaborate and detailed information concerning the individual's aptitudes and capabilities, and give guidance on the basis of such information. Vocational guidance does not involve categorical declaration that one shall be a professional while such another shall be a clerk or an engineer. It is only a hypothesis and a suggestion that has its own limitations. What the guide says is simply that such and such person should choose a particular profession, and there is much greater possibility of success in that profession than in any other for that individual.

Personnel Selection

It was the National Institute of Industrial Psychology that commenced research on matters concerning vocational guidance, and its results have been used much by all big industries. Every productive unit has a large variety of functions which can best be performed by individuals having different kinds of ability and training. Now, the selection of separate individuals for each of these jobs is called personnel selection. And this personnel selection is based upon vocational guidance. Hence, it is essential that the distinction between personnel selection and vocational guidance be well marked and known. In both it is essential that the qualities fit for different jobs be present in the person being considered for selection or guidance, as the case may be. But, in personnel selection, the quality required for some particular function is remarked, and one person out of many applicants is selected to perform that function, of course care being taken that the best of the applicants is thereby selected. In vocational guidance, the qualities of a person are gauged and he is accordingly advised to take up some vocational training or adopt a particular profession that suits him and is likely to bring him satisfaction. Vocational guidance and personnel selection are two branches of vocational psychology. Both these branches are interdependent since the provision of the right man for the right job and right job for the right man requires, on the one hand, analysis of the individual, and an analysis of the job on the other.

The Western nations have done much work concerning vocational guidance, particularly in the United States of America, personnel selection is itself a specialised job now. Considerable modernisation and improvement are being carried on to improve the techniques of collection of information regarding the professions and the method of selection. A Directory of Occupational Titles has been prepared to search for thereby providing information concerning vocations that are open to individuals. Then, an Occupational Code has been prepared by classifying the vocations according to the qualities that they require in the man according to their different levels. Detailed information regarding every profession is collected. Job description, which is an important organ of the information concerning every profession, provides a detailed and exhaustive account of the various factors such as conditions of work, wages, responsibility, etc., that are operative in the industry or vocation. The first dictionary included details of

75 per cent vocations and occupations, and it comprehended some 90 per cent of working population of that country. This directory went through additional and improved editions in 1942, 1944 and 1945 while in its 1959 revised version some thousands of professions were detailed, and job analysis in 1942 was confined to 16 professions.

Vocational Guidance in India

In India, vocational guidance is not easily available, as there are few other technical and specialised services. In 1945, the Training and Employment Service Organisation Committee headed by Shri B. Shivarao suggested that occupational information be selected and published. As a result, during the Second Five Year Plan period a project was prepared to set up 50 vocational guidance centres to supplement the efforts of the employment exchanges in their personnel selection. There have been certain appointments in this connection but the actual achievement is not very noticeable. And the books on occupations that have been published are not scientific research material but merely constitute a description. Besides with the efforts of the Government of India, the state governments have also opened some centres, while this in turn has been supplemented by certain non-governmental agencies. Among them the Y.M.C.A. and the Rotary Club have achieved things that deserve mention. As is apparent from the above rather short account, the progress in the direction of vocational guidance for a large country like India, is not worthy of praise. It need hardly be pointed out that much of this failure is to be attributed to the lack of organisation.

List of Abilities and Traits

Much important research and modification work has been carried on in connection with finding out the qualities and traits required for different professions. The National Institute of Industrial Psychology of England has prepared a list of approximately 20 psychological abilities and traits. On the basis of this list, an industrial survey was undertaken. In this survey, the specialists and senior officers working in the different occupations were requested to supply information as to the qualities and traits required for their respective functions. Specialists of different occupations effected a rating from three standpoints — average, high level, and a very high level. Now the specialists of the National Institute took the average of the ratings made available from some 80 occupations. This average was categorised in the form of a table. And on the basis of this table, it is possible to determine whether a particular individual is suitable for a specific profession or not. For example, this table, clarifies the qualities that are requisite for the medical and the legal professions and the qualities that are quite desirable.

Another bit of important research work in connection with various professions and mental abilities was carried on by R.B. Cattell. Cattell tested some, 1000 adult persons and found out their average intelligence level. This average indicates the approximate level of intelligence required by a person wishing to join some particular profession. This is made apparent in the following table :

S.No.	*Profession*	*No. of Trained People*	*Average I.Q.*
1.	Teachers of universities and intermediate colleges	30	151
2.	Doctors and surgeons	25	146.5
3.	Teachers of government schools	50	145
4.	Civil engineers	20	142
5.	Mechanical engineers	18	140
6.	Teachers of primary schools	90	137
7.	Managers of industry	20	137
8.	Stenographers	57	129
9.	Clerks	54	127
10.	Travelling representatives	24	123
11.	Nurses	250	122
12.	Telephone department employees	52	115
13.	Workers doing minute work	19	114
14.	Workers doing gross work	—	106 to 78

Tests by Devorak and Dodge

Devorak and Dodge also conducted tests upon employees of different professions, on persons successful and unsuccessful within one profession, of people working in the same profession but in different capacities. This testing was based upon a wide variety of authentic psychological testing techniques. These tests revealed considerable differences between the abilities of motor mechanics, successful or unsuccessful clerks, and other people. But these tests were neither extensive and comprehensive to be applied to a majority of professions nor concentrated enough to have completely distinguished one profession from another. In this manner, it is essential to exercise the greatest care in applying the conclusions in these tests. Dodge himself has acknowledged this fact.

Minnesota Occupational Rating Scales

In Minnesota University six mental abilities and their extent was determined for 430 professions and occupations. And even in this, the ability was individually divided into four categories — *a, b, c, d.* These six mental abilities were Verbal, Mechanical, Sociability, Clerical, Musical and Artistic. And these six abilities were divided into four classes each for different professions. For example, the Minnesota Occupational Rating Scale concerning the ability of verbal efficiency can be understood from the following table :

Class Level of Intelligence	*Necessary Ability*	*Example*
(a) High level	Highest university education, creative ability and power of argument.	Professors, authors, scientists, advocates, etc.
(b) Higher than average.	High school and college level of education.	Clerks, photographers, foremen, etc.
(c) Average level.	High school level of education.	Typists, mechanics, etc.
(d) Below average.	Junior high school or eighth grade education.	Labourers, porters, etc.

PROCESS OF VOCATIONAL GUIDANCE

The preceding description of vocational guidance must have made it apparent that it requires two kinds of information or subject matter to be collected, the first concerning indispensable information about the individual, and the second pertaining to knowledge of the industrial or occupational aspect. In this manner, vocational guidance has two aspects :

1. Study of the individual.
2. Study of the occupational or professional sphere.

Study of the Individual

Before any vocational guidance can be rendered to an individual, it is essential that adequate information concerning his education, level of intelligence, mental abilities, aptitudes, interests, physical development, health, nature, personality characteristics and economic status be gathered, because variations in any of them will necessarily require change in guidance.

1. Education. Individuals need differing levels of education in order to enter into and succeed in different professions, as for example, the highest education is required for advocates, professors, engineers, doctors, and other such professions whereas a general and lower level of education can serve the purpose if the profession is of clerk, overseer, mechanic, compounder, teacher, etc. Besides these there are certain other occupations in which the medium level of education suffices, *e.g.*, business salesmanship. In such professions, only the basic necessities of literacy must be fulfilled, as much else depends upon practice. It is only because of this importance of various levels of education being relative and relevant to different professions that most advertisement for applications for jobs contain specific instructions regarding the educational qualifications. For example, a person teaching students at the high school and intermediate level need only be a graduate while no mere graduate can teach the college or graduate level. Doctors require medical degrees while in order to qualify as an engineer, it is essential that one passes an engineering examination.

2. Training. Education does not merely imply the degree obtained at the end of a session by passing a prescribed examination. Nowadays, most occupation units make it obligatory on all new entrants to be trained in addition to be educated, and this is being carried to the extent that only a trained individual is allowed to fill the post of a high school teacher. Certain occupations need training inevitably, for example the occupation of an electrician, stenographer, chemist, compounder, etc. In certain professions, the individual after having entered it, the training is oriented for a period of few weeks, and only then he is allowed to handle work on his own responsibility.

3. Level of intelligence. Besides differences in education, different professions require differing levels of intelligence. For example, the medical, technical, legal, teaching and administrative professions require the highest intelligence level, while, on the other hand, the peon and the domestic worker can be selected from people with a much more lower level of intelligence. Other professions require only the average level of intelligence, so that, evidently, before a person can be told of the profession that suits his natural endowments, it is essential to now the level of intelligence to which he belongs.

4. Special mental abilities. Individuals differ not only in respect of their intelligence but also in respect of their special mental abilities. For example, all people do not possess mechanical ability to the same degree and neither is verbal felicity shared by all in equal degree. Different professions require differing mental abilities, verbal ability being required by advocates and teachers, etc., mechanical ability by doctors and engineers, etc. Hence prior to the selection of a profession, it is essential for the individual to be aware of his mental abilities.

5. Aptitudes. Success in a particular profession seems to depend to some extent upon one's aptitude for it. If a person lacks artistic and creative aptitude, there is not much likelihood of his succeeding in the role of an artist, and one need not expect of it. As a general rule, it is advisable for every person to join the profession for which he has any natural aptitude. Hence, knowledge of a person's aptitude is also essential before he can be given any vocational guidance.

6. Interests. Interest helps to increase the possibility of success in a profession. Interesting work is done enthusiastically and patiently while uninteresting work tends to fall upon most men, and requires very conscious application to be carried through. Success in work requires that serious interest be taken in the work, or that interest in that kind of work be created, and this is possible. Interests are mutable, and it is possible to create interest in work that was once repugnant. But, hardly be repeated as a slogan is, that a knowledge of the person's interest is essential before any vocational guidance can be rendered.

7. Health and physical development. As a general rule, proper health and physical development are necessarily taken into consideration in every profession, but in certain other occupations, success depends almost solely upon these factors. For success in the armed forces or in the police department, health and good physical development are quite indispensable. In the absence of these factors, the presence of no other qualities of ability will bring success to the individual. Hence, physical development, constitution and health are additional factors that must be taken into consideration when the question of vocational guidance comes up for consideration.

8. Nature. Different people show very pertinent and obvious differences in their nature, some being introverted while others more extroverted. And, different kinds of people can successfully settle down only in some specific professions that suit their nature. An extroverted personality, for example, is essential if one wants to succeed as a salesman, agent, administrator or even as a leader, while on the other hand, gifted introverts make great artists, authors, scholars, scientists, specialists, etc. If choice of a profession is contrary to one's natural grain then one is not happy and enthusiastic in his work, and these conditions are not conducive to progress and success. Hence, before vocational guidance can be ventured upon, it is necessary to judge a person's nature also.

9. Personality characteristics. It is a fact generally known that different qualities of the personality are required in such widely separated professions as teaching, artistic creation, selling, labour work, etc. Hence, choice of profession should also be made with due regard for the qualities of the person's personality.

10. Financial status. As a general rule, it is improper and unnecessary to take into consideration a person's financial status before making a choice of profession, but in a country like India where scholarships are hard to come by, the economic status of the student also plays an important part in his choice of the future that he wants to shape for himself. Now, a person with middle-class status is in no position to afford a technical or medical education for his child because either of these two special courses involves the expenditure of a considerable amount of money. And it is unnecessary and improper to advise a poor and needy person to go in for higher education when he cannot afford it. It is equally useless to advise such a person to choose a profession in which high education and specialised qualification are desired. Hence a person should be recommended only to that profession for which he can afford to gain education and any training that may be essential. He must have the means to gain such training. It must also be remembered that economic or financial status can be a bar to entering some professions only under certain circumstances. There are many examples of people who came from poor families having gained very high education and improved their lot in life. The truth or crux of the matter is that instead of discouraging a student from entertaining thoughts of a profession for which he apparently has not the economic means, the psychologist should expend his effort in arranging scholarships or other facilities whereby he may be able to attain the goal for which the former is striving, as he stands great chances of success. In India, these things are still unexplored, and many individuals fail to gain satisfying and rewarding positions in life that conform to their abilities, interests and aptitudes, for no reason other than that they were born in poor families.

11. Other important factors. In addition to all the elements pointed out above, it is necessary to keep in mind certain other factors concerning the individual before giving vocational guidance. Age of the person, for example, is another factor that must be taken into account since many jobs and occupations set the maximum and minimum age limits on all applications so that people not qualifying for them in this respect cannot enter these services. Hence, there is hardly any point in advising them to take up such a profession. Sex of the person is another consideration in vocational guidance upon which much depends because occupations are more suitable to the male individual while others are within the capacities of the female, and for these she is eminently suitable. Nursing and caring for the diseased in hospitals is one function that can safely and even desirably be allocated to women, while in the armed forces and the police, most of the jobs, with very few exceptions, are suitable only for the male.

Study of the Professional World

Having collected all the necessary and desired information regarding the individual under consideration, it is necessary to be true to another aspect of vocational guidance, that is of studying the professional world. While the psychologist must necessarily have enough information concerning the person to whom he is imparting vocational guidance, it is equally important that he be well informed on its professional and occupational aspect. Only then can he provide proper and effective assistance. It is not enough for the psychologist to be knowing the number and kinds of professions but also the kind of education, training, intelligence, mental abilities, interests, aptitudes, personality, etc., that are desired as well as the conditions of work that prevail therein.

Occupations have been classified in different ways, according to the viewpoint adopted in trying to know all the professions from one point of view and can be selected from among them. This has the two-fold advantage of narrowing down the range from which the selection is to be made while at the same it provides a number of alternatives. It will be advantageous now to glance at these various professions.

1. Classification according to interest. Professions have been divided into the following classes on the basis of interest :

(a) Occupations concerned with child life,

(b) Mechanical occupations,

(c) Computational occupations,
(d) Scientific occupations,
(e) Occupations concerned with change,
(f) Artistic occupations,
(g) Literary occupations,
(h) Musical occupations,
(i) Occupations concerned with sociality,
(j) Clerical occupations.

In each of these classes, there are professions belonging to five levels, depicted in the following classification.

2. Classification on the basis of education level, mental ability, or skill, training, age and social respect. This classification of the professions is the work of Beckman, which is as follows :[2]

(a) ***Executive, managerial and professional*** : This class includes the following three kinds of occupations :

(i) Verbal such as advocate, judge, educator, auditor, professor, etc.
(ii) Scientific, such as doctor, engineer, scientist, accountant, etc.
(iii) Executive or managerial, such as the various kinds of managers and executives, etc.

(b) ***Business and sub-professional*** : This class includes the following two kinds :

(i) Business such as trader, salesman, agent, etc.
(ii) Sub-professional, such as actor, photographer, designer, etc.

(c) ***Skilled occupation*** : This class includes the following two kinds of occupations :

(i) Physical labour, such as an electrician, dyer, machineman, and press mechanic, etc.
(ii) Intellectual such as clerk, supervisor, stenographer, cashier, etc.

(d) ***Semi-skilled occupation*** : Such as policeman, bus conductor, driver, guard, etc.

2. Beckman, R.O., "A New Scale for Gauging Occupational Rank".

(e) ***Unskilled occupation*** : Such as labour, peon, night-watchman, etc.

3. Classification according to the form of work. Professions have been divided into the following four classes according to the nature of work done by them :

(a) ***Social occupations*** : These professions require that the person be possessed of social qualities and a high degree of sociability because he comes into contact with many individuals. Examples of such professions are advocate, leader, trader, salesman, agent, administrator, manager, teacher, etc.

(b) ***Occupations of manual skill*** : In these professions tools are used for work that requires a high-degree of manual skill, examples being carpenter, mechanic, mason, binder, overseer, engineer, etc.

(c) ***Occupation concerned with offices*** : This class includes all people concerned with office organisations such as clerks, cashiers, peons, etc.

(d) ***Intellectual and scholarly occupations*** : In this class comes the professions that require acumen and love of academic work of the individual, examples of which are philosopher, author, inventor, poet, scientist, etc.

Job Families

From the above classification of occupations, it becomes evident that there are many professions that are similar in respect of their nature of work done, conditions of work, desired skills, interests, mental abilities, and personal qualities, etc. When such similar families are put together, a job family is constituted. In one job family the work can be carried out on different levels such as high, medium or low. Evidently, then, the individual will first have to select a job family, and then the level of that family on which he is capable of functioning.

Sources of Information regarding Occupations

The question that may be justifiable intriguing the beginner is the source of all this comprehensive information regarding a profession. The following are the sources from which such information is forthcoming and can be gathered :

(a) Through Papers and magazines.

(b) Through information published by government organisations.

(c) Through radio discussions.

(d) From employment exchanges.

(e) From information broadcast by industrial and commercial institutions.

(f) Through lectures delivered by specialists.

(g) Through examination of factories and people working in them.

(h) By working in any particular profession.

(i) From guidance psychologist and vocational adviser.

Significant Facts in Vocational Selection

After gathering information regarding the professions from one or more of the above-mentioned source, it is possible to select one's profession but before committing oneself finally, as has been pointed out before, the following things must be taken into consideration and made note of :

1. Nature of work which includes the kind of work, charge, responsibility, duty, interest, etc.
2. Working conditions, which include both psychological and physical needs.
3. Necessary personality traits such as nature, adeptness in behaviour, power of leadership, etc.
4. Level of intelligence.
5. Mental abilities.
6. Interest and aptitudes.
7. Necessary education and training.
8. Income, chances of promotion and permanency of work.
9. Procedure of entrance.
10. Necessary physical development and health.
11. Social prestige.
12. Demand of the job.

In this manner, a profession is chosen after analysing the individual on one hand, and the various occupations on the other. Analysis of the individual reveals the abilities and qualities present in him while analysis of the job or profession reveals the desired qualities and abilities. Now, all that remains to be done is that the person who possesses abilities and qualities requisite for a particular profession should be prompted to join it.

Steps of the Vocational Guidance Method

Vocational guidance, as in the case of all other forms of guidance, can be given by two methods — the individual method and the collective method. And, in these methods, the steps are the same as were described in the case of educational guidance. In this manner, vocational guidance will involve the following steps :

1. Orientation talks.
2. Psychological testing.
3. Collection of data from the school.
4. Collection of data from the family.
5. Interview.
6. Formation of profile.
7. Achievement, besides the above important steps in vocational guidance, which means that the psychologist, along with providing vocational guidance, also helps the individual to attain to the desired profession. For this, he keeps in contact with employment exchange offices and social workers.
8. Follow up studies.

QUESTIONS FOR EXERCISE

1. Discuss the scope and purpose of guidance, keeping in view the limitations of group instructional method.
2. What are the main objectives of guidance? Distinguish between vocational guidance and vocational selection?
3. Write short note on Personal guidance.
4. Distinguish between educational and vocational guidance.
5. Explain the concept and kinds of guidance. What is guidance?

16

PERSONNEL SELECTION : JOB ANALYSIS AND WORKERS ANALYSIS

PSYCHOLOGY IN INDUSTRY

Psychology is seen to be present in whatever sphere of human life that boasts of human relationships or human endeavour. In the sphere of industry, the relations between the labourers and the proprietor present a large variety, and one comes across many specimens of behaviour. Industry has many problems, including those of human conduct. For example, cases of labour unrest and dissatisfaction are not uncommon. Many causes culminate in unwillingness on their part to cooperate with the management, and in the desire to coerce the management into paying wages out of all proportions to the work achieved. They indulge in such inflammatory practices as occasional or frequent strikes that lead to factories being closed, ultimately causing loss to the management, and equally to the nation. On the other hand, bosses and factory owners are reputedly callous of their unconcern for the welfare of their employees. The least disturbance finds them indulging in lockouts, a process that has disastrous results as the piece-wage employee knows to his detriment. The country loses at the same time. Basically, all these problems are problems of human behaviour, and hence psychology is required to solve them.

Difficulties in Production

Greater and better quality of machinery is an undeniable requirement, but it is no less important that it be operated by skilful and, moreover, willing hands. How can this skill be gauged? There being a vast variety of functions and occupations in a factory, how can one discover the most adequate person for a particular job? Of the many hundreds of individuals who apply for jobs in factories, how is one to select the people who will prove to be the most efficient? For high levels of production, it is essential that the machines should be designed so as to avoid fatigue to the operator as much as is practicable. Lighting should be adequate to avoid inconvenience, accidents and unnecessary strain upon the eyes of the workers. Often, individuals lose their enthusiasm very soon for a routine kind of work. How is their interest and attention to be sustained and recreated? What should be the proper plan of a factory so that accidents are avoided? Psychology can help in the solution of all these problems that face the industry.

Problems of Distribution

With production, the work of industry does not come to an end. What is equally important is that these produced goods be sold, and sold at profitable rates. If the industry does not meet with success in this direction, all production is worthless, whatever its inherent quality. And for goods to be sold in the market, it is essential that the common buyer be acquainted with the commodity, with its quality. But for anything to happen it is necessary that there should be the necessity for a demand for the commodity, and that the consumer be aware of this need. Here, advertisement pays good dividends. And successful advertising is based upon psychological appeal. Evidently, psychology is no less important for the purposes of distribution.

Conditions of Work

In industry, the conditions under which work is undertaken has an important influence upon the labourer. In healthy conditions, the labourers are healthy, and a general atmosphere of well-being and satisfaction pervades the community. If, on the other hand, labourers are required to work in bad conditions, the number of casualties through accidents increases and this leads to dissatisfaction among the labourers. Conditions of work include many tangible and intangible factors such as proper sanitary conditions, arrangements for good air and water, provision of adequate resting places, peaceful atmosphere, good climate, proper lighting, and cordial relations between the workers and the bosses with smooth liaison between the two. Guidance from the hands of the psychologist brings about the best results in each case. The psychologist must cooperate with the opthalmic surgeon to decide the best angle of lighting. Colour combinations within the factory premises are known to affect the efficiency of the worker, experiments having revealed that a smoothing combination of colour effects improves general efficiency and also reduces the accident rate. And it is for the psychologist to pronounce judgement as to when the machines and general factory premises should be painted.

Human Involvement

Having chosen the right man for the right job in the factory is not the end of the problem, as it is necessary, for high levels of production, that the efficiency of the worker be maintained and even improved if his optimum has not been achieved. Labourer is a human being, and not a cog in the wheel. If his talent is to be exploited, it is necessary to keep in view human motives and human psychology. Psychology can easily help to solve all the human problems that crop up in an industry.

Field of Industrial Psychology

The foregoing description should have convinced the reader that psychology pervades every aspect of industry, and can do good. Its actual importance for the modern era can be gauged by the knowledge that application of psychology to the field of industry has led to the emergence and development of a separate branch of psychology, known as Industrial psychology. In the words of Blum, "Industrial psychology is simply the application or extension of psychological facts and principles to the problems concerning human relations in business and industry." Human relations in industry came into the limelight. Under extensive investigation after the Industrial Revolution in Europe. Realisation of the magnitude of the problem led to the development of Industrial psychology in the twentieth century, a science which tells of the capability and interest of an individual for a particular function. It helps to select the correct person for specialised jobs. It defines the principle whereby proper conditions can be created to achieve the maximum efficiency with the least possible amount of exertion and fatigue. One important aspect of Industrial psychology is Job Analysis. Every factory and mill provides various kinds of work, all of which are analysed by the psychologist who then lays down the qualities that are required of the individual who is to perform it. In a factory, there must be constant supervision of the labourers' work. And Industrial psychology effects improvements in the methods of supervision and observation. It helps to maintain an atmosphere in the workhouse which promotes cordial relations between the workers and the boss. It puts forward constructive suggestions for improving the efficiency in order to provide a check on his progress or failure. It has been pointed out earlier, and is fairly evident, that industry today has much need for effective and strong advertisements and propaganda. Nowadays, Industrial psychology has extended its function to include advice on the manufacture of machinery that can help to minimise fatigue and improve production.

Humanist Thought in An Industry

In the present era, there are many factors promoting the development and increase of humanist thought in the field of industry, reputedly a mechanised giant not amenable to human approaches. No longer is the labourer looked upon in the light of a small cog in the wheel of progress, a mere tool in the massive production machinery. Realization that industry is benefited by the happiness and satisfaction of the labour class has dawned, and industrial progress has been allied to labour welfare. This humanization of industry is a state of human thought for which psychology must be praised. It is due to the prevalence of such enlightened thinking that the capitalist class can be persuaded to think of the welfare of their workers. Stress on the alliance between the physical and mental aspects of human labour is the contribution of psychology. It contends that efficient physical endeavour is not possible in the absence of mental satisfaction. This fact must be kept in mind while improving the methods of work in the factory.

In this manner, an industrial is rendering valuable assistance in the entire field of industry. As knowledge of the human individual increases in the domain of psychology, the importance of psychology in the sphere of industry will grow.

Difficulty in the Selection of Workers

Modern psychology has by now undoubtedly established that individuals differ from each other in respect of their abilities, qualities of the personality, capabilities and interests. On the other hand, different functions within various industries require particular qualities and abilities in the individuals obliged to perform them. Hence, for this, it becomes essential that for a particular function only that person should be retained who possesses the requisite qualities and abilities, a requirement that leads to the problem of selection. This problem has a positive as well as a negative aspect. In its negative aspect, the activity of selection consists in sorting out the undesirable individuals from among all those who have applied for the appointment to a particular post, while in its positive aspect it consists in selecting one individual from all those who, *prima facie,* seems to qualify for the job. Such selection must take into account the interests, requirements, abilities and attitudes of the applicants.

Why is Personnel Selection Essential?

The main cause of the necessity of personnel selection is the fact of individual differences. Many experiments have led to the establishment of the fact that abilities in individual beings differ considerably as a consequence of hereditary differences. Certain qualities are innate and cannot be improved upon much through training. An individual's attitudes, mental tendency, etc., become fairly evident even in his infancy, and in greater or lesser degree they remain the same throughout his life. These attitudes have considerable importance for an individual's life. Generally speaking, any work that one can perform best is the one in the direction of which one has a mental tendency. It is not in the mental make-up of every individual to be a successful and skilful engineer, and neither is every man made to be a giant tycoon of a business. Some children evince great interest in manual work of a skilled nature and in science, and it is these children who usually develop into good engineers or scientists. All these psychological facts go to prove that any individual can be fitted into any job and that training can prepare an individual for any function are wrong. Hence, personnel selection is very much in vogue in every industry in the modern world.

Two Aspects of Personnel Selection

Personnel selection has two aspects : one, which is the analysis of each and every particular independent function in an industry in order to establish the qualities required for the individual performing it. The second function of this selection is to examine all candidates and determine the qualities and abilities that each of them possesses. The first function is called job analysis while the second aspect is called worker's analysis.

JOB ANALYSIS

Aims of Job Analysis

It has been pointed out before that the main objective of job analysis is the selection of personnel. But it can also have other objectives such as improvements in the methods of working, training of employees, promotion of employees, obviating accidents and protection of health, etc.

What is Job Analysis?

Defining job analysis, Blum has remarked, "A job analysis is an accurate study of the various components of a job. It is concerned not only with an analysis of the duties and conditions of work, but also with the individual qualifications of the worker." It is evident that job analysis will reveal the duties of individuals in a particular job or profession, as also the conditions in which they will be required to work. It will also bring out the qualities required of an individual aspiring to perform some definite function or a piece of work. According to J.D. Hackett, in the process of job analysis, the fundamental elements of a job are established and clarified, while simultaneously the abilities desirable out of the worker are known, the abilities that will help him to perform his function skilfully. Thus, job analysis has two aspects, one analysis of duties and conditions of work, and the other, the analysis of qualities desired in the worker or an employee.

Advantages of Job Analysis

Job analysis confers many advantages. On the basis of 401 essays concerned with job analysis, Zerga pointed out twenty advantages and utilities of job analysis. One is the increase in efficiency, as well as increase in the mutual feelings of the workers since everyone is happy to be employed in the job he cherishes. Job analysis can help to determine the salary or wages accruing to the employee for a particular function performed by him. Job analysis helps in the classification of professions and occupations; it thereby becomes possible to determine the qualities required for them. Through job analysis it also becomes possible to determine the extent of training necessary for a specific individual to be given a particular job. Job analysis determines the duty of everyone in his own job by determining the responsibility inherent in any kind of work.

Various Components of Job

Now, the first thing to be mentioned in connection with job analysis is the presence of various components in a job. Headings of information collected in this connection are as follows :

1. Identification of the Job.
2. Number Employed.
3. Statement of Duties.
4. Machines Used.
5. Analysis of Operations.
6. Conditions of Work.
7. Pay and Incentives.
8. Relation to Other Allied Jobs.

9. Opportunities for Transfer and Promotion.
10. Time and Nature of Training.
11. Personal Requirements :
    (a) General — Age, Sex, Nationality, Marital Status.
    (b) Physical.
    (c) Educational.
    (d) Previous Experience.
    (e) General and Special Abilities.
    (f) Temperamental and Character Requirements.

As is evident from the above list, there is an extensive collection of data regarding job analysis.

Methods of Job Analysis

Of the many methods employed in job analysis, the main are as follows :

1. Individual Psychographic Method.
2. Questionnaire Method.
3. Job Psychographic Method.
4. Job Analysis by Text.
5. Motion Study Method.

These methods will now be described in brief.

1. Individual psychographic method. In this method, the mental peculiarities of an individual, successful in a particular kind of job, are examined, a list of these peculiarities prepared and this list is transcribed in figure form on graph. This provides some standard of judgement in future recruitments for the same job.

2. Questionnaire method. A list of questions is prepared on the basis of the different qualities of personality concerned with the job. This list is then provided to the individuals doing that job, and they are asked to answer these questions. An analysis of the answers received helps to reveal the special qualities necessary for the job, a list of which can now be prepared. This, too, helps in the future selection of candidates for the job in question.

3. Job psychographic method. According to Viteles, there are three things essential for job psychographic method :

(a) Accurate classification of mental qualities.
(b) Valid methods of evaluation.
(c) Direct examination or analysis by trained examiners.

In this manner, in this method, some specialist analysts study the work, and they evolve a valid and standard method of evaluation. They prepare a very accurate list in which the various mental qualities required for the job are properly and reliably classified. A graph of these qualities is prepared so that selection of candidates for the job may become easier.

4. Job analysis by test. In the test method, some reliable and valid tests are performed on the basis of essential qualities and abilities. The candidates are tested for selection and suitability by these tests.

5. Motion study method. Under this method, the speed of individual worker in performing some job and the time consumed therein are both noted. Similar examinations are performed on the other individuals doing the same work, and the results obtained are compared. Such a study of speed and time helps in job analysis and classification of the workers.

Job analysis can be done by any one or more of these methods, the choice of method being governed by the situation or circumstances.

WORKER'S ANALYSIS

Essential Elements in Worker's Analysis

The second step in personnel selection is that of worker's analysis. In worker's analysis, as is apparent from the term used to denote it, detailed information regarding the applicant's qualities, abilities, experience and other factors is obtained. Roughly speaking, worker's analysis requires information under the following heads :

1. Age,
2. Caste,
3. Sex,
4. Nationality,
5. Physical health and characteristics,
6. Education and training,
7. Experience,
8. Level of intelligence,
9. Mental abilities and their level,
10. Interests and aptitudes,
11. Personality traits.

Having gathered the above information regarding a particular applicant, it becomes possible to determine the kind of a job he is likely to prove proficient in, and the kind of job in which he tends to be a failure. Worker's analysis also reveals the extent and nature of training that a particular individual will require; before he can successfully enter a particular profession. Worker's analysis can also help to make a rough estimate of the remuneration that can justifiably be paid to the worker, for the job in which he is expected to excel. Worker's analysis prepares a picture of an individual's personal excellence, by virtue of which it is also called as an individual's analysis.

METHODS OF WORKER'S ANALYSIS

Worker's analysis is now a matter of science, so that it has come to use certain specific methods. Broadly speaking, the following are the various methods used in worker's analysis :

1. Application Blank,
2. Letters of Recommendation,
3. Academic Record,
4. Psychological Tests,
5. Group Tests,
6. Rating,
7. Interview.

It is not essential that all the above methods be used to analyse the abilities of any individual worker, a selection of any one of them being required to meet the need in a particular case. It will be in keeping with the context to glance briefly on these methods.

1. Application blank. Nowadays, the first step in the worker's analysis is the filling in of a blank by the applicant. This application blank can be designed to reveal much information of a varied kind, sometimes being so successful as to reveal the individual's entire background. In the application blank, the individual provides information regarding his age, sex, caste, nationality, earlier or past level of education, training, personal experience, history, etc. What kind of information should be provided in the application blanks is determined differently in different professions. Professions that are likely to be influenced by the worker's attitudes, mental inclinations, interests, etc., require that information regarding them should also be provided in the application blank. Many advertisers do not make a detailed report of what the applicant is expected to include in his application; they make a brief mention of a very few things. Application blanks of this kind do not qualify for scientific consideration. An application blank should preferably contain detailed inquiries regarding all important facts and details. Research in this direction can help to form outlines of application blanks for various professions, and according to that outline, blanks can be provided to the various applicants and aspirants. Often, evidence is required to substantiate the acts detailed in the application.

2. Letters of recommendation. Letters of recommendation also help in worker's analysis. In this method, the aspirant produces various recommendations, recommendations from his previous employer, the Principal of his school or college, or from some respected stalwarts of society, etc. In these letters, in addition to the natural commendation, some degree of ability is also evidenced, but often these letters are seen to contain many confusing and incorrect pieces of information regarding the individual. One of the simplest ways of misleading the intended employer is to include many qualities that the aspirant does not possess, or to overemphasize the qualities that he is fortunate enough to possess. As a general rule, such letters of recommendation usually prove to be hindrances rather than helps to the process of job analysis, but if they are valid and reliable, they can definitely promote job analysis or worker's analysis.

3. Academic records. Different professions require different levels of education as an essential qualification. Academic records are evidences of the individual's educational progress and proficiency. These sometimes include cumulative records of the universities.

4. Psychological tests. But the most important and valid method of worker's analysis is that of psychological testing in which the applicant's mental ability, interest, personality and particularly attitude are tested. Results of these tests should be employed with exemplary caution since they can also lead to very serious mistakes,

5. Physical tests. There are some jobs that require physical fitness of various kinds as an essential pre-requisite, for example, the eye-sight of a railway guard should be normal and not impaired. And for satisfaction on this point, different physical tests have been devised to suit various professions and their requirements. Nowadays, physical or medical tests have become an essential part of examinations for governmental jobs.

6. Group tests. There are some professions in which many workers have to work collectively but even if they work individually they are constantly thrown together in the process of their work. Hence in their case, it is essential for them to possess certain group qualities which are otherwise not taken into consideration. And it is with the intention of evaluating such qualities of collective behaviour in the individual that the employees or applicants are tested in the group. In other words, their conduct in the group is judged.

7. Rating. One of the many aspects of worker's analysis is the rating given to the individual by his Principal in school or college or by psychologists. This rating is sometimes taken into consideration by the worker analyst.

8. Interview. Finally, in most of the industries today, the applicant is personally interviewed by the employer and some other specialists, during which he is questioned by them on various topics so that they can form some estimate of him as an individual. Every examiner or individual of the board of interviewers asks some or the other question, but even while the applicant is engaged in answering it, the rest of the board is very minutely observing his reactions and conduct. Interview as a method of judging personality has advantages over other methods in that it reveals certain aspects of the individual that cannot be brought to light otherwise. It helps to form an estimate of the individual in respect of his self-confidence, self-control, response to discipline, presence of mind, dynamicity, interests, manner of dressing, conduct, behaviour, manners, attraction of personality, if any, etc., besides many other intangible things that make an impression on the mind of a viewer. But for this method to yield valid and desirable results, it is essential that the interviewers themselves be educated, trained and unbiased since, otherwise, such an interview can lead to many misunderstandings and misjudgements.

The method of personnel selection is fairly evident from the detailed description of its two aspects, job analysis and worker's analysis. Following job analysis and worker's analysis, all that remains to be done in the way of personnel selection is to provide the individual with work for which he has been found and pronounced to be most able.

QUESTIONS FOR EXERCISE

1. What are the important methods of personnel selection? Explain any two methods.

2. Distinguish between job analysis and worker's analysis and describe briefly how either is carried out.
3. Estimate the value of vocational guidance and selection in industry.
4. Discuss briefly the methods of personnel selection and give the merits and demerits of each.
5. What is job analysis? Illustrate it and discuss its importance.
6. Discuss the social and economic importance of vocational selection.
7. Discuss the importance of scientific methods of personnel selection in industry.

17

INDUSTRIAL WORKING ENVIRONMENT

In different factories, offices and other professional premises, the worker is compelled to work under certain conditions, examples of which are innumerable. He may be required to continue his effort, of a definite kind, in some specific place. His health stands to be influenced greatly by virtue of the fact whether his place of work is adequately and properly ventilated or not. Provision of adequate lighting is an essential condition, and one which justifiably occupies the worker's mind, since it will influence his eye sight, thereby his fatigue and consequently his efficiency and the quality of his output. It is well known that noise can be a disturbing element, and may put one off one's work. One of the conditions of work is that there be little, if any, noise; hence this must be taken into consideration. Temperature or the climate is another factor that influences the potential of a worker as it is known that in certain temperatures, a worker cannot work well, while in a more moderate or suitable temperature, his work takes a turn for the better. Temperature, also, must be taken into consideration while looking out for the place of work. In addition to these physical conditions, there are many other psychological conditions that also influence the worker and consequently his work. Of these, some are the behaviour of those in authority, mutual relationships among the workers, their respective family lives, incentives to work, etc.

In this manner, the conditions of work can be divided into two classes :

1. Physical conditions,
2. Psychological conditions.

PHYSICAL CONDITIONS OF WORK

Of the physical conditions, the main ones are :

1. Intensity, location, distribution and colour of light,
2. Temperature,

3. Ventilation,
4. Noise,
5. Working hours,
6. Rest pauses,
7. Music,
8. Other physical conditions.

Of the psychological conditions that affect work, the main are :

1. Behaviour of the Authorities,
2. Mutual Relations of the Employees,
3. Security,
4. Satisfaction of Needs,
5. Incentives.

1. Intensity, location, distribution and colour of light. The kind and intensity of light differ with the occupation that employees have adopted. As a normal rule, individuals over 35 require light of a greater intensity than their younger counterpart. If the objects handled are minute, then, naturally, the light must be fairly bright, while in work where objects handled are of a large size, and the workers are fairly young, intense light is not necessary. Light provided should never be so intense as to cause glare, and never so dim as to cause strain in concentrating upon an object to be worked. Work that requires light of high intensity also requires the use of special protective glasses, as is the case with welding, where the light of a very high intensity is produced by the welding flame. Protection from its harmful effects is achieved by the use of coloured glasses.

The source of light should be so located as to avoid falling directly upon the eyes; instead, it should fall on the instrument that is to be manipulated and then also in a manner as to avoid all reflection into the eyes of the person handling it. Hence, light should be evenly distributed and for this, tube-lighting has been found to be superior to bulb lamps, which are now considered obsolete.

Daylight is naturally uniform in its distribution; it is only when the work is done at night that the problem of uniform and even lighting arises, and it is a problem that requires expert handling and planning.

Besides the intensity and location of light, it is necessary to pay attention to its colour. It has been uniformly experienced in a large number of cases that, light that resembles daylight is very nearly the best and most beneficial. Hence, white light has been considered the most superior. And in coloured light, the best is yellow but a healthy yellow and not a sickly pale yellow. All other coloured lights harm the eyes in some measure.

2. Temperature. Temperature of the working premises has considerable and direct influence on the worker's health. It has been found that working in too high or too low temperatures leads to disease and accidents. Proper temperature maintains good health in the workers, and reduces the number of accidents as external conditions do not divert the attention of the worker and thus reduce his efficiency. H.M. Vernon found that in the British mines, where the temperatures are above 750 Fahrenheit, there were greater number of accidents while the perception and sensitivity of workers were also adversely affected. Extreme temperatures in working areas cause discomfort to the worker, so much so that the quality as well as quantity of his output are reduced. Temperature further influences the ventilation in a room, as it is essential for proper ventilation and flow of air to have only an adequate temperature.

3. Ventilation. Inflow of fresh air is essential in a place of work, as its absence tends to increase the fatigue and laziness or drowsiness of the workers. Air easily becomes contaminated in places where a large number of individuals work together, such as mines, factories and offices. For this, the use of exhaust fans is particularly desirable. Transport should be freely and easily available in places of work. Health is adversely affected if the percentage of oxygen in air is varied even within very narrow limits. According to Poffenberger, when the percentage of oxygen in air tends to fall below 14, the workers show signs of adverse effect. Ventilation also influences the body temperature of the workers, and if the body temperature varies it leads to fatigue and drowsiness. Another important factor is the presence as well as the percentage of humidity in the air. Excessive humidity is undeniably very harmful.

4. Noise. Excessive noise normally distracts attention and obstructs smooth working. It is for this reason that in every industry now attention is paid to the noise produced, and efforts are made to curb noises that distract attention. But noise of a continuous nature is often to be more soothing than disturbing, and when it is discontinued it disturbs the attention of people used to it. The truth of the matter is that only excessive noise is harmful and has the worst effect on the auditory system. Keeping in mind these observations, efforts should be made to regulate noise.

5. Hours of work. Professions in which the hours of work are so long and so badly planned that the worker is completely fatigued by the time he stops working, find themselves confronted with the problem of continuously decreasing efficiency among their staff. In addition to this, these professions become prey to all kinds of very serious problems of human relationships. When a worker is compelled to work for long hours beyond his physical endurance limits, he becomes diseased and loses his efficiency. Besides, his irritability increases. For this reason, in most progressive nations, the government promulgates certain orders whereby the hours of work for different occupations, for individuals of different ages and of different sexes, are determined. If need for more work arises, the employer is faced either with the alternative of indulging in illegal activity or remunerating the worker for his extra labour. But if he chooses to evade these laws, he incurs the displeasure of the law, and this is never to his advantage.

6. Rest pauses. Whatever the ability and endurance of an individual, even if he be abnormal in this respect, he cannot work continuously for long periods of time. After a certain period of time he feels the need for a rest, and his need has been found to have psychological justification, as it has been found that better results can be obtained by working in shifts and periods than by working continuously. Increases of between 10 and 20 per cent in production have been found to occur as a result of provision of rest in between work. The length and frequency of rest that are required depend upon the nature of work, the endurance and age of the worker and the general conditions of work. Hard work requires relatively longer and greater number of rest pauses. Similarly women, young children and old people require longer and greater number of rest pauses than young men. Nowadays, in practically every profession and occupation, rests of 15 minutes to an hour, are provided once or more so that the worker may be able to take refreshments and restore his vitality. Rest in between hours of work not only removes fatigue, it also eliminates the elements of monotony and boredom, thereby regenerating enthusiasm and vitality.

7. Music. One of the conditions of work taken into consideration is music. From their experiments W.A. Keir and H.C. Smith concluded that music has a beneficial and desirable influence upon the mental condition of workers, and thus it helps to induce some increase in their productive capacity. And one often sees people singing at their work, a phenomenon particularly obvious in the case of Indian women working at the grinder or in the fields or even when at their domestic chores. The rhythm in music has a beneficial effect on the rate of working. Tatas in India provide music in their various factories. In Western countries, particularly in the United States, the use of music in factories and other working places is steadily on the increase. Through a questionnaire H.C. Smith collected the views of one thousand workers regarding the provision of music in working places, and found that as many as 98 per cent of them were in favour of it, as they found considerable pleasure in it. The influence of music on routine work is as yet under extensive study.

8. Other physical conditions. In addition to these conditions, there are other physical and material considerations which influence the worker and his work. For example, if there is good provision of clean urinals, latrines, bathrooms, refreshments rooms, canteen, etc., the worker's time in the office becomes more pleasant, and many of his difficulties are removed. A place of work should not be foul smelling, neither should it be dirty or dusty, as any of these conditions disgust the worker.

PSYCHOLOGICAL CONDITIONS OF WORK

Of the psychological conditions of work, the more important have the following influence :

1. Behaviour of those in authority. A worker's mind is very susceptible to the behaviour of his boss. If the behaviour of authorities is desirable and good, the worker's enthusiasm and interest in his work are maintained, but if their behaviour is bad and inconsiderate, it is potentially a dangerous state as it can lead to conflict and unnecessary tension that has the worst effect upon production. Good behaviour does not imply laxity in administration and in dealing with the workers, as in such circumstances it is inevitable that the lazy and designing individuals in the organization will have a field day and do no work at all. It is essential that constant attention be paid to the worker's performance, but tact and diplomacy should be employed if it becomes necessary to point out his shortcomings. Senior officials and employers who are in the habit of constantly haranguing and bickering with their staff, are very often faced with continuous conflict and non-co-operation. Employees are not inclined to respect and work for people who are irritable, highly inflammable and ingratiating types. Working under a considerate individual not only keeps the worker happy but also inspires him to work more and work better.

2. Mutual relations of workers. One of the psychological conditions of working is the nature of relations that exist between the workers themselves. Where the number of workers is fairly large, and the nature of work demands their constant co-operation, better results are obtained if the workers have happy relations. If the relations are not happy, work suffers. And particularly the work that requires comparative effort suffers too much if there is no co-operation.

3. Security in profession. If the worker is confident that he is secure in his job, then his work shows definite improvements. If a profession that offers no security of employment, or in a position in which one can never be confident of remaining safe, a worker cannot work with enthusiasm or with his mind on the work. Hence, a profession must offer security of future employment. After a certain predetermined period of service has been completed, the worker should be made permanent in his position, as is now done in all government jobs and many private firms. Even most governments in many countries have made laws regarding such employment procedure. Besides this minimal security of profession, other inducements are insurance during unemployment, old age insurance, and security of insurance in the event of accidents that render the individual incapable of further work. Nowadays, in all progressive states, government and other general employers make provision for these benefits, as in their absence it is only natural for the worker to spend time in wondering about his future and making efforts to secure it, efforts that enfeeble him for his regular work.

4. Satisfaction of life's needs. Every individual has some personal and other family requirements, such as adequate food and housing for his family, and purchasing power to the extent of his other reasonable needs. Besides this, there are certain needs that foster self-respect, and these, too, cannot be neglected. Progress has made it necessary for employers to pay attention to these aspects of the human personality also. Consequently they have to initiate and finance certain schemes of labour welfare that involve some expenditure, which provide many direct and indirect benefits to the worker that place him in a very favourable state of mind. Their needs being fulfilled, they are inclined to respect and obey their employers, to work for their better prospects in turn. They have confidence in their employers, and thus they are never inclined to work contrary to the interests of their employers.

5. Incentives in industry. Motives have an important place in the life of a man. In the absence of a motive, no individual can either work hard or do anything better in his life or improve his work in any way. Inspiration of this kind is available to the individual in his trade in the form of various kinds of incentives such as increase in wages, praise by authorities, promotion, bonus, etc. Incentives are now an important part of any well geared up industry. In most progressive nations, the workers stand to benefit through bonus if the production rises, and thus improve their earning, their morale goes up. In most professions, an individual is promoted to a senior position if he shows satisfactory work. If the people in authority are sensible, they will always praise the extra efforts of their subordinates. Their wages can also be increased so as to provide an extra inducement.

All the aforementioned physical and psychological conditions have considerable importance for commerce and industry. And psychologists have now seriously drawn the attention of the industrialists to this aspect. It is necessary not only with regard to economic or fiscal gain, but also with regard to humanity that the workers should have the opportunity to work in beneficial conditions, both physical and psychological. Workers, being part and parcel of the fibre of the nation, the government also should take steps to have such conditions created. When such a system is in existence in industry, the conflicts are reduced and the production increased, with the result that the employer, the employee and the state all benefit.

CHANCES OF PROMOTION

Every employee wishes that at various stages of his service he be given chances of promotion and progress. Promotion involves change in status or position of authority within the official structure. In every profession and occupation, the services are graded in one definite order. In administrative service, for example, the deputy collector supersedes the tehsildar while he in his turn is superseded by the collector. Above the collector is the commissioner. Similarly, in the army, there are various posts, such as second-lieutenant,

lieutenant, captain, major, lieutenant, colonel, etc. In every profession, the higher post or status carries better salary as well as greater authority with a correspondingly greater responsibility. Hence, it is only natural that every individual should wish to occupy as high a post as is within his grasp.

Kinds of Promotion

But promotion should not be taken to imply the gaining of a higher post. Although that precisely is the sense in which it is usually interpreted, yet the term should be more properly used to include all increases in pay, increase in leave, improved conditions of work, increase in respect and honour, etc. Walters has described the following eight kinds of promotion :[1]

1. Increase in wages, salary or remuneration,
2. increase in position, authority or responsibility,
3. increase in leave or decrease in hours of work,
4. transfer to a better place or department,
5. improvement in place of residence or of working,
6. opportunities of gaining training and experience becoming available,
7. greater security of position of benefit,
8. increase in the period of service.

In this manner, then, if the worker's salary or remuneration is increased, he will be deemed to have been promoted. He will equally be deemed to have benefited in the same manner if he is given a higher position, greater authority or responsibility. He may be allowed to work for fewer hours. Or, in other words, time available for recreation will have been increased, whereby he stands promoted. As an indication of promotion, individual may be transferred to a better place or to another department considered better. Services or employments that involve transfer of employees from one place to another make use of this device to promote their personnel. Seeing that a particular person is good at his work, he can be shown signs of favour by improving his working conditions or by improving his place of residence. Employees who work well are given chances of gaining further training and obtaining additional experience. In almost all services, if the employee continues to show improvement after his appointment thereto, his post is made permanent and secure. Security of employment is

1. Walters, J.E., *Applied Personnel Administration*, Wiley.

another form in which promotion may be indicated. When individuals show a consistently good record of work, their period of service is increased. In many cases, people are re-employed after having been officially retired from service.

From among the various forms or kinds of promotion described above, different individuals favour different kinds, relative to the various professions. Some people place the highest premium upon economic gain while others find more value in increased respect and honour. Improvement in the conditions of work is another mode of promotion that is dear to some individuals. And it is equally inessential that in some specific context only one form of promotion may be awarded. In very many cases, promotion leads to increased wages, authority and responsibility as well as better conditions of working. In this manner, often the employee gets his promotion in more forms than one.

Bases of Promotion

In every profession there are some definite laws governing promotion, just as there are definite ways of selection and appointment. One of the commonest methods of promotion is that of seniority in which every employee is promoted after he has put in a definite period of work in one situation. But, equally, in almost all services, attention is paid to the individual's ability when he is being considered for promotion, over and above the extent of his service. It sometimes occurs that an individual's ability and efficiency are so great that he is given promotion by superseding other senior officials. Private business lays much stress on work as well as on ability. The employer stands to gain something if his employees work better and more, so that he is easily enabled to enhance their wages or to give them a greater share in the profits. But in certain occupations, inside and outside the government structure, where the employer himself does not superintend the work, or where there is no objective or concrete employer himself, or where the employer is of the ingratiating type, promotion depends more on pleasing authority than upon seniority, ability or results obtained. In professions in which there are no definite laws and rules governing promotion of the workers, promotion takes place through the whim of those in authority.

From the above description, it is evident that promotion depends upon the following factors :

1. Seniority,
2. Ability,

3. Better and more work,
4. Kindness of the authorities.

Promotion on the Basis of Seniority

In most occupations and services, wages of the employees increase somewhat every year, and thus seniority is a basis of promotion common to almost all occupations. Seniority as a basis of promotion has psychological sanction, as every worker wishes that in view of the greater period of service rendered, he should be given a post above the newcomers. Absence of any definite rules regarding promotion on the grounds of seniority leads to discontent and people lose interest in work. At the same time, they show no inclination to stick to any one profession. Naturally, the profession as a whole tends to suffer through such vagrancy as every new entrant takes his time in learning the ropes and if the old ones keep running away, much efficiency and effort are lost. It is for this reason that in every service, wages improve with seniority, and in most cases promotion also takes place on the same basis. But it is incorrect to consider seniority the sole basis of promotion. Just as the senior individual desires promotion, the more able and efficient also desires promotion and better prospects. If his talent is allowed to lie dormant, and if he has to wait a number of years before he comes into authority, or if he is required to constantly serve under a less efficient man, he is inclined to lose patience and become dissatisfied. His mind wanders out of the periphery of his work, and he feels imposed upon if asked to obey the less able individual who is in authority. And this insubordination leads to defective administration. Hence, ability should be taken into consideration along with seniority when the question of promotion comes up.

Promotion on the Basis of Ability

The second major basis of promotion is the individual's ability that takes very young people to the tops of their professions in very short periods of time. And if seniority be the sole basis, then an individual starting at the lowest rung can never reach the top. For this, ability, and consideration of ability, are very essential. Yet, for this reason alone, it is not safe to completely discount seniority, as many occupations place the premium upon experience. Secondly, having put in years of hard and honest service, the employee desires that he be given some token of appreciation for his selfless service, because if he is not promoted he becomes dissatisfied. And, there can be no general rule regarding the alternate propriety of seniority or ability as the basis of promotion in any individual case, or any single profession. Generally speaking wages or salary should be commensurate with the years of service put in. But before a key post, or a position that wields very wide authority can be handed to a person, it is essential to inquire into his antecedents and evaluate his abilities.

Promotion on the Basis of Results

Those in authority everywhere, whatever the profession, whatever the service, desire subordinates should give off their best. Where private business is concerned, the employer is interested in one thing exclusively, that is, results in terms of work, both as regards quantity and quality. Hence, in such cases, promotion is also dispensed on the basis of results obtained by the individual under review. This particular method of promotion gives very good results in a large majority of cases since it not only satisfies the instincts and interests of those interested in efficiency and ability, but also appears inducement to those not so inclined. It leads most people to emulate others, and very good results are achieved all round.

Promotion on the Basis of Kindness or Recommendation

Recommendation or kindness of authorities is perhaps the worst method of promotion. Yet, it is very much in vogue in this enlightened age. In government and semi-government organisations, it is the ingratiating type of individual who figures the highest on lists of promotions as he makes his presence felt by grovelling to the authorities, by entertaining officers, by making judicious presents to them and to members of their families or by benefiting them in other respects. Lacking this effusive sociability, even the most efficient, honest and hard-working individual with a good seniority remains in position without any hope of progress. Cases of this nature also present very bad examples to other workers, with the result that the best part of their energies are wasted in pleasing the authorities rather than in working.

Modes of Promotion

The above description of the bases of promotions also reveals the mode of promotion. In fact, an individual has to be selected for promotion in much the same manner in which he is to be selected for appointment. In both cases, much care and understanding should be used in making the selection. What more usually happens is that the care taken in selecting an individual for appointment is far greater than the attention paid to his promotion. And in most cases promotion is done on the basis of seniority, one of the most prevalent methods. Promoting an individual on the basis of his ability is none the worse. Another good, and fairly reliable, method of promotion is the one based upon efficiency and results obtained in previous position. But to promote an individual on one's whim, on recommendation, on one's pleasure, is not at all a good method, but a thoroughly undesirable one. It is unscientific, unethical and harmful also.

Importance of Promotion

Promotion is an important aspect of every profession. Its propriety is based on the psychological fact that every employee wants promotion and improvement on the basis of efficiency, ability or years of service. Promotion is also an important inducement to the employee to work better and to work more. Promotion gives the worker enthusiasm and confidence, encourages him to produce even better results. Existence of definite rules of promotion induces a sense of security in the employee, as then he can decide on the method he has to follow in order to benefit and gain promotion. Under these conditions, they are not only discouraged, but are even inclined to try even harder. For this reason, it is essential that in every establishment the rules of promotion be definite and precisely laid down, so that there be no cause for complaint. Seniority, ability and the quantum of work done form the propriety of promotions. Promotion based on recommendations or personal likes or dislikes, or because of considerations of personal gains is completely improper and unjustified. Such behaviour kills the initiative of other workers, and their efficiency falls. Evidently, promotion in any service is as important for the employer as it is for the employee. The employer can use that as a basis for selecting good workers, and thus his work benefits. The worker's incentive to continue his effort is maintained. He is even inclined to improve the quality of his work. But promotion is actually beneficial only when its rules are observed, and are so known to every employee. Its best use can be made only if its basis is correct, proper and scientific.

QUESTIONS FOR EXERCISE

1. Citing relevant studies, discuss the influence of noise on industrial output.
2. Citing relevant studies, show how physical conditions of work affect the worker and production.

3. Describe the effect of noise and music on industrial efficiency.
4. Distinguish between the physical and psychological environments of the worker and state the importance of latter.
5. What are the organizational and psychological climates in the many and varied industrial environments? Discuss the importance of psychological climates in industry.
6. Attempt an analysis of the basic criteria that should be taken into account in evaluating working conditions in industry.
7. Distinguish between the physiological and psychological factors of working environment and discuss their interrelationship.
8. List the physical aspects of industrial environment that affect efficiency of work and discuss any two of them fully.
9. Show how rest pauses and noise affect the efficiency of work.

18

Efficiency, Time-Motion Study and Therbligs

Quality and quantity of work, in any factory, industry or office do not depend upon the machines alone. Whatever the quality of mechanical equipment existing in the factory, for a very high level of production, it is essential that the individuals operating the machines be experts, and highly qualified. Hence, Industrial psychology makes a detailed study of the factors and problems influencing efficiency. Psychologists have also suggested various measures for improving and maintaining the efficiency of working personnel.

WHAT IS EFFICIENCY?

What is this efficiency? How can it be discovered or determined? Efficiency is the individual's skill in any specific job, by virtue of which he can perform that function well. Efficiency is not a general quality because no individual can do everything efficiently. He can be highly skilled in only a couple of functions. Different individuals have skill in different kinds of jobs while people who are skilful in the same work differ in the degree of skill. His efficiency, or a statement of it, must be qualified by the function in respect of which he is acknowledged to be successful. A skilful person can perform some definite function better and quicker than the average worker. Hence, efficiency is measured or reckoned by the quantity of work done, and the time taken in doing it. If mere saving of time is effected, the person cannot be said to be skilful because he must also maintain the quality and quantity of work in that reduced time. Similarly, skill as a quality cannot be attributed to any individual who merely does a lot of work. Evidently, efficiency requires more and better work to be done in less time. If a person possesses all these three qualities, in connection with some definite form of work, more than other individuals doing the same work, he will be said to be more efficient. Evidently, then efficiency is a relative term. Individuals are efficient as compared to one another. But this efficiency is not affected at all times and between all individuals. Normally, when an individual is said to be efficient, it is implied that he does more work than the average worker in the same unit and does it better in the same time.

DETERMINANTS OF EFFICIENCY

In order to maintain and improve upon the efficiency of individuals, psychologists made a detailed study of the conditions or determinants of efficiency. Efficiency is a psycho-physical state in which both mind and body are directly involved. Hence, its determinants can also be roughly divided into the internal and external. External conditions are the following :

1. Rest,
2. Work period,
3. Health,
4. Climate.

Now these various external conditions will be described in some length :

1. Rest. In the foregoing chapter of fatigue it was mentioned that a person becomes tired if he works without rest, and his skill decreases proportionately : hence it is evident that rest is one essential factor of efficiency. In an experiment Sheppard put twelve college students on the chest-waist machine for eight hours, the work to them being repeated but with intervening periods of rest. This experiment illustrated that uninterrupted work reduced the worker's efficiency. Watt's experiments showed that work done with adequate provisions for rest led to an increase in efficiency of up to 9.3 per cent. Vernon and Bedford studied workers in an electricity plant or power house who worked both with rest and then without rest. They came to the conclusion that work done without rest does not produce very good results. Other experiments have proved that where the work is of a purely mental nature it is best to relax for a period of five minutes after every hour of work, while a ten-minute break is better. Of the entire hours of work in a day, the workers should be given 16.6 per cent as rest.

It must also be kept in mind that providing unnecessary periods of rest has no real benefit, but is instead prone to cause loss. Too long a period of rest leads the worker's mind away from his work completely. Ten minutes are enough under normal conditions. But it is wrong to imagine that lunch time is a period of rest.

During the period of rest, the worker must not be given any physical or mental work. Another important thing in this connection is that the time of rest should be predetermined as its uncertainty is harmful because of the tension created by it. As it is, the existing tension is not reduced. The time required for rest in a particular form of work is something that cannot be laid down with any severity. There can be no general rule. As a general rule, some rest is required in every form of work, but normally more tough or difficult work requires longer periods of rest.

Rest creates mainly the following benefits :

(a) Production increases in quality and quantity.

(b) Accidents in the industry decreases.

(c) Boredom and disinterest are eliminated.

(d) Relaxation reduces tension and provides comfort.

2. Time of work. Another important determining factor of efficiency is the time of work. If the period of work required from the employee is unnecessarily long, it will be natural for the worker to feel exhausted with the result that his efficiency will fall. Many experiments have proved that the labourer should not be compelled to work for more than eight hours. Forty hours in the week is quite sufficient and adequate. As the hours of work increase beyond this, the worker's enthusiasm, efficiency, health, strength and capability, etc., steadily fall, the ultimate outcome of which is harmful for the employer. Hence, the salvation of the employer as well as employed lies in the fact that the hours of work should not be increased beyond well-defined limits.

3. Health. A good health is another requirement for high efficiency. If the worker does not enjoy good health, he will be prone to fatigue and low quality of work done. The importance of health in industry is evident from the development of a new branch of science, the Industrial Hygiene. It makes a study of all conditions and circumstances that influence the worker's health, and helps in the creation of conditions that will favourably influence it. The advent of industrial hygiene led to the improvement in the health of workers as well as in the quality and quantity of work produced by them. According to industrial hygiene, in order to maintain a good standard of health among workers in industrial centres, the following facts should be attended to :

(a) Every industrial centre should be equipped with a good doctor who can immediately attend to a worker falling ill.

(b) Special attention must be paid to the prevention of contagious diseases from spreading among the workers. Immediately as some worker contracts any such disease, he should be quarantined, and put under expert medical care.

(c) As far as possible, alcoholic and other stimulants should not be available to the workers, and even the ones addicted to it should be helped to get rid of their addiction.

(d) Workers should be given essential information on matters of health, and on the prevention of some common diseases.

(e) Special attention should be paid to workers physically, mentally or financially backward, and special facilities provided to reduce the degree of backwardness.

4. Climate. Climatic conditions of the place of work also influence efficiency. Many of the important things in this connection have been mentioned in a previous chapter entitled Psychology in Industry. Modern factories that are scientifically designed have special arrangements for controlled lighting, ventilation, running water, cleanliness, temperature, sound, etc. If this is not done, the health and ultimately the efficiency of the worker suffer.

In addition to the external conditions, efficiency is also affected by some internal conditions, which are as follows :

1. Motivation,
2. Monotony,
3. Application,
4. Emotional adjustment,
5. Aptitude and personality differences.

1. Motivation. Motivation is intimately concerned with efficiency. If it is lacking, the presence of all physical comforts cannot induce any efficiency. But if is present, and most other comforts lacking, efficiency is maintained to a fairly large extent. And ways of providing motivation in industry have been studied in a previous chapter. For motivated working in industry, it is essential that the needs of worker be fulfilled, his health be maintained, his future be fairly secure, and that he be promoted and otherwise rewarded adequately for efficient and skilful work. If promotions come as a result of ingratiating behaviours towards the authorities, even the most efficient worker loses motivation. If the people in authority do not behave properly, the worker loses his-motivation. All these things have been studied.

2. Boredom. Boredom is another factor that has an adverse effect upon the efficiency because in it the mind and body both lose their vigour. Hence, psychologists have conducted many experiments towards discovering the nature of this phenomenon of boredom, and have tried to analyse its causes. The following means can be employed to reduce or prevent boredom in work :

(a) ***Variety in work*** : According to Poffenberger, one cause of boredom is the repetition of same kind of work. It is a matter of common experience that one tires of the same work if persisted in, and this fact does not need the endorsement of a psychologist. Hence, if interest in the work is to be maintained it is necessary that the work presents some variety to the worker. This variety can be used to reduce or even prevent boredom.

(b) ***Rest along with work*** : If there is no adequate arrangement for rest along with work, an individual becomes exhausted and tends to become bored. Hence, it is desirable to have some definite arrangement for rest along with work, if boredom is to be avoided.

(c) ***Short hours of work*** : If the hours of work are very long, the worker becomes bored and tends to remain fatigued most of the time. Hence, it is essential that the hours of work be not long.

(d) ***Arrangement of recreation*** : Recreation refreshes the individual, hence it is most essential for removing boredom. Therefore, it is now a common practice to provide the workers with all kinds of equipment with which they can amuse, and refresh themselves. It creates novelty as well as a diversion that helps to recreate interest in the worker.

(e) ***Motivation*** : To keep boredom away, motivation in the work of the worker should be maintained by various means. He should not be allowed to work under heavy pressure of any kind. He should be encouraged to develop his own motivation for the work he does.

(f) ***Selection of work according to intelligence, personality and abilities*** : If any work that the individual does, does not conform to his level of intelligence, qualities of his personality, his capacity and special abilities, then he will gradually become increasingly bored. Hence, it is essential that the person chooses his occupation with due regard to his own personality and its complication.

3. Application. Another important and essential internal condition of efficiency is the undisturbed and undivided application of the employee to his work. For this, it is necessary to remove noise and other obstacles or interferences. Sometimes the absence of motivation is another cause of indifference to work. For efficiency it is essential that all internal as well as external diverting factors be removed from the sphere of activity, and the worker encouraged to pursue his work undisturbed and with the fullest application.

4. Emotional adjustment. A study of most accidents reveals that they are caused by inattention, lack of interest, laxity or mental conflict. And all of these factors have emotional maladjustment at their root. Hence, another important condition of efficiency is emotional adjustment. In order to maintain it, generally the conditions of work of the employee should be good. In addition to this, individual guidance should be available to them in order to help them to solve some of their personality problems.

5. Characteristic interests and personality traits. Finally, efficiency also depends to a large extent upon the individual's own characteristic interests and personality traits. If his occupation conforms to them, his efficiency is maintained but in case of an adverse choice of trade, his efficiency lies unexploited. Secondly, there is a certain class of individuals in the case of whom it is very difficult to maintain any definite level of efficiency, though efforts can achieve some degree of success in this direction.

From the above account of the various conditions and determining factors of efficiency, it would be apparent that industrial psychology has made considerable headway in its research on this aspect, and that continuous efforts are being made to discover systematic law. Such an effort can only have the most desirable results for both employer as well as employed.

TIME-MOTION STUDY

Taylor's Studies

Study of time and motion in industrial psychology has revealed many important things regarding efficiency. In 1910 Taylor carried out certain experiments concerning motion. In this study he divided a single function into numerous component parts, and noted the time taken in the performance of each part. After this, he increased their wages, and, reducing the time taken in the performance of each component task, he studied the results. Following motion study there was time study.

Gilbreth's Studies

But the most important study on this aspect was by Gilbreth.

Symbol	Name of Symbol	Symbol	Name of Symbol
	Search	#	Disassemble
	Find	0	Inspect
	Find		Pre-Position
∩	Grasp		Release Load
	Transport Loaded	∪	Transport Empty
		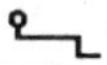	Rest for overcoming Fatigue
9	Position		Unavoidable Delay
#	Assemble		Avoidable Delay
U	Use		Plan

Fig. 18.1. Therbligs Chart

Through a study of time-motion Gilbreth tried to discover the method by means of which a worker can do the greatest amount of work possible in less time than normal. For this, he observed that maximum economy in this could be effected only if all unnecessary activities were eliminated from the function, and only the absolutely essential or inevitable activities were allowed to remain. Conducting experiments of this nature on labourers who haul bricks, Gilbreth concluded that, if all unnecessary movements were excluded, the work normally done in twelve hours could be completed in five, while, instead of moving 120 bricks in an hour it is possible to displace some 350 bricks in the same time. In his study Gilbreth made use of the cyclegraph for studying movements. Stop-watches were used to record time. In a time-motion study, all the movements required in any function are divided into the smallest invisible units. Then, analysis reveals the unnecessary and the necessary activities, the unnecessary or superfluous being eliminated. At a later stage, motion came to be studied with automatic cameras, and with tri-dimensional cameras even later. Nowadays, besides noting the length, breadth and height, it also records the time. This complete picture is known as the stereo-crono-cyclegraph. With its help it is possible to study all the motions of any one piece of work at the same time.

THERBLIGS

In addition to studying motion, Gilbreth also tried to validate them, and for doing so he determined the symbols of various movements, and he started using those symbols to describe those particular kinds of movements. Gilbreth formed seventeen such symbols of various movements.

These symbols are called therbligs. This work contains all letters that Gilbreth's name includes, only their order is reversed. A simochart prepared with the help of these therbligs. In the simochart, using the diagrammatic or plotting method, the motions of the various parts of the body are filled in, keeping a definite scale and the due proportion between themselves, and their relative therbligs indicated thereon. The simochart reveals the activity that the specific part of the body has to do for a specific time in performing a specific function.

Advantages of Time-Motion Studies

Time-motion study has proved of immense value to the industry. On one hand, it helps in job analysis, while on the other it helps to discover the method by which a maximum work can be obtained in the shortest period of time by eliminating all unnecessary movements. Thirdly, studies of this nature also indicate the nature of training to be imparted to trainees intended for certain specific functions. Another benefit deriving from this study is that it helps to fix the value of a particular function, and thereby the salary payable to its performer.

QUESTIONS FOR EXERCISE

1. What is efficiency? Describe its determinants.
2. Explain Time and Motion Studies.
3. Write short note on Therbligs.